Hill Towns of Italy

ITALY

LUCY LILIAN NOTESTEIN

Hill Towns of Italy

Illustrated by
DAVID GENTLEMAN

LITTLE, BROWN AND COMPANY · BOSTON · TORONTO

FIRST AMERICAN EDITION

Published simultaneously in Canada
by Little, Brown & Company (Canada) Limited

PRINTED IN THE UNITED STATES OF AMERICA

*To my sister Margaret
and my brother Frank,
companions whose delight
in hunting hill towns
never wanes*

Contents

Preface

THE essence of travel is discovery. It is a personal adventure in curiosity. 'The bear went over the hill to see what he could see.' If 'the other side of the hill was all that he could see', it was his own fault, for the other side of the hill may be bare, it may even be ugly, but it is sure to be different, at least in the view it presents. This book is but an introduction to Italian hill towns. There are hundreds of other hill towns worth exploring, and it is my hope that the reader of this book will be inspired to set out for himself to see what is on many a hilltop and on the other side, in the Pistoian Alps, for instance, or to the east of Florence by Poppi, in much of the Marches, in the Abruzzi, in Latium, in Calabria, Apulia, and Sicily. Italy is inexhaustible. There are ancient peoples with whom to get acquainted, personages of the Middle Ages and the Renaissance, painting, sculpture, architecture, regional customs, and always views.

There are, however, certain admonitions and advices in order. This book presupposes that the traveller goes by motor car. This is not necessary—trains and taxis are available—yet it is advisable. One should be equipped with at least two, and different, road maps, not only because they wear out quickly from being folded and refolded but because road maps put out by different publishers show variations in the small towns and small roads marked. Second-class roads are nearly always more desirable than those shown in red; there is much less traffic on them; there is usually more to see. Even third-class roads marked in white are usually hard-surfaced, and some that look like goat trails on the map are often possible. But do not travel on Saturday afternoon or on Sunday unless before noon, and don't get caught in a deluge in the hills on any road. For towns, local maps of streets and the location of buildings are available at almost any hotel in a given town, or, if not there, at a local bookstore or even general store. Incidentally, one should remember that public buildings, including churches, are closed during the long siesta period from twelve to three or four o'clock, and, incidentally also, one should carry a good flashlight, for museums and churches are often dark.

Hotels—many Italians hardly understand the word hotel but rather *albergo*—are of all sorts of course. Some are excellent. I have mentioned a few by name in instances where the hotel itself is worth seeing. The Jolly chain of hotels built in recent years in Italy—there are new ones appearing almost every year—has opened up for travellers, particularly in southern Italy and Sicily, many places where formerly the tourist could not go, save as he found a large center and went exploring only within the travel-reach of a single day. Every year there is a new edition of the Michelin hotel guide for Italy. In this one can get all the information one needs about where to stay. Some of the very simple hotels are clean and comfortable. If one telephones or writes ahead one can usually even engage a bath in those shown in Michelin as 'two-housers'. The concierge will gladly do the telephoning for one.

The reader may be surprised that I have omitted Perugia and Assisi. These are towns included now in every general guidebook of Italy, and in nearly every tour. There seemed no need for me to duplicate here. Assisi, the town of St. Francis and of Giotto's great frescoes in the church on the brow of the hill; Perugia with its magnificent town hall, its national gallery of Umbria, its Fonte Maggiore, its Etruscan remains, its dark alleyways, are of course towns that no one who visits Italy should miss.

I have many persons to thank: first of all my father, a Latin professor who loved his Italy, and my mother, who took me, my sister also, with them for a year in Italy when I was but a youngster. We walked miles following aqueducts across the Roman *campagna*, climbed the old Triumphal Way to the top of Monte Cavo, picnicked all over the Alban and some of the Sabine hills, sat on the rubble at Ostia, hunted out the old Etruscan Veii, and visited many hill towns such as Narni when visiting hill towns was still something of an adventure. It was then that I began to love Italy and its hill towns. I have been back many times since and always to the hill towns.

I have also to thank my sister Margaret who first suggested to me the need of this book and kept urging me to write it. She has helped all the way through with suggestions and in many other ways, relieving me of various responsibilities and allowing me to go ahead. To my brother Frank also I owe many thanks, for he has worn out several pairs of shoes tramping with me over the pavements and cobblestones of Italy; his photographs on our various trips form the basis of the illustrations, and he has helped endlessly in the final details of getting the manuscript ready for the press.

My thanks go also to several friends who have aided and abetted me in the project, Mr. and Mrs. Robert Izant, Mr. and Mrs. Allen W. Wilber, Mr. and Mrs. Ross Thiele, Mrs. Harold Golder, Mr. Howard Lowry, Miss Caroline Rogers, Mrs. Robert Wallace McClenahan, and Mrs. Paul Angert.

Finally, I owe my thanks also to Smoky, our German shepherd dog, for his patience and philosophic attitude that have made possible our various long absences of four or five months at a time. Like the wolf of Gubbio he seemed to know that there must be some reason behind it all.

LUCY LILIAN NOTESTEIN

1

Why See the Hill Towns

'A walled city is like a veiled bride.
What is one about to embrace?'

MAURICE HEWLETT

THERE was once a village, according to an old Italian fable, on a hilltop so steep that the people tied sacks under the tails of their hens so that the eggs would not roll downhill. The village bore the name of Pocopaglia, meaning Littlestraw. One can think of any number of Italian towns to which the fable might be applicable, for from the earliest days of history, or before, the people who lived in what is now called Italy built their towns on the hilltops. From a point on the west side of Lake Maggiore one can count twenty-six villages clinging to the mountainsides. As one follows a winding valley road almost anywhere in central or southern Italy one looks up on either side at every turn to the tops of hills crowned with villages, gray villages sometimes and sometimes brown, of stone usually, of brick occasionally, with towers and often a dome cutting the skyline. One usually sees also an ancient wall, or part of it, which circled the town, and a gate or two just wide enough to admit the traffic in a day when that meant pedestrians, oxen and donkeys, armed horsemen, and possibly wide-wheeled chariots of war. Down on the slopes are the vineyards punctuated with mulberry trees, and the olive orchards, and the pears, possibly also some persimmons, golden in the fall, and still lower the little fields of artichokes and lettuce, beans, corn, and yellow pumpkins for the pigs. Seen in a sunset light the villages are blue, lavender, and gray, and as the lights come out, winking up the hillside, they have an air of mystery as of a fairy tale. But in the morning they look solid and substantial, fortresses rather, where men and women of this day are living, the descendants of men and women who lived there a thousand years ago, or two thousand, or in some instances probably three thousand years ago.

Their forbears had found it safer to go to the hills which could more easily than valley towns be defended against marauders. Then every tribe warred with every other, and every town was a potential enemy. So around their cluster of houses they raised thick walls and at the entrances put heavy gates, often with double or triple arches, that could be locked and barred. Besides, from these high sites those who were leagued together could the more easily communicate; signal fires or banners from towers could give warning of an enemy. There may, too, have been other reasons. The air in the summer was less hot and humid up high than in the misty, sometimes swampy, valleys. For some reason they did not know, they were probably healthier on the hills, not subject to chills and fever as those living at a lower altitude. In medieval days they liked to build their churches as near to heaven as they could get them; the people gathered around the church, for in it their whole life was centered. There were their accustomed rituals, there in the paintings on the walls much of their education, there the discussions between neighbors and in the earliest days even the court of justice, and outside on the piazza, possibly the only level place in town, were their festivals. So the hills became their homes.

On the same piazza as the *duomo* in the hill town one usually finds the town hall called *palazzo communale*, or *pubblico*, or *palazzo del ragione*, or *del popolo* or *dei priori*, with a tower as high or higher than that of the church. Indeed there was sometimes rivalry between the two, the church and state, so to speak, as to which could raise the higher tower. Then usually there was on the same square the bishop's palace and that of the *capitano del popolo*, the local governor, occasionally some other palace. Somewhere there, too, is often the *pozzo*, the cistern with its stone coping and ornamental wrought-iron top from which a chain and bucket are suspended. Since shallow wells were hardly feasible on hilltops, cisterns of rain water were necessary, especially as a siege was always a possibility. Of course aqueducts were sooner or later built from the higher wooded hills and water piped to

fountains throughout the town. There the women gathered to talk and fill up their copper jugs for household use. In many places one still sees this procedure, the women carrying the jugs home on their heads. In a few instances one finds the pavement of the main piazza patterned, as in Siena, or Arezzo, or Pienza. Pavements, however, of piazzas and streets are ordinarily of large rectangular blocks beautifully fitted together. How the blocks were brought there nobody knows, but probably they were sledded up the hillside behind oxen or donkeys. It may be in some instances that the stone came actually from the hill on which the town was built.

Streets everywhere are narrow; at their widest they allow of but two small European cars to pass—if their paint is thin; at their narrowest nothing but a Vespa and a couple of pedestrians could get through, and even so the pedestrians would have to flatten themselves against a wall when the Vespa passed. Into some of these sun may never penetrate for any distance; into others possibly for a few hours a day. Many streets are stairways only. Washings, a colorful display, are strung across from window to window overhead and draped along the balconies.

The buildings are all of stone, or brick where that is more readily available. In the piazzas or along the main streets one finds the medieval or Renaissance palaces, themselves often works of art by famous architects of their day, one of the Sangallos, or a Rossellino, or Sansovino, or Michelozzo, or some other, with overhanging eaves and cornices and beautifully designed, sometimes carved, windows. Sometimes along the base is a stone bench where retainers sat or from which one could mount a horse. On the walls above are iron rings for banners and torches. Over the massive and impressive doorway is a coat of arms, and within usually a courtyard, certainly a commodious entrance-way and a stairway of marble or travertine; occasionally this is so sweeping and easy that a horseman could ride up it. These palaces undoubtedly belonged originally to the landowners whose retainers worked the fields below, getting their share of the produce according to the age-old system of *mezzadria* (share-cropping).

Along the narrow back streets, one looks through wide-open doors into ground-floor rooms, often below the level of the street, where there may be chickens penned and clucking, occasionally ducks or rabbits, or in Sicily even a goat, a family meat-supply. Along the wider streets are, of course, the shops that supply the town, the butcher shop with bloody carcasses hanging at the open door or just inside—the calves, goats, hogs, the hares with the fur skinned halfway down, the pheasants, the lanky chickens and ducks, and the little songbirds, that are the delight—and the disgrace—of every Italian hunter. These birds even if served whole and unplucked would each hardly make a mouthful. The groceries are a more refreshing sight with their pears, apples, *pomodori* (tomatoes), huge peppers, red and green and brilliant yellow, lettuce, dried *ceci*, and rice, *funghi* (mushrooms) and chestnuts, *pasta* in all forms, *salami*, cheese and crackers, and on the shelves behind some cans of this or that. Of course there are the bakery and the pharmacy and the cobbler's shop, the dark cellar where the wood-worker is busy with his saw and lathe making or repairing furniture, the smithie's shop where he hammers out the iron and copper, and of course the wine shop. Wine and bread, *pasta*, *polenta*, and chestnuts, today as long ago, are the mainstay of the diet of the Italian country-man. Every town, too, has an *albergo*, or *locanda*, though one would not always like to stay at it, and two or three *ristoranti* or *trattorie* of varying descriptions. At their best they are very good with delicious soup or *pasta*, or *vitello* (veal) cooked in at least half a dozen different ways.

Yet if these hill towns were as nearly all alike as here described, one or two at most would satisfy one's curiosity. But each is different, has its unique distinction. One never knows quite what to expect. One rarely happens into a hill town without finding something that makes the trip worth while, a fountain perhaps, some lovely view out between two ancient walls as at Preci, a quotation from Dante underneath a shrine. Arcola, for instance, has no great art, but an old pentagonal tower, narrow winding streets that dive like ground squirrels under houses, and a view that you keep remembering when you shut your eyes. So, too, looking across the bay of La Spezia from Lerici one discovers Porto Venere rising straight from the sea up the hillside. It is scarcely mentioned in guidebooks, though well known to Italians as one of the enchanting spots of Italy. To it one goes back and goes back.

Just south of Florence is a district where pottery is made. Nearly every farmhouse has its kiln. Its walls are topped with terra cotta garden pots and finials in many designs, shapes, and sizes, or these are lined up under its olive trees. In Impruneta also is a fourteenth-century church with two beautiful della Robbias and a cloister. This is the home of the legend of the St. Luke Madonna which used in time of impending disaster to be carried into Florence in long procession; it now presides over the beginning of the grape harvest. There, too, a donkey- and cattle-fair takes place on the eighteenth of October.

Or one may make a pilgrimage because of some familiar lines or some association, to Vallombrosa, for instance, in the hills east of Florence, where, in the fall, maples blaze and beech are golden. Of it John Milton wrote:

> 'Thick as autumnal leaves that strow the brooks
> In Vallombrosa, where the Etrurian shades
> High over-arch'd imbower . . .'

> (*Paradise Lost*, Book I, ll. 302–304)

On the way one may discover little Etruscan Pelago, high on its hill among the olive groves. It was the birthplace of Lorenzo Ghiberti who spent years making the bronze doors of the baptistry in Florence.

Nearly every hill town claims some famous son. Pietro Vannucci, of Città della Pieve, as a boy was led by his father across the valley to Perugia and there set to study painting in the studio of Benedetto Bonfigli, who was painting the frescoes in the communal palace. He became in time the great Perugino. Norcia back in the Apennines was the birthplace of St. Benedict, founder of the Benedictine Order. Horace had his villa, his Sabine farm, almost in the shadow of Licenza. Raphael was born in Urbino. Todi boasts of Jacopone, whose *laude* were sung all over Italy. Palestrina gave its name to a musician known the world over.

Yet often what draws one to a hill town is rather some association with the Romans or the Etruscans, a bit of megalithic wall, some painted tombs, a fine collection of Etruscan cinerary urns, churches that once were Roman temples; sometimes it is a legend as that of the wolf of Gubbio; sometimes it is the beauty of a great cathedral, a lovely Lombard campanile, frescoes by some famous artist; the magnificence of Renaissance palaces; or a grouping of medieval towers against the skyline; often it is a combination of many things.

As you go up and down and in and out you are often conscious of a pride of place in the people of these hill towns. There are local festivals:

the great Palio in Siena; the Joust of the Saracens in Arezzo; the festival of the Ceri in Gubbio. Every village, be it one of no more than five thousand persons, has its own art gallery, *pinacoteca*, for art and craftsmanship are part of their proud tradition. So here they have collected whatever they can find, first of the work of local artists, but also that of others in some way associated with them, for the great artists travelled far and wide painting frescoes in the churches, carving fountains or pulpits on order. In these small art galleries one often finds an Etruscan collection, figurines, and vases, cinerary urns dug up in nearby fields, and broken bits from Roman temples or a yard or two of mosaic from a Roman pavement. If in their town they possess some great art work by a native son, they are sometimes very jealous, one is told, of its being removed, even temporarily, for display elsewhere. It is definitely theirs.

Usually on the walls of the town hall, either outside or inside, are displayed the armorial bearings of all the governors of the commune. And though they rarely honor their distinguished sons by naming streets for them—it is rather the great men of a united Italy, Cavour, Garibaldi, Mazzini, who are so honoured—they put marble plaques on the walls to mark the homes of their local artists, architects, philosophers, or mathematicians, or occasionally a statue in the middle of a piazza. So Certaldo in this day has put up a statue to Boccaccio, and a plaque over the door to his house, to Boccaccio whose bones several centuries ago they dispersed as unworthy of lying in their church. (Later they regretted this action, and ordered the construction of a new tomb.) If a native son was great enough, his house may now be set up as a museum; and one is shown, for a few hundred *lire*, his birthroom, the kitchen with its ancient fireplace for cooking, a bench or two, possibly a table, a few of his rough drawings or a page of manuscript. Marble plaques, too, may mark the *ringhiera* where possibly Dante at one time addressed the citizens or where Savonarola thundered forth.

These people like to show you the way to their treasures; their faces light up when you admire the town or tell them that the view is *bellissima*. This has been their home for many generations and every stone and shrine is part of their communal memory. A taxi driver may look out over the valley of the Trasimeno from the top of the hill at Cortona and discuss the battle when Hannibal routed the Roman

Flaminius, and tell of the bones still being found down there when men are plowing (probably those of medieval battles). These people have a pride of place, yet there is no stuffiness in their local loyalty, no flag waving; one might almost call it an inherited attitude. Browning once wrote:

> 'Open my heart and you will see
> Graved inside of it, "Italy".'
>
> *'De Gustibus'*

But it's not just Italy that these people are thinking of; it is Cortona, or Monterchi, or Gubbio, or Colle di Val d'Elsa, or whatever town they call their own.

Perhaps a corollary to this is the friendliness of these people. Ordinarily they show the stranger every courtesy. Once while we were taking pictures just below the village of Serra I dropped my glasses and found my loss an hour later down below in Lerici. We went back of course, and as we were ogling the ground where we had stopped, a group of peasant women came up the hill, each with a load on her head. Was I hunting my glasses? they asked, and being answered in the affirmative they announced with evident pleasure that I would find them in the store to the right just inside Serra. Find them there I did. How the word had been spread so that these women coming up the hill were aware of it, I shall never know. High in another village an elderly woman stopped us to ask where we came from, and hearing, was all friendliness. She had lost a husband in the last war, and so, alone, she had moved here from Trieste to be near relatives. The government was giving her two hundred *lire* a day (thirty-two cents). We remarked that she would live high on that, and she laughed. She was not begging. One other day in another town we were photographing the doorway of a fine old palace. Presently an aristocratic-looking woman came out and introduced herself. Would we like to come into the garden courtyard and see the ancient fountain and take a picture there? Of course we went, saw the fountain, a lovely bit, and there we met her husband and her children. Soon they were taking us up the long marble staircase to see the old palace and the frescoes on its walls. Their surname, we found, was that of the owner of the palace when it had been built in the 1500's. Once when I had been too long in hill towns and was greatly in need of a shampoo and set, I inquired of the hotel owner and manager in another ancient palace, and he offered to take me to a private house where his wife went for such services. It was a simple place, with no running water. The water, heated in the kitchen, was poured on my head from a pitcher with a sprinkler top, but the place was clean and good. When I left, the owner-operator came to the door with me, shook hands, and sent her maid to see me back to the hotel and to carry my raincoat. One Sunday noon, driving into Viterbo, I was desperate to find our hotel, the Nuovo Angelo. There had been a confusion of one-way streets and I had found myself driving up a steep and narrow way with the whole populace, it seemed, walking slowly in front of me and beside me, as usual paying absolutely no attention to an approaching motor car—horns are not allowed. All I could do was to go in low and race my engine as a warning signal. When I finally arrived in a level piazza, practically sweating blood, I stopped still. The piazza was a solid mass of cars, and of people having their Sunday gossip. There was still no sign of the New Angel. But there was a *carabiniere* in full Sunday regalia, white gloves and all, and I beckoned to him. He slipped through the crowd and came, and with great graciousness showed me the way, even moved people out of the path of the car. *Carabinieri* are almost everywhere gracious to strangers in Italy. Above the Camollia Gate at Siena there is a legend, *Cor Magis Tibi Sena Pandit*, which being freely translated reads: 'Wider than her gate Siena opens her heart to you.' A similar legend might well be inscribed over the gate of many a hill town.

2

Florence and the Hill Towns

'And bells say ding to bells that answer dong.'
Folgore, *Sonnets of the Week*
as translated by
DANTE GABRIEL ROSSETTI

FLORENCE lies in a valley, yet one thinks of her as the mother of all
that one finds in the hill towns of Tuscany and Umbria. To her one
goes first, and then out to the hill towns, the better to appreciate and
understand them. Or one visits the hill towns and then goes into
Florence, and here is the summing up, the climax of all that one has
seen: the art, the architecture, the sculpture, the bronze work, the
wood carving. But Florence is more than the Uffizi, the Pitti, San
Lorenzo, Santa Croce, and San Marco, more than Brunelleschi's dome,
or Giotto's campanile, the Bargello or the Palazzo Vecchio, more than
Masaccio's frescoes in the Carmine, or Benozzo Gozzoli's in the
Riccardi Palace, more than the *David* of Michelangelo or Cellini's
Perseus, more than the Archaeological Museum or the Stibbert
collection of medieval armor, more than the story of Dante, Savonarola, or the Medicis, more than the Boboli Gardens, Bellosguarda, or
the house of the Brownings. Florence is all this, but more, much more.

Florence is the bells in the morning, the moon coming up over San
Miniato, the narrow streets that are hardly more than slots, the overhanging eaves of the palaces, the clop-clop of the donkeys coming in
to market in the gray dawn. Florence is the smell of roasting chestnuts
in the fall, the fragrance of wistaria hanging over villa walls in the
spring. Florence is the fishermen lined up along the banks of the

muddy Arno on a Sunday morning with their shouts of joy over catching a tiny fish. Florence is the artisans on the left bank in their veritable holes in the wall. Florence is the shrines at street corners under the wrought-iron lanterns; the flower stand behind the Strozzi Palace, the strawmarket under its loggia, and the bronze boar in its bronze swamp, just beside the loggia. Florence is the little linen shops gone commercial, the tourist bait along the Ponte Vecchio and the Lungarno, the boys on bicycles carrying carved unfinished chairs, the hand-carved frames of mirrors, not yet gilded, the tooled leather. Florence is its great factories hidden fortunately from the casual visitor by some sort of superzoning. Yes, Florence is even the food, the various *pasta*, the tender *cipollini* that are so delicious, the artichokes and *finocchio*, the *risotto* and the *bel paese* cheese. Florence is the meeting of the stunningly dressed women of an afternoon at Doney's for tea or *cinzano*, or a concert in the Sala of the Cinquecento of the Palazzo Vecchio. Florence is the flower pots on the walls of the villas that climb the hills around, the view from the Piazzale Michelangelo at dusk with the lights just coming on over the domes and towers and roofs and bridges, the reflections in the Arno of an evening, the purple shadings in the sky. Florence is its festivals, the caging of the crickets in the Cascine on Ascension Day, the Easter lighting of the *Scoppio* before the *duomo*, the 'futball' games. Florence is the happy commingling of the present and the past, of history and legend. So, too, are the hill towns.

Pelasgian, Umbrian, or Etruscan in their origins, they were already old behind their walls when Florence was an unprotected cluster of houses by the river, a place of barter only. For centuries from these earliest days, Romans, Goths, Lombards, swept past and over and all around through Tuscany and Umbria, leaving not only immediate devastation, but also, as some stayed to colonize, baths, temples, theaters, churches, campaniles, an architectural style, or a sculptural motif. Then came Charlemagne in the late eighth century (crowned in 800), establishing a feudal system. Presently the communes emerged, giving fealty to emperor or pope, and gradually winning greater and greater independence with their consuls or *priori* elected by the guilds, their *podestà* or *gonfaloniere* and *capitano del popolo*, their communal palaces, and their *bargellos*. To untangle the course of history of the

Italian communes, to trace the changing affiliations of town with town, even of parties within a given town, and of the struggles with outside invaders is a job only for experts, and I shall not attempt it here.

Meantime, Florence, a thriving city of merchants already by the year 1000, had become by the end of the twelfth century a great city-state that was influencing life and customs throughout Europe as well as those in all the country round, shipping their textiles everywhere, from London to Turkey, combing Italy and far places beyond the mountains and the seas for the materials of manufacture, setting up a banking system that has persisted to this day.

From time to time it subjugated neighboring cities, Arezzo, Cortona, Pisa, Volterra, even Siena, besides smaller towns. Guelf in sympathies, it formed the Tuscan League and forced into town the nobles living in their lonely *castelli* surrounded only by their retainers. There these new citizens built towers often two or three hundred feet in height and fortified them against their enemies—so that the skyline bristled as it did in many a hill town, as it does today in a greatly modified degree in San Gimignano. Later they were required to lower these to no more than one hundred feet. Towns were Guelf or Ghibelline according as the dominant element supported pope or emperor, and their battlements told the tale; those of the Guelfs were straight across the top; those of the Ghibellines were forked. Many were the wars between the cities. Florence and Siena particularly came to blows. Once only in the wars Siena worsted Florence, at the battle of Montaperti. So it was also between families. Woe to the Ghibelline who dared to marry Guelf, or the Guelf who eloped with Ghibelline.

To explore the streets of Florence, to ask the meaning of their names, to find out who lived here and worked there is to stir one's curiosity and to re-evoke for oneself something of the life and atmosphere of those centuries, twelfth, thirteenth, fourteenth, fifteenth, and sixteenth, when Florence was the mercantile and artistic center of all this north-central part of Italy. There is of course a Via Guelfa and a Via Ghibellina, though they are not at right angles as in Cortona. More significant, for they are in the old city, are the Via de' Cimatori, dei Calzaioli, Via Calimala, Corso dei Tintori, Piazza del Lana, Via Condotta, dei Malcontenti, Borgo Allegri, Via del' Orivolo, dei Velluti, delle Conce, Via Pelliceria, Piazza del Tiratoio. Each has its

story—the street of the sheep shearers, of the hosiery makers, of the guild of finished cloth, of the dyers, the piazza of the wool guild, the street of the pack mules, the street of the unhappy on their way to execution (an understatement if ever there was one), the Borgo of the happy, of the clock, of those who first developed silk velvet from whose name the word velvet is derived, the street of the tanneries, of skin and leather dressing, of the fulling mill.

One sees in imagination the flocks of sheep being driven by their herders into town from the high pastures of the Tuscan hills. Perhaps even the boy Giotto may have occasionally come along from those hills by Vespignano. (There, it is reputed, Cimabue once saw him watching sheep and drawing on a rock the figure of a lamb and brought the boy back to his studio in Florence and so started a great artist on his way.) One visualizes the dyers (*tintori*) at their cauldrons mixing dyes from plants and lichens brought from everywhere, from the fields of Italy, from France, from the Levant. Fortunes were made in Florence from dyes and methods of dyeing. Even a war with Volterra was once fought for possession of the alum, a mordant found in Volterra's hills.

As one walks through the Borgo Allegri, one likes to think of Cimabue, and Ghiberti, and Antonio Rossellino, all with studios on the street; but one likes still more to remember the legend that when Cimabue finished his *Madonna* and it was carried through the streets to be placed in Santa Maria Novella, the populace rejoiced so mightily that ever afterward the street was called the Borgo of the Happy. No doubt, as on other such occasions, shops were closed, the church bells rung, and the great procession was accompanied by the sounding of trumpets. Unfortunately for the story, the Allegri family also lived on this street. There must have been great rejoicing, too, on that March day, the fifteenth, of 1352, when the great clock of the Palazzo Vecchio first struck the hours for everyone to hear. It had been made on the Via Orivolo, a corruption of Orologio, meaning clock. As yet only a few had watches or clocks. The matin bells of the churches had rung the men and boys to work; the vesper bells had told them it was time to quit.

One might suppose that all who could would flee away from the Via delle Conce, yet here, tradition says, the Medici themselves came to live during the plague, seeking protection in the salutary air of the tanpits. Why it was salutary is anyone's guess; perhaps the acid tanbark discouraged rats, and rats with their fleas, though no one knew it then, were carriers of the plague. Though there is no street sign to indicate the fact, one remembers, too, that until Cosimo dei Medici gave possession of the Ponte Vecchio to the goldsmiths and jewelers, the bridge was lined with butcher shops, some forty of them.

One might follow other streets named for great Florentine families, whose palaces once lined the street, leaders in their guilds. The Acciaiuoli made their fortune in iron, and were of the blacksmith guild, those men, who, like 'Il Caparra', made the lanterns to hang at the corners of palaces, the brackets, the cistern tops, the wrought-iron gates, the brass, the copper, and bronze vessels. (Some of the Acciaiuoli were bankers, too.) The Bardi, the Mozzi (both on the far side of the Arno), the Cerchi, the Albizzi, all were banking families. They and their successors in a sense ruled all Europe economically in the thirteenth and fourteenth and fifteenth centuries, the men whose money counters (*banchi*) gave the name to a world-wide institution, whose £. s. d. have left their symbols in English currency. They were of one of the seven ruling guilds of Florence. This guild was the strictest and most religious of them all. Their members attended mass regularly, had prayers in the family in the morning, opened the day at their counters with religious services. When they had made their peace with God what difference did the rate of interest make!

In the late Middle Ages Florence was, as today, the fashion center of its world, at least so far as finished goods were concerned. It not only developed woollen goods from raw materials, but it 'finished' woollen goods, as many as ten thousand pieces a year, brought from England and Flanders and France. Each piece sent out bore the 'Calimala' stamp, the guarantee that it had been weighed, measured, inspected, and was true to specifications. A high ethical standard was the tradition of the guild; members were forbidden to bet or swear or take part in games of chance after dark. Every boy when at sixteen he joined the guild was soon taught his responsibility as a craftsman and as a citizen. At the height of their activity in Florence the wool and Calimala and related guilds numbered better than thirty thousand members. There were pools where wool was washed, one in front of Ognissanti. There were carders, weavers, fullers, those who skillfully

combined silk with gold and silver thread in fine lacework, those who
wrought brocades, who painted designs on muslin or appliqued gems
on linen or on lace. There were dyers. In the narrow streets all the way
from Via Calimala to Ponte Carraia from the windows of the upper
stories, wool or fabrics were hung out drying. Colors were magnificent, all those of an autumn sunset sky, rose and green, gold, scarlet,
storm-cloud blue and sky-blue, olive and ivory, yellow, oyster-white,
and brown. Wagons and donkey carts, mules with their packs and
drivers streamed across the bridges bound for little boats, perhaps at
Signa, or ships at Porto Pisano. Others were bringing back from
everywhere loads of materials to be worked on.

One can surmise how all this business activity must have reacted on
the country around. Though not all the towns were similarly organized
by guilds, they had their own artisans of various kinds: blacksmiths who
wrought their own lanterns of local design, wellheads, and brackets;
their own goldsmiths; workers in copper, brass, and bronze; their own
stone masons and potters; their own tanners and leather-workers.

Yet Florence, too, must be supplied not only with food from the
fields, but with wool, so far as possible, with linen or raw flax, with
silk thread from the cocoons, with mulberry leaves to feed the silkworms, with dye stuffs and plants, with oak bark for tanning, with
wood for staves and hoops, for barrels and vats, and hammer handles,
as well as wood of various kinds for fine inlay work on doors, and for
the carving of choir stalls or wooden crucifixes, with simples for
apothecaries, with furs and hides for making boots, buskins, and
galosce, and for binding books, with reeds and straw for plaiting
baskets, with stone and marble, with iron from Elba and adjoining
Tuscany, with tin, gold, and silver from overseas.

The monasteries had early taken to growing flax in their garden
plots, and had filled their cupboards with fine linen. They taught the
peasants also to grow the flax, to make it into linen thread, and weave
it into garments. Then the nuns in the convents taught the women of
the aristocracy how to fashion lace. Soon women in various hill towns
were making laces of local design, so that even today laces of Assisi
differ in design from those of Borgo Sansepolcro (not a hill town
though with the character of one), those of Orvieto from those of
Arezzo, or Camerino, or Aquila.

By the end of the fourteenth century Florence was importing from the valley of the Rhône silkworms and the leaves to feed them; and so it passed a statute that on every *podere* (the plot of one peasant in the farm of a large landholder) five mulberry trees must be planted yearly until the total should come to fifty. So doubtless began the custom, still prevalent, of planting mulberry trees among the vines, the leaves for silkworms, the trees for support for grapevines. The agricultural workers and the local transportation workers must have played a heavy part in Florence's prosperity, as did the navigators and the bookkeepers.

Meanwhile Florence, as also the hill towns, had been blooming intellectually and artistically. Architects, sculptors, painters, woodworkers, poets, prose writers, statesmen, patrons of art, made Florence their home and intermittently the scene of their work: Dante, Boccaccio, Machiavelli, Cimabue, Taddeo Gaddi, Filippo Lippi, Ghirlandaio, the della Robbias, Michelozzo, Michelangelo, and others. Sometimes they went away, occasionally spending months or years executing some order in another town. Giotto travelled to Assisi to paint frescoes in the church of San Francesco, went also to Urbino and other towns. Gozzoli painted frescoes in Montefalco and San Gimignano, where Ghirlandaio also painted. Fra Angelico was called to Orvieto. Sangallo built palaces and churches in many places, notably at Montepulciano, and the della Robbias left their ceramics up and down the land. So also other artists from other towns came and went, sometimes even to Florence; Luca Signorelli from Cortona, Maitani from Siena, Mino da Fiesole from Poppi, and the great Arnolfo from Colle di Val d'Elsa. It was as if a spark that had lain long buried in the ashes, only now and then showing a bit of life, had finally glowed and then taken fire.

There were reasons, of course. As trade had flourished, raw materials had become more abundant: gold, silver, tin, iron, copper, stone, marble, and the materials for mixing paints and glazing ceramics. Then, too, many men now had money; they could afford to build palaces, to decorate them with frescoes and (later) paintings, with carved and hooded fireplaces, with beautiful windows such as those in the Florentine Bargello, with statues all around the courtyard, and loggias where one could sit and take the air. The greater guilds, too, had money, especially the wool and Calimala guilds, who for a time financed much of the building of the *duomo*. The men of Florence had decided, too, to order new bronze doors for the baptistry and sent out word all over Italy for artists to assemble for a competition. When they came, seven only were accepted as sufficiently skilled to enter the trials, and of the seven, five were men from the hills.

Whether this spark that now blazed in Florence and across the Italian hills had been there in its ashes from Etruscan days, quiescent until such time as trade had flourished, raw materials had become abundant, when men had wealth, were travelling, reading, being subjected to new ideas, we shall never know. What we do know is that Florence was ringed about with towns once Etruscan: Fiesole, Pelago, Arezzo, Cortona, Perugia, Chiusi, Chianciano, Sarteano, Montepulciano, Volterra, Todi, Orte, and probably many others long since vanished. We know, too, that the Etruscans were accomplished artists, that they chiseled, and painted, and fashioned ceramics, made gold work such as no one since has known, that everything they worked with was made beautiful, safety pins, mirrors, goblets, lamps, amphorae, and braziers. Beauty was in their blood, was of their tradition. Italians ever since have been true to this tradition; even their commonest pieces of equipment are made with an eye to their beauty as well as to their utility.

The spark in these men of Italy was so potent or perhaps their training so fundamental in the *bottegas* of their masters that artists could work in various mediums. Michelangelo was a sculptor and an architect. Giotto painted frescoes and built a campanile. Brunelleschi was a goldsmith yet he built the dome of the cathedral of Florence and carved a wooden crucifix for Santa Maria Novella. Verrocchio was a goldsmith, a sculptor working in both bronze and marble, and a musician. Buontalenti was an architect, yet he laid out a great portion of the Boboli Gardens and painted scenery for one of Tasso's pastorals. Donatello worked in marble yet he could carve mirror frames. Leonardo da Vinci could paint a *Last Supper* and design a bridge. Vasari, the architect of the Uffizi, in his *Lives of the Painters* once wrote: 'We seldom find a man distinguished in one art who cannot easily excel in other arts.'

Yet despite the flourishing of art, life in Florence as elsewhere in the thirteenth, fourteenth, fifteenth, and sixteenth centuries, was austere at best, and dangerous. Even palaces, elegant as they were, were not built for comfort. Plagues swept off thousands in a single season. Droughts succeeded floods. Feuds were a commonplace. At night one never knew, on venturing out, what enemy lurked in the shadows around a corner with his knife or bludgeon ready. *Amici—nemici Parenti—serpenti Cugini—assassini Fratelli—coltelli* (Friends—enemies Relatives—snakes Cousins—assassins Brothers—knives) read an inscription on one of the palaces on the Corso dei Tintori. One has but to read Benvenuto Cellini to know how cheap life was. Wars were a summer occupation. As husbands, fathers, or sons failed to return, wives and mothers mourned, singing a song grown familiar through many years of women's grieving:

> 'Gather up his tools and bring them
> With his apron of brown leather.
> Father, wilt thou not be going
> To thy work this summer weather?
> Father slain and brother wounded—
> They have struck them down together!'
>
> Refrain of folksong of old Florence[55]*

Merchants travelled far as they went about their business, yet brigands ambushed highways and pirates raided ships at sea. Infant mortality was incredibly high. The ordinary workman got a pittance as wages. It was not unusual for one fourth of the population of Florence to be on relief.

The houses of the people in the cities were for long usually of wood, occasionally of stone; their roofs were merely thatched. Conflagrations were not uncommon. Other than the fires of the kitchen, the smoke from which was carried up through a hole in the roof, no one had heat in winter, save possibly as today they may have used *scaldini*, small receptacles filled with glowing charcoal. Sometimes windows were boarded over to keep out cold, or covered with oiled silk or linen to let in light. Furniture was sparse. The tables from which they ate were boards on trestles, the seats were benches, except for the master of the

* Numbers refer to the bibliography beginning on page 249.

house who had a chair. Husbands and wives often ate from the same slab of bread, which served as a plate. Chickens strolled in through the open door and often had to be shooed away.

Sanitary arrangements were few, though in the palaces one may see occasional attempts at such. In the street there was usually a shallow ditch where slops were thrown. Children and women squatted where they could; men sought a convenient corner, and dogs, as ever, found substitutes for grass. Only a heavy rain must have made streets tolerable. Yet there were in Florence, and probably elsewhere, some sanitary laws. Diseased animals must not be 'allowed to drink' from 'public fountains'. In the inns plates and eating utensils must be clean, and pots must be polished. Swallows in the streets were for some reason protected; maybe they helped to reduce the swarms of flies breeding there on refuse.

But life was not altogether bleak so long as one could eat and play, take vengeance on one's enemies, and receive absolution for one's wicked deeds.

To be sure, the ordinary man never had an elaborate diet. Millet and chestnuts, later corn and wheat, had always provided his daily bread and many stomach-warming stuffs. Hares and birds that he could snare, the little fish in streams, eggs and cheese, pine nuts and fruit, wine and oil, sometimes clover juice and 'herbage' of various kinds supplied his other needs. At the inns where the spit turned constantly, browning ducks and geese, pigeons, pheasants, and larks, perhaps one could have a thick soup, a *polenta*, or a *frito misto*, made of bits and pieces, possibly similar to our hash (though today it is something quite different).

Yet while the simple man ate simply, the rich often held great banquets, vying with each other in display, especially when marrying off a daughter or entertaining some visiting dignitary. On such occasions there might be eels, or kids 'boiled in white wine', geese stuffed with quinces and garlic, molded jellies of fruit or wine. When Pius II once stopped in Mantua on his travels, he was presented with three fat steers that had been 'fed on turnips', 'washed' regularly in 'warm water, combed every day and bedded down on clean straw'.[19] He relished that meat and noted it in his *Memoirs*; he had never tasted 'sweeter'. Of course vegetables were available, marrows, leeks, cabbages, artichokes among them. There were nuts of various kinds and many fruits. Cucumbers were an appetizer, usually eaten outside before the banquet began. Guests, after a preliminary bath in the Arno, entered in the order of their rank.

In the market places of an evening men and boys could gather round the storytellers. There were occasional fables then as now. Both children and grownups loved them. There had been a woman, so the story went, who had over her door a bas-relief of a hen to show that she sold eggs. She always had eggs—no shortage ever—till people began to wonder how she came by so many. One day a neighbor entering found her away, and decided to investigate, as neighbors sometimes will. In a cupboard a hen was clucking, and it said:

'Cocode! Dear me!—Where can Furicchia be?
Cocode! Furicchia mine—Bring me some warm red wine,
Cocode! These eggs I have laid. Cocode! now six for your
          trade.
Cocode! Now these are mine. Bring me quickly the warm red
          wine.
Cocode! Take them away; Many more further will I lay,
And thou wilt be a lady grand, As fine as any in the land;
And should it happen that anyone, Drinks of this wine as I
          have done,
Eggs like me she will surely lay; That is the secret, that is the
          way.
Cocode! Cocode.'[55]

The prying neighbor quickly helped herself to the warm red wine on the hearth, and hurried home. Presently she too was clucking—but you know the rest. Perhaps it was amusement they found in that story, and perhaps it was a warning. Who knows? There were many kinds of stories.

In the piazzas, too, there was often music, sometimes wandering minstrels, for there were many who went about, or possibly a group of *laudesi*. Often there were festivals of the saints with processions of priests in gorgeous vestments, carrying candles and sacred insignia.

There were the annual celebrations of the guilds with games and processions and banquets, carnivals in the Piazza of Santa Maria Novella, tournaments in the piazza before Santa Croce. At home or in the inns men played backgammon or chess perhaps.

Of course children had fun of their own devising, though by city law they could not spin tops on the street or throw stones at fish in the Arno. A game they liked was Guelf and Ghibelline. Two self-appointed captains, linking hands, gathered in friends or casual persons passing on the street and lined them up according to their party affiliations. (In the Middle Ages in Italy it was always as if election year.) At the end a mighty tug of war ensued.

But what did the women do for amusement? Their work was never done, tending babies, giving the children their Saturday bath, looking after household duties, helping friends in trouble, praying in the churches, carrying water from the fountains, washing in the cold water of the public washing basins. Doubtless they stopped at the fountains to pass the time of day, but probably they found their recreation mostly sitting outdoors in the shade in the summer or in the sun in winter, knitting, weaving, winding silk from the cocoons, plaiting straw, and chatting with one another.

In the hill towns life was probably much the same as in Florence. There, too, were the *nobili*, the *popolani*, the donkey-boys, and artisans, plus many an agricultural worker who went with the morning light, came back at dusk carrying his scythe or pruning knives, or digging tools, or slowly trudging behind his oxen up the hill. Of course these little farmers shared the harvest with their landlords, the ownership of the oxen also. The landowners in turn paid the taxes, the hire of supplementary labor, the cost of stables, sheds, cottages, and their maintenance. Both men and women on the farm had their routine. The women did what traditionally has been women's work. They cared for the chickens, geese, ducks, gathered the eggs, collected the down. They looked after the bees, extracted the honey, made beeswax and candles. They churned the butter, molded the cheese for home consumption. (Much of the cheese for Florence actually came from outside Tuscany, from as far away sometimes as Sardinia and Sicily.) They grew sage and other herbs and whatever flowers they had. They prepared the silk from the cocoons, the thread from the flax, and no doubt wove it into tunics and shirts for their menfolk, into skirts and simple dresses, often of canvas, for themselves.

But the women of the upper classes, how did they employ their time? Besides the ordering of their households, watching from the windows what was going on in the street, and visiting with their friends, they no doubt spent much time in the planning and execution of their wardrobes. In the fourteenth century in Florence and in many other towns both men and women were indulging in luxury in dress. Sumptuary laws were consequently enacted to curb this extravagance and to promote democracy. These regulated fashions forbade, for instance, buttons on one's garments, fringes, ermine, or any display of jewelry. On those who dared to disobey heavy fines were imposed. Yet women were quick to find ways of evasion. A half-button was no button, they argued, and often got away with the argument. A fringe on a hood was detachable, and therefore only a wreath. A ribbon to tie on some artificial flowers was a necessity, not a luxury. (One can almost see them whispering their secrets to one another.) Civil authorities and the dignitaries of the church may have thought that things had gone too far, yet they could not altogether prevent what they deprecated. They finally all but gave up, for 'what the woman wanteth, God wanteth, and what God wanteth, cometh to pass'.[56] What wonder indeed with all the wealth of elaborate textiles that Florence had been producing!

Benozzo Gozzoli painting in the chapel of the Medici the procession of the Magi showed Cosimo, Piero, and Lorenzo dei Medici in such costumes, their horses caparisoned in gold. Giotto, Perugino, Pinturicchio, even Fra Angelico, monk though he was, and many others had seen such stuffs. Luca Signorelli, Vasari reports, loved to wear fine clothes. So did Bacci (Sodoma). One has indeed but to walk through art galleries in Florence or Siena or any town to see them for oneself in countless paintings of the fourteenth, fifteenth, and sixteenth centuries: jackets elaborately conceived and brocaded, fur-trimmed perhaps, or adorned with lace ruffles; velvet hats and toques; silken tights; soft buskins for the feet or leggings heavily overcast with gold. The men indeed were robed as royally as the women. These silks, satins, and velvets catch the light and shimmer; they look soft to touch, like dogs' ears; they fall in folds, and sometimes, as in Botticelli's paintings, they flow away as gracefully as summer clouds. Always the Madonna is queen of heaven, rarely a simple peasant girl caught unaware in a role she had not dreamed of. The friars in their habits of muted colors are still elegant. The robes of angels have frequently a band of rich embroidery. Did Florence export its textiles to heaven? Or had the angels been shoplifting when they came to Florence?

But what did the simple people wear? The paintings show the men of the fields and hills in coarse wool or linen tunics, belted, their legs and feet bare, or if not bare, shod in heavy leather *galosce* or in moccasins, even in wooden shoes, the hair of their heads all ruffled up. The artisans at their benches were by no means all simple men (though many were), but while at work they may have worn a costume. The goldsmiths, we are told, wore gold-colored smocks with their leather aprons. What better advertisement of their wares!

All the sophistication of the Renaissance had been building up gradually over several centuries and came to its climax in the fifteenth and sixteenth centuries. The hill towns had felt its impact as had Florence; they had, as the major cities, their quota of educated men, not just artists and artisans, but men who wrote books and treatises and poetry. Arezzo, perhaps, had had more than most. Besides Vasari, it claimed Petrarch, who actually, though he had been born there, had lived his life elsewhere. As early as the eleventh century Guido d'Arezzo (Monaco) had developed a system of musical notation which became the basis of our modern scale. Fra Guittone d'Arezzo of the mid-thirteenth century was one of the early Tuscan poets, a writer of sonnets, love poems, and letters. Cenne della Chitarra was a minstrel of considerable repute. Pietro Aretino was a well-known satirist. Poets had been flourishing in Italy; indeed many everyday people were writing verses. Folgore of San Gimignano in the thirteenth century was one of the gayer Tuscan poets. St. Francis of Assisi himself went through the country begging and singing as he went. He is known especially for his 'Canticle of the Sun':[3]

'Praised be my Lord God with all his creatures; and specially our brother the sun, who brings us the day, and who brings us the light; fair is he, and shining with a very great splendour; O Lord, he signifies to us thee!

Praised be my Lord for our sister the moon, and for the stars, the which he has set clear and lovely in heaven.

Praised be my Lord for our brother the wind, and for air and cloud, calms and all weather, by the which thou upholdest in life all creatures.

Praised be my Lord for our sister water, who is very serviceable unto us, and humble, and precious, and clean.

Praised be my Lord for our brother fire, through whom thou givest us light in the darkness; and he is bright, and pleasant, and very mighty, and strong.

Praised be my Lord for our mother the earth, the which doth sustain us and keep us, and bringeth forth divers fruits, and flowers of many colours, and grass.

. . . .
. . . .

Praise ye, and bless ye the Lord, and give thanks unto him, and serve him with great humility.'

Jacopone of Todi, also,

> 'That son of Italy who tried to blow
> 'Ere Dante came, the trump of sacred song'
>
> MATTHEW ARNOLD, *Austerity of Poetry*

was a popular poet of the Franciscan order. Yet it was not simply the writing of verse that evidenced the general intellectual awareness of men. Cecco d'Ascoli Piceno, though he, too, dabbled in verse, was an astrologer, mathematician, and physician, burned at the stake in Florence in the fourteenth century for his supposed scientific heresy. In Colle di Val d'Elsa, Cennino di Drea Cennini, pupil of Agnolo Gaddi, though no great painter, wrote a long treatise on color and the methods and vehicles of painting. The great Leonardo, born on a hilltop near Vinci, in Tuscany, was an inventor, painter, architect, and sculptor.

Education was widespread. Even in the twelfth century boys at home were being taught their ABC's, learning the stories of Greek and Roman mythology, singing Latin hymns. Many of them were sent to school in monasteries, which having been the guardians of knowledge through the Dark Ages, conducted schools open to both men and boys. It had been the custom in these monastery schools to teach many things, not only literature, philosophy, government, but calligraphy, architecture, and the more practical arts of roadmaking and agriculture. There had been cathedral schools as well, those conducted by a priest or clerk, or someone who set himself up as a schoolmaster.

Besides, universities had been growing up in many parts of Italy. As early as the eleventh century the University of Salerno was well known for its medical school, for in southern Italy men had learned much from the Saracens of the practice of Arab and Greek medicine. There even the dissection of pigs was practised in an effort to discover the purposes and processes of various organs. Frederick II of Sicily had established in the University of Naples a chair of anatomy. Physicians were using cold baths for reducing fever, and sending patients off to mineral springs for various ailments. It was quite usual for the rich of Florence to frequent the baths in valleys near Siena. In the north there were universities in Milan, Padua, Modena, Vercelli, Vicenza, later at Arezzo, Siena, Perugia. But the greatest of them all was that of Bologna which specialized in civil and canon law, though it included also training in the trivium (grammar, logic, and rhetoric), and quadrivium (music, arithmetic, geometry, astronomy). As early as 1200 ten thousand men were already students at Bologna. They came not only from Italy but from all Europe.

Perhaps there remained in this northern country a kind of literary tradition that harked back to Rome. Arezzo was still proud of Maecenas, a native son, who at his home in Rome entertained Horace and Virgil and was a friend of the great Augustus. The younger Pliny of Como on the lake had encouraged education in terms reminding one of those of today. In his *Epistles* he tells of establishing a library; he arranged what we would call scholarships for students; for the setting up of a university at Como, he offered a challenge fund, one third of what would be necessary provided the parents of prospective students would give the other two thirds.

In the towns, of course, the public meetings in the piazzas and the churches furnished all the education that many of the people had. High-born women undoubtedly had some schooling. In the fifteenth and sixteenth centuries it was not unusual for a woman to make formal addresses or write poetry not only in Italian but in Latin or Greek. From the early days of the University of Bologna some women had been employed as instructors in law, mathematics, even in anatomy. Ordinarily, however, the girls, unless admitted to convents, had very little training except that thrust upon them by the round of daily life. The paintings in the churches, the frescoes depicting Bible stories or the lives of saints were their education, and that also of those illiterate persons who worked the fields and drove the donkey carts. The stories that came down to them from days long gone were passed around, of Santa Fina perhaps, of Santa Margharita of Cortona and her little dog, of St. Francis, of St. Jerome, and St. Augustine and many another, or of the founding of the order of St. Benedict at Vallombrosa.

San Miniato, built in the eleventh century, stands on a hill across the Arno amid orchards of 'silvered olives' and great pointed cypresses. Surrounded by its *campo santo*, it is a quiet place and very beautiful. From it one looks on Florence in its valley, and on the higher hills around, to west, north, and east. Much undoubtedly through the centuries has happened there that men remember, but one story, part history, part legend, that has its setting there, gives it significance. It happened that in Florence one Giovanni Gualberto had a brother whom he dearly loved, and this brother was killed. As was the custom, Giovanni swore vengeance on the assassin. One evening not long afterwards as he was climbing the hill of San Miniato toward his father's home he met the murderer unarmed. The man knelt at his feet begging mercy and reminding Gualberto that this was Good Friday, that even Christ upon the cross had prayed for them who crucified him. Gualberto, stricken with compassion, struggled with himself. Then he 'held out his hand, raised the suppliant from the ground and embraced him'; and went again on his way. Entering San Miniato 'he knelt down before the crucifix' and begged of Christ forgiveness; whereupon looking up he saw the head of Christ bend toward him. At once desire for worldly things fled away, and against the wishes of his wealthy father he entered the monastery and took the vows of a Benedictine. Several years later the abbot died and Gualberto was chosen to succeed him. He refused. Instead, he took himself to the hills to what is now Vallombrosa, built himself a hut, and became a hermit. Gradually others associated themselves with him. Finally he felt constrained to gather them into an order and imposed upon them the rule of St. Benedict, imposing also the rule of silence. In later years the rulers of the Vallombrosa order were members of the Senate of Florence. To the poor they distributed scores of thousands of loaves of bread and on the mountainsides all around they planted thousands of beech trees. In the fall today the beech trees of Vallombrosa glow in the sunlight and as they fade they take on that peculiar yellow that means Florence to the visitors that love her.

Yes, Florence is its churches and its down-to-earth activity, a commingling of past and present, of history and legend, a blending of man's handiwork and natural beauty; and the hill towns of Tuscany and Umbria, and even of the Marches, are a reflection of what she was and is.

Tuscany

3

Volterra

'From lordly Volaterrae,
Where scowls the far-famed hold
Piled by the hands of giants
For godlike kings of old.'

MACAULAY

DRIVING along a country road in Tuscany on any rainy day one's
eye is caught by the great grass-green umbrellas, with red
handles, carried by the people as they trudge along behind their
donkeys. These are almost a symbol of Tuscany, especially in the
west. Though Italy is not a large country, except from north to south,
it is divided in many ways, by mountains and by valleys. We are told
that 'only one fifth of Italy is flat land', and most of that is along the
wide river valleys in the north. As one moves from province to
province or from valley to valley, one encounters not only varying
dialects and traditions, but varying local ways of doing common
things, different patterns of strawstacks, different methods of supporting grapevines, or of hanging up the yellow corn to dry. To watch
for these is one of the delights of following country roads, particularly
back roads. In Italy 'over the hill' is often 'far away'.

It is fun, for instance, to go straight from San Gimignano to the
high Volterra road, instead of going around the usual way by Poggibonsi. One crisscrosses fertile valleys, where the gray and green of
olive leaves all but twinkle in the wind, where in the fall blue grapes
in bunches measuring often eight to ten inches in length hang on vines
festooned from mulberry tree to mulberry tree. The steeper hills are

covered with chestnut and ilex trees and the banks are purple with heather. Once on the asphalted road one is soon in a different countryside. The woods, orchards, and vineyards are gone. There is a high, rolling plateau, and a relatively desolate country. An occasional lonely tower stands out, centuries old and crumbling, and now and then a clump of trees to mark a farmhouse surrounded by its fields. The beehive strawstacks so familiar in northern Tuscany have given place to great rectangular yellow stacks, lacking only doors, windows, and chimneys to make them seem like houses. They have pitched roofs of straw, and eaves, and across the ridgepole from side to side run ropes weighted down at either end with rocks. This bespeaks a windy country. Then all at once across a valley rises gray Volterra with its fortress and battlemented towers, and walls.

Most people, however, will go to Volterra direct from Florence along the winding road past the American war cemetery under its pine-clad hills and through Poggibonsi, a center of Chianti wineries. If one should be coming from Siena instead, one should make a point of driving half a kilometer off the highroad to visit the medieval village of Monteriggioni, its walls and fourteen towers intact, its cistern in the center of its broad piazza, its single twelfth-century church. Dante mentions the town in his *Inferno*. Built originally as a bulwark in Siena's wars with Florence, it passed from one to the other and back again. Today it is occupied by the workers in the fields around. It has little but a smithie, a general store, the public laundry-place, old stone houses decked out with flower pots. Through the high narrow gate by which one enters and leaves there is a lovely view across rolling fields.

Some have called Volterra grim; others have referred to it as 'one of the most majestic and awe-inspiring sites of Italy'. Its position and its history make it so. The ancient Etruscan Velathri, it was probably settled soon after Vetulonia and Tarquinia in the ninth or eighth century B.C. Its walls of huge blocks of rock, unmortared, were then, it is estimated, five miles around. Its population may well have been made up largely of metallurgical workers. In the third century B.C. it fell to the Romans, after a long siege. Its proud boast indeed is that never save by starvation or some sort of double dealing has it been conquered. During the second Punic War it furnished to Scipio timbers

Volterra

for ships, and grain. Centuries later it became for a short time a residence of Lombard rulers. Though a commune in the Middle Ages and Ghibelline, it became in effect a pawn in the struggles between Florence and Pisa. For a while it paid a heavy tribute to Florence. Later Lorenzo dei Medici took Volterra over as he took so many towns. It was then that the great fortress, built in the fourteenth century on an Etruscan foundation, was greatly enlarged.

Perhaps it is the countryside around that makes people call Volterra grim. Perhaps it is that forbidding *fortezza*, now a prison, and the high walls that nearly surround the town. Perhaps it is the great psychopathic hospital close by that sheds its aura on the city, as if there were a subtle sympathy between men's deranged minds and the barrenness of nature.

One does not here look out on many pleasant vineyards and olive orchards as in so much of Tuscany. The land is largely gypseous, a clay soil useful for many purposes, satisfactory for grain but unsuitable for the growing of grapes and other fruits. The wine from grapes grown on such soil is usually acid and ill-flavored. Just to the south is a range known as the Metalliferous Hills, with which undoubtedly the Etruscans were familiar, as they were with the similar metal deposits of Elba. And for miles around for a thousand or two thousand years there have been quarries for alabaster, salt, sulphur, and alum. This earth is indeed still yielding the raw materials of manufacture. On any clear day plumes of steam can be seen rising from Lardarello. It is the site of a modern borax plant. Near Casciano to the north there have been mineral springs known supposedly from Roman days, and developed possibly by the Countess Matilda in the eleventh century. Along the river valley from Cecina are old salt diggings and also mineral springs.

Yet far more grim and threatening to Volterra than this rather sterile countryside are the *balze* to the north of the town, ugly jagged chasms, landslides really, that are slowly eating away the town itself. To be sure, it was these that first uncovered in the 1700's the Etruscan necropolis, but they carried also to the valley below two churches dating from the seventh century, a monastery, and houses. Gradually through the years the town is slipping down the hill; it is as if a slow curse lay upon it.

Yet as one approaches along the parkway underneath the walls and comes into the main piazza, one becomes aware rather of a beautiful medieval city, unspoiled by too many tourists. On the east side stands the Palazzo Pretorio of the thirteenth century with its open arcades on the ground floor where markets are held, its simple twin-light, round-arched windows with slightly pointed bearing arches, its heavy Porcellino tower, supposedly named for the sculptured animal on the bracket high above. Lower, on the southeast corner there is a small unmistakable pig. Directly across the piazza backing up to the cathedral is the Palazzo dei Priori (1208–1254), with its clock, its slender tower in two stages, its heavy cornice and battlements, its façade adorned with coats of arms of the many *podestà* of the town, its Florentine lions at the corners. Inside, in a room to the left of the entrance, there are many more coats of arms, and upstairs is the local art gallery, worth seeing for works of Luca Signorelli, Domenico Ghirlandaio, Taddeo di Bartolo, Mascagni, Stefano di Antonio Vanni, and various other Florentine, Sienese, and Volterran painters. If one has zeal to climb the bell tower, one can on a clear day see as far as Elba to the southwest and to the La Spezia promontory to the northwest. The other palaces around the piazza are all of the Middle Ages, though somewhat restored, and all beautiful. There is the bishop's palace—for years Volterra was ruled by bishops—the Palazzo Incontri, housing the Cassa di Risparmio of Volterra, and the Palazzo del Monte Pio, in which is the modern Ristorante Etruria.

Around the corner, in the Piazza San Giovanni, are the cathedral and the octagonal baptistry, neither of great beauty, though having interesting features. The *duomo* was first consecrated in the twelfth century, done over in the thirteenth century by an undetermined architect, probably Pisan, for in its blind arcade it shows strong Pisan influence. Its façade is chiefly interesting for its beautifully carved marble doorway with geometric mosaic designs in its lunette.

Inside there is much more to see, especially the pulpit (*pergamo*), with its supporting columns resting on two lions and two creatures of generally bovine persuasion, in quite the Lombard manner. The special works of Mino da Fiesole are also to be noted; the carved pyx on the high altar (figures of the Christ Child, of Faith, Hope, and Charity), and the kneeling angels atop the two spiral columns on either side of the altar.

Outside, the baptistry seems unfinished; only that side toward the *duomo* was ever faced with marble, and that is in green and white stripes. It is perhaps unorthodox to say so, but the building makes one think of nothing so much as a man in a strange and unbecoming dinner jacket. Once again the interior is more interesting. There is the carved baptismal font (1502) to the right of the altar, the work of Andrea Sansovino. He was primarily an architect from Monte San Savino, a hill town on the uplands between Arezzo and Siena. There is also a holy-water basin said to have been adapted from an Etruscan *cippo*, that part of an Etruscan tomb, a round pillar, that often protrudes above the turf.

Perhaps before leaving this district one should go to the bishop's palace. There in the museum of sacred art are a della Robbia and various other works in silver and enamel. These any enthusiast for this sort of thing would hate to miss. Besides, there is a lovely view of the Priori tower through the arches of the cloister.

To get the feel of the city, to see its medieval palaces and houses, it would be well just to walk about through some of the streets, down Via Roma and Via Ricciarelli, Via Buomparenti, and Via dei Sarti, then back to the main piazza and down the Via Porta all'Arco to the only Etruscan gate remaining in the city. It has been so supported and built about with Roman and then medieval walls that one must walk through the deep gate and then look back to see the great slabs of stone that made it up originally. On the face of the arch are three great lumps of stone, once Etruscan faces, but so carved through twenty-five hundred years or more by wind and rain and cold and dust as now to be unrecognizable. Some think that they may well have represented three Etruscan gods, Tinia, Uni, and Menrva, who correspond to Jupiter, Juno, and Minerva of Roman mythology. Here as in many other places in the hill towns one has a chance to see how readily a town such as this could be defended in the days of horsemen, swords, and pikes. Men, women, even children, on top of the wall could hurl down rocks or boiling oil or whatever came to hand upon the heads of the assailants beneath. It would take a Trojan horse to get inside, so long as food and water held out.

Once having studied the arch one should walk back through it uphill and to the left along the Via Fornelli (the street of little ovens) for the far views across the rooftops of the street immediately below, to the hills beyond. These rooftop scenes in the hill towns are often memorable; nothing weathers more beautifully nor blends more subtly with the blues and greens of Italian hillsides than the dull reds and browns and cinnamons of tile roofs.

Along the streets, particularly Via Fornelli, one sees, usually a step or two below the pavement, through open doors, men and boys sawing and carving alabaster; for fashioning alabaster is this city's chief industry. There are various larger shops where the tourist will be welcome to see and to buy; and buy he will unless he has strong sales resistance. There are bowls and jugs, platters, bird baths; there are figurines of all sorts, birds, goats, cats, dogs, and deer; there are donkeys braying, balking, donkeys maternally eying other smaller donkeys, donkeys with a wicked eye, donkeys beneficently inclined; there are Madonnas, too, and all the saints; there are fruits carved and painted so realistically that one is almost tempted to bite into them. These are perfect for a decorative fruit bowl or for a della Robbian Christmas wreath.

One should go farther still, out to the point beyond Santa Chiara to see the *balze* for oneself, and the Etruscan walls close by the church. In another direction, walking out from the Porta Fiorentina one can see the excavations that mark the Roman occupation of Volterra. It is, however, in the Etruscan museum on Via Don Minzoni that one sees the best that has been found of local archaeological interest, both of the Etruscan and Roman eras of the city.

This museum is a must. There are many Etruscan museums in Italy, that in Florence and those in Rome of course the best. Perugia, however, Orvieto, Chiusi, Tarquinia, Arezzo, and various other places have smaller collections often notable in some respect, and in some of these places there are also Etruscan tombs worth visiting. It is surprising how these museums complement one another. That of Volterra is almost entirely a collection of cinerary urns, six hundred of them, organized in rooms according to the subject matter of their bas-reliefs. In this district of Italy cremation was the custom among Etruscans.

Even a casual inspection of these reveals the fact that urn-making on standardized patterns must have been a business in Etruscan days, just as tombstones today are turned out on a mass-production line.

There are identical battle scenes, sacrificial scenes, scenes of souls being conducted to the nether world, purely decorative designs with standardized flowers, or the familiar Etruscan rounded dish, with the thumb-knob in the center, that souls apparently carried with them on their long journey. Some of these are in travertine, others in the local alabaster. As sculpture they may not be noteworthy, but if one is interested in Etruscan civilization one cannot afford to miss them.

For the Etruscans are the great mystery story of Italy. They occupied at one time much of the northern part of the country, even as far as Bologna. They had ports on the Adriatic coast, Adria (whence, presumably, the Adriatic derives its name), and Spina in the lagoon district south of Venice, near, probably, to the present town of Comacchio. They were a loose confederation of cities, with a general assembly held once a year. At one time they held the district south of Rome as far as Naples and a little way beyond. They had mines in Elba, and towns all along the Tyrrhenian Sea north of Rome. Indeed the Greeks knew them as Tyrrhenoi. Yet gradually both Greeks and Carthaginians pushed them back, and finally the Romans struck their deathblow when they conquered Veii just north of Rome in 280 B.C. As a people under Roman domination, however, they continued into the early Christian era. Much they gave to the Romans, kings first of all, the Tarquins, but also the chariot, the royal toga, fasces, sceptre, and the Cloaca Maxima, which drained the Forum. Even the Roman wolf, though without the nursing twins, is said to be of Etruscan origin.

Yet though Virgil writes of their expert horsemanship, and Livy and various others speak of them in their contact with the Romans, no one to this day knows who the Etruscans were or whence they came. Herodotus, writing in the fifth century B.C., says that they migrated from Lydia in Asia Minor to the western shores of Italy. Dionysius of Halicarnassus (54 B.C.–A.D. 7) thinks rather that they were a tribe native to the Italian peninsula. Some others suggest that they came from the north across the Alps, perhaps across the lower passes to the east, settled in the north of Italy and spread from there. Each thesis has had its advocates, but no one yet has proved his point. Perhaps there may be some truth in each, for wherever they came from, they must have mixed with native tribes; and there just could have been migrations of the same people by different routes at different times.

There is much to suggest, however, a Near Eastern origin, their stylized beasts, for instance, their leopards and lions—the Etruscan and the Hittite lion are identical, at least to the amateur eye. If one looks closely one finds occasionally in the bas-reliefs the double-edged Mycenaean axe. The double flute, so common in these sculptured bits, was used also in Lydia and Phrygia. Their arts of divination through the entrails of beasts, even the shaping of their tombs, find their counterparts in Near Eastern practices. That they were familiar with Grecian mythology, with the tales of Ulysses, of Troy, of Agamemnon, of Helen and Paris, we know also from these urns. Other bits in other places show strong Grecian and Egyptian influence. That they traded with Greece and Egypt, with Cyprus, with the Phoenicians, and Syrians, there is no reason to question.

Books of a sort they seem to have had, for we can discover them in an occasional sculptured detail, but they left no recorded history. A few inscriptions, short and factual, names of persons and of places, do exist, one of the longest in the museum at Perugia. From these scholars have become familiar with the alphabet, but as yet have gained no clue to the actual language. So the mystery goes on, and will perhaps forever. Or possibly someday in some Near Eastern diggings they may find the clue or the actual story of the migrations themselves.

In the meantime we study urns, sarcophagi, and painted tombs, and all the multitude of household appliances and decorative objects found in the tombs, and from them build up for ourselves a picture of Etruscan civilization. Once in a while we see representations of their temples, and are surprised to find Doric, Ionic, or Corinthian columns. We see men indulging apparently in human sacrifices. We see men taking off to a land beyond earth's horizons, often being driven forward by winged angels, their Harpies, presumably; and we see the various means of transportation to that land: the horse-drawn chariot, no doubt for the élite of the community; the covered wagon, remarkably reminiscent of that used by the western pioneers in America; the boat across the narrow water, piloted by the Etruscan Charon, whatever name he bore. Occasionally the traveller goes by foot. Sometimes the pilgrims start off to an accompaniment of horns or other musical instruments, with friends and family standing by, as if they were surely bound to some fair Elysian fields.

To judge from the majority of carvings we would suppose that most men were warriors; but that they entertained themselves in many ways is evident, with wrestling, swimming, gladiatorial combats, with fishing, boar-hunts, bull-fights, and with gay banquets elaborately served. In the early Etruscan period the men wore beards. Later, apparently, they had bare faces, but often, not always, with long hair to their shoulders. One sees them wearing at times a kind of toque on their heads.

One of the rather startling discoveries made by visitors to an Etruscan museum is the high position held by Etruscan women. One finds almost more recumbent figures of women on the sarcophagi than of men. In a few instances men and women are shown together. One sees women helping their husbands to put on their armor; one sees them at the banquets lying on their couches in complete equality with their menfolk. The women of the Etruscan upper classes—and one assumes that those depicted in the paintings and on the sarcophagi were of the aristocracy—are beautifully robed with flowing gowns. Embroidery may run the length of the sleeves. Deep ruffles now and again fall from the knees to the floor. Their coiffures may be elaborate braids or high pointed arrangements. On their feet they were known sometimes to wear red leather, pointed slippers with bejeweled clasps. Indeed it must be that their husbands lavished their substance on them. Their rings and ear-rings, gold and amber necklaces and bracelets, their buckles and clasps like golden safety pins four to five inches long, would make a modern woman envious. They had tiny ivory combs sometimes edged with carved birds or animals. They had mirrors of metal engraved on one side, highly polished on the other. They had compacts and jewel cases.

The Etruscan goldwork indeed is like nothing that we know. Tiny hollow golden tubes have been covered with gold granulations, small as or smaller than actual grains of sand; or threads of gold have been laid lengthwise along the tubes and somehow made a part of the tubes. If one wishes to see this goldwork at its best one should get permission to be shown through the treasure room in the Florence Archaeological Museum, though in the Villa Guilia in Rome there is an excellent display.

In many museums one sees Etruscan household equipment better

than at Volterra. They had great pottery amphorae, sometimes delicately carved, for storing grain or oil; they had jugs of bronze and sometimes of silver, fluted bowls, pitchers with spouts that would pour; they had lamps of many kinds, small ones to handle and others that stood upon the floor; they had braziers for heating, others for cooking. They had goblets, iron beds to sleep on, needles, and a wealth of decorative figurines and vases.

They loved animals, had cats and dogs—one in a carving greatly resembled a dachshund—spirited horses and the more sober donkeys. Horses appear more often than other animals. They are always prancing. Their tails are arched, their heads flung high. Perhaps the idea that horses were aristocratic animals, held through all the Middle Ages and even to this day, came from the Etruscans. They never appear as work animals; they draw chariots; they carry horsemen, often in armor; they run races; they never draw a plow. The Etruscans depicted, too, mythological creatures: griffins, marine horses with dragon tails, mermaids. In their painted tombs one sees stylized trees, flowers, ivy vines as if forming the frame of the picture. Evidently they liked color, greens and reds, blues and yellows.

It is an illuminating and salutary experience to follow through Etruscan museums and tombs and to meditate on how little there is that we have today that they did not have four hundred, five hundred, or six hundred years B.C. In the Etruscan excavations near Bolsena there was once found a skull having gold bridgework and a gold crown to a denture. Here was an ingenious and artistic people, expert metallurgists, expert potters, artists and artisans of high quality. Yet they have faded from the scene. No one knows who they were or whence they came. But their inheritance undoubtedly lives on in Italian veins. Even names persist, as that of Cecina (Ceicna). There are not only a town and river of that name, but a bishop of Volterra of that name died, it is said, only two hundred years ago.

4

San Gimignano

WHEN during the last war the report came through in the news-papers that San Gimignano had been destroyed, many a lover of Italian hill towns was heartsick. That lovely town of towers and palaces, a medieval monument, was gone. It just couldn't be. Fortunately, it wasn't.

Perhaps San Gimignano himself had once more saved the town from northern invaders, as tradition says he had in A.D. 550 when Totila, the Goth, and his raiding army stood outside the Porta delle Fonti. Then the people of what was then Castel della Selva (fortress in the woods) had prayed the saint, a one-time bishop of Modena, to hurry to their rescue. Suddenly, the story goes, a light from heaven had shone brightly on their fortress and the saint in shining armor had appeared in threatening mien. Totila paled in fear before this supernatural manifestation and fled away. Thereafter Castel della Selva became the town of San Gimignano, and has been ever since. Today there is a small statue of the saint, protected by a penthouse roof, over the arch leading to the courtyard of the town hall; and in the art gallery upstairs in the palace the visitor will find a fifteenth-century painting by Taddeo di Bartoio of the moustached and bearded saint holding the many-towered town in one hand while his other hand is lifted in blessing.

In San Gimignano's heyday, the thirteenth and fourteenth centuries, the towers, it is estimated, numbered fifty to sixty, possibly more, a veritable forest of stone. To the visitor of the twentieth century, the thirteen or fourteen still standing, seen against a Tuscan sky, are like something remembered only in a dream. They are square and massive with occasional narrow windows and many smaller holes a few inches square. In these the rooks that circle high above the city morning and evening take refuge at night. Grasses and small flowering plants grow and bloom in the crevices.

The legend is that two young Romans, Silvio and Muzio, first built fortresses on this hilltop, no doubt bent on raiding the countryside about. There is much evidence, however, because of tombs found just outside the town and other underground structures nearby, that Etruscans had occupied this hilltop before the two young Romans. Anyhow, in very early days there was a village here which became a town with first one circle of walls and in later days a second.

Of the actual history of the town we know but little until about the beginning of the thirteenth century when, with local patriotism running high, it was warring with its neighbors. Intermittently for twenty years it fought with Volterra, but finally it brought its banner home in triumph, the white lion on its red and yellow field. San Gimignano had won its place as an independent commune. Even then the town was drawn into the perennial struggles between Florence and Siena. Besides, both Guelfs and Ghibellines were strong. The leaders of these rival factions, the Ardinghelli and the Salvucci, each had their friends and supporters, and the town was torn asunder. Streets and walls were often stained with blood, and few men of the ruling class knew peace even in their hearts. Finally, in the mid-fourteenth century, the town threw in its lot with Florence, and from that time on as a political entity it ceased to have great importance.

But Florence had long been wooing San Gimignano. In 1300 she had sent an emissary, none other than Dante Alighieri, to persuade her to join the Guelf League. It was a notable occasion on that eighth of May, an occasion proudly recorded in the annals of the town. No doubt the populace were crowding balconies and towers as the little procession entered the gate and moved through the streets, trumpets sounding. Behind Dante and his company on their gaily accoutered

San Gimignano

horses, there danced, probably, a horde of little Guelfs making merry. In the Piazza del Duomo Dante dismounted, climbed to the great *sala* of the Palazzo Communale, and there addressed the *podestà* and the general council in the name of Florence.

Through all the medieval period, even to the early 1500's, the town grew in beauty and distinction as patrician or wealthy merchant families completed palaces and towers. Artists, too, first from Siena, then from Florence, came and went, leaving behind frescoed walls or marble sculptures in cathedral or in churches. There were other visitors. Living in the Dominican monastery, preaching in the Collegiata (*duomo*) in 1484, Savonarola had first denounced the abuses of the church and the sins of the Italian people before ever he had let loose in Florence the blasts that were to consign him to the flames. In 1507 Machiavelli had spent time there training the local troops in the use of unaccustomed arms.

However grim at times life was for most people, for the young and irresponsible sons of the aristocracy and of the merchant princes it was, between wars of course, often a round of merrymaking. At least the town's young poet of the thirteenth century, Folgore, so represents it in his *Garland of Months*.[1] In the courtyards fountains plashed, arbors hung thick with vines, and pots of flowers adorned the balconies or wide window sills. In the winter, fall, and spring, there were fishing, hawking, hunting, with hounds and 'ambling palfreys' or 'Spanish chargers'. To own a horse in those days was a symbol of belonging to the upper crust. In winter the youth regaled themselves with feasting before roaring fires, dancing, singing, making love. They slept between silk sheets, and under fur coverlets. In summer they wore thinnest silk clothes, drank chilled Tuscan wines, and took themselves to castles in the valleys of the Alps. It seemed as if there was nothing serious in their lives. 'Never', says Folgore, 'hanker for a wife, who would spoil everything for you'; and again: 'Leave the silly priests to their gabble, for in them are too many lies and too little truth.' Folgore would have been sympathetic with Pier della Vigna at Frederick's court in Sicily, who wrote:

'The life of holy prelates is abominably funny,
   Their hearts are full of venom while their tongues are dropping
                                                                honey;

They pipe a pretty melody, and so approach discreetly,
And offer you a cordial, mixed with poison, very sweetly.'[50]

This all sounds like a tale out of Boccaccio, a tale of youth who feared
lest the sun should not rise for them tomorrow.

'Fair is youth and void of sorrow
But it hourly flees away.'

So wrote Lorenzo dei Medici (quoted by Derek Patmore in *Italian
Pageant*, p. 86) at a somewhat later date. Though undoubtedly the
picture Folgore draws was true to a large degree of the smart set in all
of Tuscany, the dream of delights here envisioned may be somewhat
too crowded. Folgore, after all, was one of the group known as the
'Brigata Spendereccia' (spendthrift club) with headquarters in Siena.
Dante mentions this in his *Inferno* (Canto 29). He notes by name
Niccolo of Siena, and especially Caccia of Asciano (a hill town southeast of Siena) 'who wasted his vineyard and his great wood'. No
wonder, when they squandered their florins on cloth from Russia, new
musical instruments from Germany, and 'lemon-flavoured candies'
from Gaeta (a hill town on the shore between Rome and Naples)—in
the thirteenth century!

Yet as Folgore belonged to San Gimignano, so also did the blessed
Santa Fina. Poor child, she went out one day to draw water from the
fountain, a little girl of ten. There a youth who thought her beautiful
gave her an orange, a precious fruit in those days in Tuscany. In all
innocence she accepted it and took it home, telling her mother of the
incident; whereupon her mother scolded her roundly, dwelling on the
decencies of life, impressing on her that to accept such a gift from boy
or man was only a step away from losing her virginity. At once the
child was overcome with the enormity of her sin. By way of penance
she lay down on a board and refused ever again to get up, while she
prayed continuously for forgiveness. Gradually she wasted away. As
the end of the fifth year approached, San Gregorio, surrounded by
seraphs, appeared to her in a vision and told her that she would be
released to paradise on his name day, a week away. When the moment
came and her spirit fled away, as the legend goes, the town was filled

with whirlwinds. The devil and his henchmen were taking off in anger, having lost a soul to their dominion. Then in all the town the bells began to ring of their own accord. The oak board on which she lay was all at once covered with blooming violets; and indeed the whole town was filled with their fragrance. You can see all this recorded by Ghirlandaio in the Santa Fina chapel of the *duomo*. You can see there, too, her gold and white carved tomb, work of Benedetto da Maiano and his brother Giuliano.

However beset in the past with wars and feuds, however full of towers and saints, San Gimignano is today a quiet town of ten thousand persons with little but its past to live on, a town, as Henry James wrote long ago, 'presenting itself more or less in the guise of some rare silvery shell washed up by the sea of time'. The paradox is that it is communistic; yet perhaps it is not a paradox at all but a normal reaction of a city assigned to the shelf.

One could spend days there examining the architectural detail of palaces, and other days studying the frescoed stories in the churches. Not for nothing was it made a national monument in 1928. There is no need to learn the names of all the palaces, the Chigi, the Cortesi, the Mori, the Pesciolini, the Tinacci, the Tortoli, and all the rest, but one should walk along the streets and enjoy their beauty. A few of course one should identify, the Ardinghelli and Salvucci towers, the communal palace with its Torre Grossa, the old palace of the *podestà* with its clock, the Torre dei Becci, the jumbled mass of towers and ancient houses beside it, and the Pratellesi, now housing the public library.

One usually enters San Gimignano through the San Giovanni gate (1262). On the right, part way up the street, one passes what was once the church of San Giovanni of the Knights Templar, later of the Knights of Malta. Its handsome façade of travertine with its Romanesque portal flanked by twin blind arches, in the Pisan manner, is worth a glance. Above the door is the typical Maltese Cross enclosed in a circle. Farther up the street is the fourteenth-century Palazzo Pratellesi, worth a careful scrutiny. As usual in San Gimignano the first story is of stone, the two upper floors of brick. Though time has mellowed both their texture and their color, the bricks of the third story are laid in alternate courses of yellow and red. The pointed windows of these two upper stories are of two lights, each delicately edged. The slightly pointed bearing arch above the windows is bordered by a terra cotta frieze of lions and ivy leaves, and between the windows and the bearing arch is a circle. Though there are many and beautiful variations, particularly in the friezes and edgings, in the shape of arches and doorways, in the number of lights in the windows, one can look for this general pattern repeated many times in the palaces of the town.

Beyond the Palazzo Pratellesi one passes presently under the Arco dei Becci and into the lovely tricornered Piazza Cisterna with its fishbone-patterned pavement and its old well (*cisterna*) (1273). The latter is octagonal of travertine panels. Two travertine stanchions and a connecting travertine lintel carry the pulley and chain for drawing water. Several steps lead up to the well. The piazza is faced with beautiful buildings, one having a balcony gay with vines and flower pots. Next to it is a high tower. On the west side near the Piazza del Duomo are the truncated twin Ardinghelli towers, no longer impressive.

On the south is the Palazzo Tortoli, once Friani. It has Gothic twin-light windows, mullioned by white marble columns and edged with terra cotta. The *voussoirs* (the wedgelike stones forming the arch) of the Gothic bearing arch are arranged in pattern, alternately, two bricks of yellow and two of red, as in the face of the second- and third-story walls. The terra cotta frieze above the bearing arch is of flowers. Even the small round recessed window under the arch is appropriately edged.

The Albergo Cisterna, on the same side, was itself once the Casa of the Salvestrini. Of course it has been greatly altered, but one still climbs marble steps to the first floor. From its rooms and terraces one gets an idea of San Gimignano one does not get by walking through the streets; one looks behind the scenes to gardened patios where fig trees, roses, lettuces, and zinnias grow, where children with their teacher-nuns are singing in the open air or doing their exercises, where housekeepers have hung out their multicolored shirts and handker-chiefs and aprons in the sun. The whole town comes alive. One looks across the red- and brown-tiled roofs to streets far below where men and women are carrying their loads as they go about their business, and to high towers not a long stone's throw away. High up in their

walls are the narrow slits from which the crossbowmen of another day
shot their arrows. Beyond are the valley, farmhouses, church towers,
fields, and wooded hills.

If one wishes really to see San Gimignano, one will stay in town a
night or two. On a stormy night there when the lightning crackles and
the thunder booms, one feels as if in an eyrie, especially if a bolt strikes
a tower close by and all the rooks come out protesting in their raucous
way. And as one listens to the roar of water over terraces one begins
to wonder whether the slippages that took place in Volterra might be
repeated here. But in the morning all is well. These slopes are solidly
founded. The sun comes out. The dark storm-clouds, blacker than
normal in this intense light, drift off across the hills, carrying to the
valleys beneath their patterned shadows. The world is fresh and clean
and one thanks God 'for all the beauty hereabout'.

From the Piazza della Cisterna one proceeds to the adjoining Piazza
del Duomo, also paved in fishbone style. Here to the right is the old
original Palazzo del Podestà, the palace of the governor of the
commune, where he and his councillors had their offices. It was repaired
in 1239, enlarged in 1337. On the street level is a great arch giving
access to the building, but also shelter for the market on rainy days.
Around the walls of this loggia are stone benches. From the vaulted
ceiling hangs a huge wrought-iron lantern. Outside on the wall is
fastened a modern wrought-iron trash basket of beautiful design.
Atop the building rises the Rognosa Tower, one hundred and sixty-
seven feet high. On the face of the small supplementary tower is the
old clock installed in 1407.

Across the piazza a flight of stone steps, wide as the cathedral itself,
leads up to the Collegiata, a simple building of the twelfth century.
Its façade, modified at different times from that of the original
structure and damaged in the last war, has been recently restored. It was
at first a basilica, only a nave with side aisles. Later in 1456 a choir and
transepts, chapels and a sacristy were added, the work of the
Renaissance architect, Giuliano da Maiano.

In the interior one notes at once several features. Here stripes of
black and white marble are used in great restraint, only in the arches
of the nave. Probably this was one of the earlier cathedrals to adopt this
new vogue initiated by Florentine architects of the eleventh century to

add color and interest to their buildings. The frescoes, too, are note-worthy. Scenes from heaven and hell as conceived by Taddeo di Bartolo of Siena appear high up on the walls of the nave. Scenes from the Old Testament by Bartolo di Fredi, also of Siena, fill the wall of the left aisle. Those on the wall of the right aisle tell the story of the New Testament as Barna da Siena interpreted it.

All these in the early days were the Bible of the people. They were also probably their serial stories. To be sure, the priest said mass, received their confessions, and gave them absolution, but here on these walls was something they could see and understand. How they must have delighted in the colors as well as in the stories. How they must have led their children by the hand and taught them to look up to see the mysteries of the creation, the story of Adam and Eve driven from paradise, of the animals entering and leaving the ark, of Joseph and his dream, of the crossing of the Red Sea, of the flight into Egypt, of the boy Christ in the temple, of the Garden of Gethsemane, of the crucifixion and the resurrection, of the blessed received into heaven and of the wicked cast into hell. Did the people then go home to talk of these things, did their children act out these stories in their play, and did they all pray more fervently before the household shrine because they had looked at them? Or did the children wake up at night crying out in terror as they dreamed of the tortures of the damned? One wonders.

More even than to these, however, the visitor to San Gimignano's cathedral directs his attention to the chapels: to the oratory of San Giovanni, on the left, where is the baptismal font and the fifteenth-century *Annunciation* by Ghirlandaio, and on the right to the Renais-sance chapel designed by Giuliano da Maiano and dedicated to Santa Fina. There is much here to admire: the wrought-iron gate by which one enters, the white and gold tomb, the Ghirlandaio frescoes in the lunettes above. In the first one sees San Gregorio appearing to Santa Fina and telling her of her approaching death. A beautiful young girl, she lies peacefully on her oak board, her hands raised in an attitude of prayer. At her head sits her faithful nurse, Beldia, and on the other side another who also seems aware of the heavenly visitation. All three have lovely faces. The room itself of Santa Fina's home has a classical elegance in its richly adorned pilasters, its panelled ceiling, its delicate moldings and friezes, the long table on the far side, the high-backed chair, the views from the door and window. In the other lunette one sees a chapel, and beyond at either side the towers of the town. Here Santa Fina lies on her bier while the bishop reads the burial service. Already she is working miracles, having just restored sight to the boy at her feet and having made the withered hand of her nurse come alive. Before leaving the cathedral one should see also on the front wall, by Jacopo della Quercia, the wooden statues of the *Angel Gabriel* and *The Virgin*, and also Gozzoli's fresco of *San Sebastian* pierced with many arrows.

Once outside again, one faces on the right the town hall, or Palazzo del Popolo, a building of the late thirteenth and early fourteenth centuries. The plan for it is attributed to Arnolfo di Cambio. Its massive tower, one hundred and seventy-four feet high, as well as the palace itself, has recently been somewhat restored after minor war damage. The twin stairways outside lead to a speaker's platform (*ringhiera*), a common feature of communal palaces. It was here that every new *podestà* was inducted and received the keys of the town. To go inside, however, one does not climb to this platform but turns sharp right at the foot of the cathedral steps, passes under the arch and into the Piazza Pecori. Here one enters the courtyard of the palace, one of the loveliest spots in all the town. It has a brick pavement and pillars, an open stairway over which a wrought-iron lantern hangs, a roofed gallery from the walls of which vines or geraniums are dripping, a supporting arcade along one side under which are ancient faded frescoes, an old travertine well (*pozzo*) under a wide brick arch. Seen from ground level or from the gallery above this courtyard is a delight.

One climbs the stairs and then others to the great *sala* or council chamber. It is here that Dante came. The room itself is beautiful in its proportions, in its woodwork and decorations. Along the top are the armorial bearings in color of many a *podestà*. On the south wall is the *Maesta* or Coronation of the Virgin, painted by the Sienese Lippo Memmi in 1317 and retouched one hundred and fifty years later by Gozzoli, who added also several figures. From this room one enters a smaller hall with carved and inlaid seats and a tribune. Here the secret council met. Before leaving these rooms one should step out on the balcony for the view. Upstairs on the third floor is the art gallery. The most important paintings are by Pinturicchio and Filippino. Lippi, though there are some by Taddeo di Bartolo, Bartolo di Fredi, by Gozzoli and others including two local painters, Vincenzo Tamagni, a pupil of Raphael, and Sebastiano Mainardi, a pupil of Domenico Ghirlandaio.

One can go on climbing to the tower, for a wide view extending to the Apuan and Pistoian Alps, and including all the villages between and to the south as far as Colle di Val d'Elsa, Casole, and beyond. However, if one does not wish to climb so far, one can be content with views out the various windows of the art gallery. Beside the old Palazzo del Podestà is the Chigi palace and then the beginning of the Via San Matteo. Just beyond are the twin Salvucci towers and the square Pesciolini tower, and still farther the greens and blues of the Tuscan hills. Past the *duomo* below one looks down on the Piazza del Erbe, and if one is lucky, one will be there on a market day when the *contadini* from all the farms around have brought in their fruits and flowers and vegetables, their cheese and eggs and chickens. Both piazzas are then full of people moving about among the baskets and the donkey carts, talking and bargaining. There is even a team—or maybe two—of white oxen standing in a corner. And now and then a woman in her simple dress and heavy shoes, a scarf or handkerchief tied round her head, climbs the long flight of steps and slips inside the house of prayer, possibly to make confession or entreat the Virgin. Looking down thus over piazzas and towers, it is not too hard in imagination to thrust back the centuries and to re-create for oneself something of the scene it must have been in medieval days.

But there is another nearer view that one must not miss, and to find it one must get one's feet on solid ground again, follow along the right side of the *duomo*, turn left behind the apse on the Via Monte Staffoli, then to the right again, and climb a little stairway to a small tower, to which a *custode* gives one entrance. Here is a marvellous vista of the towers of the town and the hills beyond, and, in the fall, of Virginia creeper flaming on the walls. One looks down at one side into an old convent garden of tremulous olive trees and old cypresses, and an ancient wellhead in the center. It is another of those views that one carries away engraved in memory.

Returning to the Piazza del Duomo, the visitor should proceed
down the Via San Matteo, slowly, inspecting every building to see what
of beauty it has to show, in windows, doors, cornices, and eaves, terra
cotta friezes, long stringcourses Byzantine in feeling, or, occasionally,
majolica decoration. There are the Tinacci Palace, the Cancelleria Arch,
part of the inner circle of walls, the church of San Bartolo, with its
high blind loggia, Pisan in effect. Before passing through the Porta San
Matteo, one should turn right on the Via Venti Settembre and then
again to the left. This brings one out on a large piazza where are the
eleventh-century San Pietro, no longer open to the public, and San
Agostino. It is the latter that one has come to see. Here is the tomb of
San Bartolo carved by Benedetto da Maiano, and another *San
Sebastian*, this one by Gozzoli. At a time of plague the citizens had once
appealed to this saint for help, for no saint had suffered more himself
from the 'slings and arrows of outrageous fortune'. The main purpose
of one's visit, however, is to see in the choir the series of seventeen
frescoes depicting the life of St. Augustine and of his mother Santa
Monica. They show him as a young boy in Africa being turned over
to the schoolmaster, again at nineteen at the University of Carthage.
They show Monica praying for her son and blessing him as he starts
off to Italy; they show him landing and being welcomed, later reading
rhetoric and philosophy in Rome, again leaving for Milan, where he
is welcomed by St. Ambrose and the emperor Theodosius. There he
listens to a homily by St. Ambrose on doctrinal matters, while all the
time Monica is praying for his conversion. They show him reading the
Epistle of St. Paul to Alypius, being finally baptized. Then the story
changes from the biographical to the interpretive, for one sees him
with a child on the shore of the sea, and the child explains that 'as one
cannot empty the sea with a cup, so one cannot understand the mystery
of the Trinity'. The frescoes then go on to show St. Augustine
explaining to his brothers the rule of the order. There follows the death
of Santa Monica, the consecration of Augustine as a bishop, his
conversion of Fortunato, the ecstasy during which he is told by St.
Jerome of the heavenly joys, and finally his funeral. One notes throughout, the Renaissance backgrounds, the classical detail, the faces of the
men and women and children, especially the latter. The colors are
still fresh and lovely; and the little dog in the foreground of one of

the pictures, though put there to fill a space, is very lifelike. His ears are up, his tail also; he seems as if in a quandary. Would these priests have any tidbits, cookies, perhaps, secreted in the folds of their robes? This probably is not a point that Mr. Berenson would have mentioned; rather he would have discussed tactile values, movement, space composition, the art of portraiture just at this time being discovered in Florentine artistic circles. For instance, in this same fresco Gozzoli painted himself, with a book in his hand, the figure to the right.

When the visitor has lived long enough in the shadow of St. Augustine, he may well go out and down again to the Via Venti Settembre and follow it as it becomes Via Folgore da San Gimignano, to the very edge of town, to see a lovely little church, that of San Jacopo. It, too, is a combination of materials, the lower floor of stone, the upper of brick. Over the portal is a penthouse roof. Under the decorative cornice of green Sienese majolica (the best clay for such work was the white clay of Siena), there is a rose window of unusual design and workmanship. This church, too, has a Maltese Cross over the door, for it was an early church built possibly in the eleventh century.

If after all of this the visitor still has time—and plenty of time one should have here—he should walk downhill to the arcaded Fonti, where women for probably more than one thousand years have done their washing, where the wool from the sheep in the Middle Ages was washed before it was combed and carded. One should explore other streets for what they hold of beauty or of views, the Via delle Romite, the Via Quercecchio, the Via di Castello. At the far end of the latter is the penitentiary, once the Dominican convent where Savonarola lived when he was in town. On the wall beside the door there is a plaque noting this fact.

But one of the musts of a visit to San Gimignano is to go to Santa Maria Pieve di Cellole, four kilometers or so beyond the Porta San Matteo. Outside the gate one turns left, not on the first street, which follows around the wall, but on the next. Two kilometers or so later, the road to Certaldo turns to the right. Here one takes the left branch instead, a dirt road to the west, till one sees the sign to Cellole and turns right, up a narrow rocky trail. On this hilltop there was in medieval days a leper colony ministered to by San Bartolo. Now there is a farmhouse or two and the church all but hidden among rows of old cypresses. It is a low and simple late twelfth-century structure, all of stone, except for the wooden roof which slants from the center to the side walls. Above the lintel of the door is a rounded arch ever so slightly pointed, with Byzantine cornice. Over this is a double Romanesque two-light window and above that a Greek Cross. The windows at either side are hardly more than slits.

Within, the church is Romanesque, a nave and side aisles; the arches on each side are supported by three columns, then a pillar and two more columns. The capitals are crudely carved, Lombard in feeling. The simple apse, up two steps from the floor of the nave, is a rounded vault, unsupported save for the high arch at the front. Below the point of curvature is a succession of blind arches. The tympanum of each is intricately and rather crudely carved in Byzantine designs, each differing from the others. In the center at the rear is a long slit window flanked by columns and then by carved pilasters, each different. On the altar in the foreground is a white crucifix almost the height of the window at the back. The church is very dark and but for the *custode* who turns on the hidden floodlighting of the apse it would be almost impossible to see the carvings.

Two thirds of the way down the right aisle a door gives on a farmyard garden, laid out in walks, and full of trees and grapevines, flowers, and vegetables. One enters, turns left, unlatches a gate into an olive orchard where mint and weeds are growing underneath, and yellow crocuses gone wild. There one sees the apse from the outside, the carving similar to that within, though there is much less of it.

To the southeast one looks down on San Gimignano. Across the valley to the north and east lies Certaldo where Boccaccio lived his later years and died. To the west are wooded hills. This seems almost a hallowed place; it is so beautiful, beautiful when the sun shines and one looks up to the blue sky through the pointed cypresses, beautiful when the gray clouds roll up all around and mists close it in. The first time we went there, another car drove up soon after our arrival. A tall, distinguished-looking woman came up to us. How had we, Americans from so far away, found this lovely church, she asked. She, a Florentine all her life, had discovered it only a week before. It was so beautiful, she said, that tears had rolled down her cheeks, and now she had come back bringing friends.

We, too, have found it unforgettable.

> '. . . it will never
> Pass into nothingness; but still will keep
> A bower quiet for us. . . .'
>
> JOHN KEATS, *Endymion*

5

Colle di Val d'Elsa

IT IS irresistible, this town, brown and gold and cinnamon, with green trees climbing the hill in the foreground. Turning uphill toward Volterra from the Siena road, along a rippling *torrente*, one suddenly comes upon it to the left, Colle di Val d'Elsa, high on its long ridge. At some time a gully had cut this ridge through, leaving as if two hills, and the distance between is now spanned by a bridge. The hill, the town, the bridge, the trees, the rushing stream, tributary to the Elsa, all seem like those of some ancient yellowed print, but in color.

One rounds a corner at the top and there is the magnificent Porta Volterrana, an impressive gate for any town. The stone arch is but wide enough for a single car but the superstructure and the bastions at the side, of weathered brick and stone, are massive and forbidding. These are flanked by great circular towers, and embellished all along their length by a heavy arched cornice topped by square Guelf crenellations. A stone and brick bench projects toward the park in front. On this usually lounge several men sunning themselves.

Colle's name evokes vague memories of Italian history. Of course! Here the great battle was fought by which Florence wiped out the disgrace of Montaperti, the battle in which Provenzano Salvani, Siena's hero of nine years before, had paid with his life, where indeed his head had been carried at the end of a pike in triumphal procession. 'With him', wrote Dante in his *Purgatorio* (Canto XI) '. . . all Tuscany resounded, and now he scarce is lisped of in Siena, where he was lord when the Florentine rage was destroyed,' for, as he said: 'Worldly renown is naught but a breath of wind, which now comes hence and now comes thence, and changes name because it changes quarter.' Even though small, Colle had had need of its massive walls and gates. A free commune, to be sure, after long dependence on Volterra, it had been a pawn in the many wars between Siena and Florence and a butt for the raids of the Aldobrandeschi, feudal barons of Santa Fiora to the south.

It is a town essentially of a long single street, though once to the left and again to the right a narrower way angles off along the edge of the hill; and of course there are the *vicoli*, the little narrow alleys. Many of these lead off to or along the cliffside. Between their close-set walls of brick or stone you look out to the flickering green of olive orchards and the blue shadows on distant hills. In the foreground there is perhaps a balcony with flower pots, a wrought-iron lantern on its bracket, a woman with a basket balanced on her head, all silhouetted against the light. Along the main street are some fine old houses and small palaces, not magnificent but often beautiful in their simplicity.

Farther down is the present town hall, a terra cotta palace of the Renaissance. Over its door are the Medici insignia, the shield with six boluses. This appears in several other places in town, evidencing the period of Medici dominance, as in so much of Tuscany. (As one goes about from town to town it is interesting to note the number of boluses on these escutcheons.) The records show that the earliest Medici insignia carried eleven boluses. By the time that Cosimo became head of the family, the number had been reduced to seven. Piero, the gouty, had seven also, six red and one blue. Lorenzo and those who followed showed only six.

From the bridge that joins the two hills and the two wards, so to speak, of the upper town (Colle Alto) one looks along the walls ahead, tufted with grass and other plants. Below is virtually a cliffside, fit place for goats to climb and feed on bushes and trees that have found a footing there. Several hundred feet below lies Colle Basso, old, too, though now the business town with many modern buildings. Beyond the bridge and another arch straddled by a sixteenth-century palace with wide overhanging eaves, the road leads through the Castel Vecchio. Here is the older center, a piazza with patterned pavement, the *duomo*, the bishop's palace, and the fourteenth-century palace of the Pretorio marked by several escutcheons. One of these is that of

Colle itself, the head of a spirited horse with bristling mane. The *duomo*, undistinguished and comparatively modern (1603 but with a nineteenth-century façade), encompasses an ancient parish church. Its square campanile serves also as a clock tower.

Farther down the street one finds a charming spot where a *vicolo* comes in. On a corner building is a large shrine, a painting of the Madonna and child framed elaborately in stone with lanterns in front. It is another of those colorful bits, all blue and rose, that, when one comes upon them unexpectedly in gray Italian villages, warm one's heart. On the other side of the *vicolo* a balustraded stone stairway leads to the entrance of the local museum. One pulls the bell and climbs up. A woman and her husband, custodians, let one in. Actually there is little to see, a few dusty paintings, one obviously of the school of Perugino, hanging or leaning against the walls. In the back room there are only a fresco or two and a large replica of the Colle horse. The custodians, however, are full of enthusiasm, proud of everything, eager to tell of the treasures of the town: the work of Giuliano da Maiano (or possibly Mino da Fiesole) in the *duomo*, the bronze lectern there by Pietro Tacca of the seventeenth century, the baptismal font, the chalice of Byzantine design. In the bishop's palace, too, frescoes have been uncovered, and in the church of Santa Maria in Canonica down the street is a *tabernacolo* of Gozzoli's. One should see the tower, too, farther down where Arnolfo di Cambio had been born.

Of all this it is the birthplace of Arnolfo that matters most. It is near the far end of the street, the largest tower in town, marked by a marble plaque. Arnolfo had been an architect, the designer of many of the major buildings of Florence. His father, too, was an architect and, to judge from appearances here, must have been a local aristocrat as well. His name is variously given but probably was Jacopo Tedesco da Campione (whence Cambio), which suggests Lombard ancestry. At least we may assume that his family came from the north, from the lake country, like enough, for of the two Campiones one is on a southern branch of Lake Lugano (later, in the fourteenth century, we know this town bred architects) and the other on Lake Garda.

What Arnolfo's early training was or how he eventually got to Florence we do not know. As an architect and an aristocrat, his father undoubtedly had a horse and went about. We know that he spent time

Colle di Val d'Elsa

in Florence, was considered a maestro in his guild. He was reputed to have built the palace of the counts of Poppi with its lovely stairway in the courtyard. He undoubtedly instructed his young son in the arts of design and building, and may well have taken him hither and yon to see great buildings. There are those who think that Arnolfo had been influenced by Cistercian architects, because of his liking for pointed arches, pinnacles, gables, vaulted roofs. He may have been, for San Galgano was after all but twenty-five or thirty miles away across the hills from Colle and the abbey was still in building when Arnolfo was a youth. With a horse or even a boy's stout pair of legs it would have been quite possible for him to go there. Or he may have been enrolled there as a pupil and in some monk's *bottega* have had his early lessons in sculpture. Vasari, however, reports that he studied under Cimabue.

What we do know is that in 1266 he was helping Nicolo Pisano in the carving of Siena's pulpit. Some years later he was summoned from Rome again to help Nicolo Pisano—and Giovanni—on the carving of Perugia's Fonte Maggiore, though how much he actually did there is still a question. (There are several statuettes of his in the museum at Perugia.) In the meantime he had been studying and working in Rome and thereabouts. He had built the canopy over the high altar in St. Paul's outside the walls, had carved various statues and tombs, particularly those of Cardinal Annibale in St. John Lateran, of Pope Adrian V at Viterbo (in San Francesco), of Cardinal Guglielmo de Braye in Orvieto (San Domenico). Obviously he had been much impressed with the vogue in Rome, introduced by the Cosmati, for inlays of colored marbles in pavements, screens, pulpits, and elsewhere; in several of his tombs he used this new style.

Just when and where he won his spurs in architecture we do not know. Sooner or later, however, he became the official architect of Florence. He enlarged the Badia. Some attribute the Bargello and its tower to him, though if he built it, he was only twenty-six when he first began it. He planned and built in part—for they were not completed at his death—both the outer circuit of walls of the city and the Palazzo Vecchio. The walls were a major undertaking. Six feet thick, they carried every four hundred feet a tower twenty-five feet square and seventy-five feet high. The Palazzo Vecchio posed many problems. Its site was one, for according to a tale, probably apocryphal, it could not rest on any land that had ever been owned by a Ghibelline. Arnolfo, therefore, had first to tear down buildings, and put the new Signoria not in the center of the piazza but in a corner. He was required, too, to incorporate the already existing Foraboschi Tower, ninety feet high. This had housed the city's bells, had been known affectionately to all Florentines as La Torre della Vacca; when it tolled they said, 'the cow moos' (*La vacca mugghia*). This must be retained, be made the basis of a great new tower. Arnolfo, too, designed Santa Croce, giving it the magnificence of spaciousness. He had been asked indeed to build the largest possible church at the lowest possible cost —which sounds just like the direction of a church committee anywhere at any time. Despite its flat roof it had height, and breadth, and length, and light streamed through its high pointed windows.

In 1294, just after he had begun Santa Croce, when he was a man of sixty-two, he was given by the city the commission to turn Santa Reparata into a great *duomo*. Now he was told to build the most splendid and beautiful church possible, all of marble, and adorned with statues. Siena, Orvieto, Pisa, they were well aware, already had built or were building cathedrals larger and more ornate than Santa Reparata. Their own must surpass all these, be the grandest at least in all Tuscany. For this they voted certain taxes. So Arnolfo set to work, made his plans and built a model. It should remind the people of their cherished Santa Reparata, which probably, like San Miniato, had been faced with panels of serpentine and other colored marbles, but it should also have the newer, Gothic look, not a flat wooden roof but one of stone, high and vaulted. There should be great pointed arches, long pointed windows, in groups, capitals with rich foliage. Outside, the façade should have three doors, have gables, and pinnacles, decorated cornices, sculptured figures, much patterned marble, and mosaics shining with gold as well. There should be a cupola and lower cupolas above the chapels grouped around it. The whole should have grandeur and spaciousness to the glory of the eternal God—and of Florence. (In the Spanish chapel of Santa Maria Novella a detail in a fresco shows the *duomo* as Arnolfo is supposed to have conceived it.)

To lay the foundations he poured into the great preliminary excavation rubble and then more rubble until everything underneath was solid. Then the walls began to rise. Dante, Arnolfo's friend, it is said, day after day, sat on a stone in the piazza and watched as the building grew. People still point out the spot. By 1300 all the *signori* and the people could begin to see how great was to be this edifice, and they voted to exempt Arnolfo for his life from all taxes and assessments, since through 'his industry and genius' the cathedral promised to be what they had hoped.

But great building takes time when there are no bulldozers and no cranes, when materials arrive by donkey-transportation, when every few days some saint merits a celebration. The long walls were only partly up when Arnolfo died, at seventy-eight. So the cathedral we see today is not his. Other builders came and changed and modified, and in places enlarged his plan. Yet Arnolfo's name will always be associated with it. One feels even now a kind of family resemblance between it and Santa Croce, seeing the same great piers, recognizing the same spaciousness and airiness, the same essential dignity in its interior, the same marble panels outside. On the wall of its left aisle as one enters, there is a memorial to him, the first architect of Santa Maria del Fiore; and in Santa Croce Giotto is thought to have portrayed Arnolfo in a fresco (in that of the monks lamenting the death of St. Francis), one of two men talking together in the foreground.

Little Colle di Val d'Elsa is not one of the great hill towns, but it has flavor, charm, and memories—memories that reach even farther than the views across the hills from Arnolfo's high tower.

6

Siena

ONCE, years ago, I was standing at my window in Siena at dusk looking out across the valley. Then in the *campo santo* that crowned a low hill beyond, the lights began to wink on until it seemed that every grave had come alive. That moment has been for me ever since a warm memory, knowing that those who have gone on still have their lights shining through the night.

It is not a custom unique to Siena, though well it might be; for among the people of Italian hill towns none are more perennially and persistently alive than the Sienese. What they do they do with dash and abandon. When they fight, they fight it out, no holds barred. When they celebrate, they pull out all the stops and leave them out. They bubble over. When they build they think in terms of splendor and magnificence. When they paint they spread on gold as if it were a water-color. Not for nothing did the same wolf that suckled Romulus and Remus become their emblem. The city of Siena stands on three hills, yet seven times within its still-encircling walls the wolf reminds the passing throng of their heritage.

According to a favorite legend, Senus, after the death of his father, Remus, fled with his brother north to what is now Siena and there again set up the Roman wolf. Another story says that on their way they were hidden from pursuing enemies first by a black cloud, then by a white; and that in token of this favor of the gods, Senus chose black and white for his official shield. One sees it thus today above each door and window of the Palazzo Pubblico. One wonders, of course, whether the legend may also have influenced the builders of the *duomo* and campanile in their rather startling use of alternating layers of black and

white marble. However these things came to be, we know that Siena
was for a time a Roman colony, and the Roman wolf a familiar and
just possibly an inciting emblem.

It was natural enough, when one considers the position and
importance of their respective cities, that the wolf of Siena and the
lion of Florence should have been traditional enemies and rivals in
almost every way. To be sure, the wool trade in Florence had been
flourishing for at least two hundred years before fugitives from
Barbarossa at Milan in the middle of the twelfth century introduced
the art of wool-working to the Sienese. Actually in Siena it never
prospered as in Florence. The Sienese hills were more barren than those
farther north, not so full of swift streams to supply water necessary for
pasturage, and for the processing of wool. None the less by the thirteenth
and fourteenth centuries Siena's merchants, like those of Florence,
were going everywhere, to London, Flanders, Turkey, especially to
the great fairs of the Champagne in France. Like the Florentines they
were not only merchants but bankers; they were nimble in exchange,
and their interest rates sometimes reached sixty per cent. For a while
they may have surpassed even Florence in this field, for some of the
popes entrusted to them their funds—no small accounts. One of the
Chigis is said to have had 'one hundred branches' to his banking
operations. Moreover he possessed one hundred merchant vessels,
trading far and wide. He was but one of Siena's bankers. It was no
wonder that the city came to be filled with palaces and its towers so
numerous, as an old chronicler put it, as to resemble 'a canebrake'.
Moreover, Siena's artisans excelled in ceramics and in wrought-iron
work. The wealthier citizens wore as gorgeous clothes as the men and
women of Florence. They used tablecloths, napkins, sheets, and
mattresses. They washed their hands before they ate. Their women sat
upon rooftops dyeing or bleaching their hair. (It seems that even in
Siena many men preferred blondes.) They imported cosmetics, spices,
perfumes. They became expert in the manufacture of sweetmeats,
especially in the blending of honey, almonds, citron, lemon peel, and
other subtly flavored bits for *panforte*. These filled their cupboards and
those of many another in distant lands.

Life had its amenities and luxuries. Yet it was in no sense peaceful.
As Siena and Florence were rivals in business, so they were always

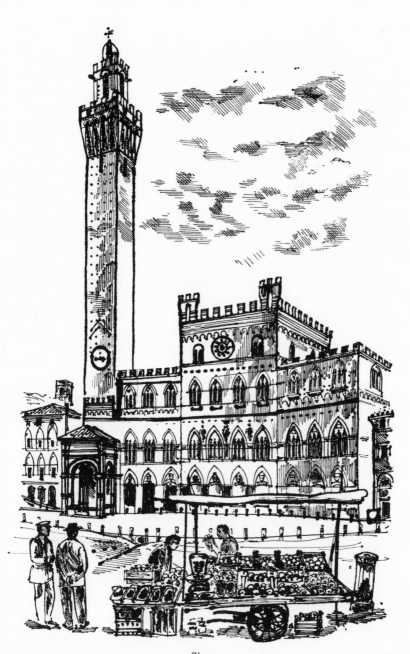

Siena

seeking to extend the boundaries of their respective *contade* (counties). They fought for dominance of all the smaller towns around, Poggibonsi, Casole, Montalcino, Montepulciano, Grosseto, Massa Marittima, Radicofani, and others. Florence was Guelf, Siena, by and large, was Ghibelline and supported the imperial cause. Every Florentine despised Siena. Every Sienese hated Florence. They had been battling each other since the 800's at least. Besides, the woods were full of feudal barons raiding from their *castelli* on the hilltops. Particularly did the Aldobrandeschi of Santa Fiora to the south harry the Sienese and their merchant trains.

Within the city there were similar rivalries. The Salimbeni fought with the Tolomei down the street, the Piccolomini with the Malavolti, the Saracini with the Marescotti, and so it went. Streets were narrow. People lived almost on top of one another. Skins wore thin. There were brawls, sometimes between one hill and another, or between rival *contrade* (*contrade* were the small parishes within a *terzo*, and a *terzo* one of the three main sections of the city). Those with the emblem of the goose might fight with those bearing the emblem of the porcupine, those of the caterpillar with those of the rhinoceros. Streets were often bloodied.

It was on one such occasion while the local Council of the Bell, the governing body, was meeting at San Cristofano (now Cristoforo) and discussing how to stop a current brawl, that two emissaries from Florence rode, uncontested, through the gate and brought to the councillors an ultimatum. The Sienese must open their gates and tear down their walls so that the Florentines might enter where they should choose; they must deliver up the Florentine exiles (Ghibelline) who had taken refuge in Siena; this they must do at once or suffer utter destruction. An army was already on its way to enforce the ultimatum. There was consternation in San Cristofano. Some were for yielding, for the army of Florence numbered at least forty thousand men, possibly many more. It had been augmented by troops from Perugia and Arezzo, from Colle, Bologna, San Gimignano, Lucca, Volterra, Prato, and other towns. Siena had but its own citizens plus the five hundred Florentine exiles and eight hundred German mercenaries sent to them sometime before by Manfred of Sicily. But one of their number, Provenzano Salvani, persuaded them otherwise. The councillors sent back word that they would give their answer in the field. The wolf was snarling.

Now the bells rang, and people rushed into the streets, especially into the piazza before San Cristofano; and at the summoning of the bishop the clergy and all the lay brethren betook themselves in haste to the *duomo*. The councillors quickly elected Buonaguida Lucari their dictator. Coming out into the air, he addressed the crowd, telling them of the great danger that beset their city. 'Men of Siena,' he said, 'let us surrender ourselves with all our rights to the Queen of Eternal Life, Our Lady and Mother, the Virgin Mary! Follow me now, all ye freemen, pure in faith, to make her this offering.'[53] Bareheaded and barefoot, he started toward the cathedral. The councillors and the people followed calling all the while 'Misericordia'. The bishop, also barefoot, was waiting at the door. When he had kissed Buonaguida, the two proceeded to the altar and there knelt; and as they did so, persons who had been enemies for years embraced one another and fell on their knees. Rising, Buonaguida laid the keys of all the gates of the city on the altar and addressing the Virgin gave the city into her keeping from 'the lions that seek to devour us'.[50] Then the bishop spoke, exhorting them all to forget their differences great and small. When all the people had taken the sacrament, they formed again in procession and marched through the streets singing hymns and calling 'Ave Maria'. So Siena became the city of the Virgin, *Civitas Virginis*, and has been ever since, for had not Buonaguida, in his final word, addressed the notary thus: 'Do thou take note of this donation that it is forever so long as the world endures.'[36]

The next morning, September the third, 1260, twenty thousand Sienese soldiers, on horse and on foot, passed out through the Porta Pispini (then the Porta San Vienne) to meet the Florentine army. Several kilometers out, by the Arbia, on the field of Montaperti, the battle ensued. It was a 'famous victory' for the Sienese. Ten thousand Florentine soldiers were dead, twenty thousand others wounded or taken prisoner. The Arbia ran red from the blood of men and horses. Yet more humiliating even for the Florentines was the loss to Siena of their *carroccio*. Among the communes the *carroccio* was 'a symbol of independence'. It was a cart drawn by white oxen in vivid trappings, and surrounded in war by men pledged to defend it with their lives.

It had a mast bearing the standard of the city and a platform on which an altar was set up. On this before a battle a priest said mass. Beside it the captain of the forces always pitched his tent, and from it the order for battle was given. This *carroccio* had been captured, and the red and white banner of Florence dragged in the dirt behind a donkey.

The next morning the Sienese soldiers returned to the city. The women met them at the gate, crowned them with olive branches. Then once more a procession moved to the cathedral. For three days the people continued praying and giving thanks to the Virgin, their protector and 'advocate'. Never have the Sienese forgotten this their greatest moment in history.

Church and city were indeed from the early days of Siena's life closely integrated. The councillors, having no building of their own until the completion of the Palazzo Pubblico in 1309 or 1310, met in San Cristofano; the *podestà* had his office in San Pellegrino. Even as early as 1200 a statute had required each citizen of the city to bring to the high altar of the cathedral a wax candle on the eve of the Feast of the Assumption. The people went in a great procession by trades each in the colorful costume of his district or of his craft. Preceding these were the nobles and the officers of the commune. On the next day, the fifteenth, representatives from every subject town or village or *castello*, every robber baron under Siena's jurisdiction, came to pay his tribute tax in money, wax, candles, or brocades at the *duomo*. There it was recorded by a municipal clerk. One village sent a committee of its citizens with a twelve-pound candle, another with twenty-five pounds of wax. Grosetto had annually to send fifty of its citizens, each with a candle, Montepulciano also. So each of the two hundred or more towns and villages that at one time or another were dominated by Siena renewed its allegiance to her at the *duomo*. There must have been on that great August feast day almost a constant procession through the gates, each delegation in their most resplendent local costume, moving through the streets with banners fluttering, each person with a lighted taper, knights and simple *contadini*. That night bonfires blazed on all the surrounding hills, torches flamed from battlements within the city, and in Il Campo barrels of tar were set on fire.

Of processions, in fact, in medieval days, there was no end, and every one, wherever it originated, moved through or around Il Campo. There was a memorable occasion when a holiday throughout the city was declared, the shops closed, and the bells rang in all the churches. That was the ninth of June, 1311. For nearly three years in his studio in Via Stalloreggi, Duccio di Buoninsegna had been working on his altarpiece for the *duomo*. Now it was ready. It was, according to those in the know, 'the most beautiful picture that ever was seen or made'.[36] In its original form it was an elaborately contrived screen with gables and steps, painted on both sides. The front panel showed the Virgin on a heavy and richly carved throne, holding her infant son. Angels surrounded her and saints. Kneeling in the foreground were the four patron saints of the city. Above at either side were half-length figures of ten apostles (Peter and John were two of the saints in her immediate entourage and so not here included). On the back were twenty-six scenes depicting the passion of Christ.

When the painting was reverently lifted from the studio, a great procession formed. There was the local band, the trumpeters, the drummers, the tambourine players, then the bishop in gorgeous vestments, followed by priests and companies of friars. Behind them came the *signori*, other officers of the commune, and the more important citizens, carrying burning candles. After these the populace fell in, and last of all the women and the children. Through the Via Stalloreggi, the Via di Città, down to Il Campo, then back to the cathedral a joyful people marched, while all the bells kept ringing. But new generations demanded new styles. Two hundred years later Duccio's masterpiece, his *Ancona*, came down. Today, what is left of it is to be seen in the cathedral museum (Opera del Duomo).

Though the *duomo* usually saw Siena at its reverent best, the streets and Il Campo sometimes saw its citizens in moods of wild hilarity. Siena loved entertaining visiting dignitaries. When Eleanor of Aragon stopped on her way to be married, a dance was held and in the street a fountain was improvised. On one side it spouted red wine, on the other white wine, and in the center—believe it or not—water. Silver cups were provided and everyone could drink his fill. In 1463 the Duchess of Calabria visited the city. For her a dance and pageant were arranged. All the young women were invited and came in their most gorgeous gowns and precious jewels. A great she-wolf had been manufactured and gilded and set up in Il Campo. Out of it at the appropriate moment came twelve persons 'right well and richly adorned, and one dressed like a nun, and they danced to a canzone that begins: "She won't be a nun any more." '[17] Then there was general dancing and singing and 'a goodly collation was provided'.

When Pius II (whom they claimed as their own Piccolomini pope, though he had been born in Corsignano) came on his way to Mantua he was greeted by bonfires, trumpets, and bells. People embraced each other on the street, as well they might, for Pius had made their city an archbishopric, had granted them Radicofani as a possession, and had demanded that the *nobili*, long deprived of it, be given a share in the city government. When he returned in February, again they dressed the city as for a festival with evergreens and flowers; and the people were singing like robins after a rain.

Then there was the day, June 1, 1343, when water was first brought into Il Campo and the Fonte Gaia (because of the joy of the people over it) began to flow. For eight days before and after the people celebrated. Every guild came to Il Campo in its own costume, the woolworkers, the tanners, the dyers, the ironmongers, the potters, the goldsmiths. They held games, feasted, and danced. At night as many as five thousand burning candles and torches moved like huge lumbering fireflies among the dancers. Such was Siena's joy at the gift of water in Il Campo. (The Fontebranda in the valley below San Domenico already existed.) Presently they unearthed from beneath one of the palaces an ancient statue of *Venus*, signed Lysippus. This they carried in procession to Il Campo and mounted it proudly atop their fountain.

Fourteen years elapsed, years of conflict and calamity. Finally a councillor suggested that all this time they had been honoring a pagan goddess; possibly their misfortunes could be laid to this account. In an orgy of fury the people tore down the statue, smashed it to bits, and the bits they buried significantly in Florentine soil.

The fountain still remained. Not until the early fifteenth century did the city commission one of its sculptors, Jacopo della Quercia, to decorate it. His was a notable work. It was a marble basin thirty-five feet long, built into the hillside. The inner surface of the walls at the back and sides he covered with deep bas-reliefs. At one end was the creation of Adam, at the other the casting out of Adam and Eve from the Garden; in the center was the *Madonna and Child.* Other niches held statues of the Virtues. But time and weather, though sluggish, are also carvers; and animals and men are often oblivious of beauty. In the 1800's della Quercia's work was replaced by a copy. The damaged originals may still be seen on the top floor of the Palazzo Pubblico.

Il Campo was also a place of games and tournaments. In the early medieval days it often saw buffalo-races and donkey-races and a 'furious game of fisticuffs'[17] involving sometimes as many as six hundred men, the Giuoco della Pugna. All these of course were forerunners of the relatively modern Palio, that pageant of medieval manners run there today in July and again in August.

This Palio is ostensibly in honor of the Virgin. On the banner (*palio*) awarded to the winning *contrada* on July 2 is a figure of our Lady of Provenzano, on August 16 a depiction of the Assumption. To give the occasion further religious significance the horse of each contestant is led, in advance, into the church of its quarter to be blessed by the priest.

Only ten of the existing seventeen *contrade* are allowed to enter the race. For days before, the preparations go on in a tumult of expectation. Each district decorates its streets and buildings with its colors and emblems. There is the wolf, of course, the goose, the eagle, the snail, the turtle, the mussel, the panther, the porcupine, the ram, the owl, the giraffe, the unicorn, the dragon, the caterpillar, the forest with a rhinoceros, the wave with its dolphin, the elephant bearing a tower on its back. Then the flag throwers are rehearsed, two for each *contrada*, and a drummer. They are dressed in medieval costume from the feather in the hat to the pointed shoes. They are as Aldous Huxley says, like 'personages out of a Pinturicchio fresco'.[30] Their flags, each of several colors, they pass back and forth, shift from hand to hand, now under a leg, now over the head, then they hurl them high into the air and catch them as they flutter down.

During the race, three times around the course, the jockeys urge on their horses by every means available. (One doubts whether they have found any means more efficacious than that medieval one mentioned by Sacchetti of putting a thistle under the tail of the horse.) After it is over, there ensues a night of bacchanalian revel. Forgetting all restraints, men have been known to dive into fountains filled for the occasion with wine.

Shaped much like a shallow amphitheater, Il Campo was laid out in 1194. Until the middle of the fourteenth century it was a soggy mess of mud in winter, in summer a field of dust. In 1346 it was finally paved with brick, the material most readily available. Streamers of travertine, radiating from a point directly in front of the Palazzo Pubblico, divided it in sections, thus symbolizing the city government reaching out in every direction. On the far side of a line of posts ran a stone roadway separating the brick center from the surrounding tangle of houses and palaces with their wooden overhanging loggias, as shown in a contemporary painting.

On this *corso* the Palio is run. There, too, one can sit out, as in the Piazza Repubblica in Florence, at tables on the uphill side and sip *caffe espresso* or *cinzano* with some *cavallucci* in the afternoon or perhaps a glass of Brolio with lunch, while one gazes upward and all around at the palaces and at the slender Mangia tower rising into the sky like a gigantic candle. In the morning against the light it is a purplish shadow; at sunset it glows against the blue.

So clean and inviting now, it is hard to realize what Il Campo must have been like in the twelfth, thirteenth, and fourteenth centuries. There pigs roamed at will, encouraged as official scavengers to nuzzle for the garbage dropped from carts on market days. Cattle, too, were brought here for periodic sales. The small tradesmen and artisans, the cobblers, the makers of sweetmeats, the bakers, and others here displayed their wares. At the time of the Feast of the Assumption a fair was held which attracted traders from Florence and beyond, and the town was filled with tumblers, jesters, ballad singers, and stray musicians of all kinds. There, too, gambling booths were set up. Occasionally there were simple pageants on a stage, representing scenes from the life of Christ. Later there came to be miracle plays with speaking parts arranged.

There were grimmer occasions. Here came San Bernardino preaching against luxury and the shamelessness of the times and implementing his words with a bonfire. Here on Il Campo the knights and foot soldiers assembled before they went forth to battle. On occasions of emergency at the main door of the Palazzo Pubblico a candle was lit;

and every man of battle age must be there ready before the candle
had sputtered and gone out. Here, too, was a usual place of the execution of prisoners.

Yet as the moods of the people swung back and forth, restless as
the plashing waters of their Fonte Gaia, there in front of them stood
the Palazzo Pubblico (1287–1309), solid, stately, and beautiful, and
above it the Torre del Mangia (1325–1345). It is one of the most
picturesque and imposing municipal buildings in the hill towns, if not
in Italy. Not even the Palazzo Vecchio of Florence, which this ante-
dates by some ten years, is more impressive. It is of gray travertine
on the ground floor and above of a weathered soft red brick. It is
distinguished further by its shape, a central mass rising to four stories
(three according to continental counting) with a wing at either side;
by the gracious curving also of its façade to the line of Il Campo itself.
Two rows of triple-light, slightly cusped windows under heavy solid
Gothic bearing arches extend the length of the building. High on its
face is the familiar monogram IHS (*Iesu Hominum Salvator*) surrounded
as if by a sunburst. Their own San Bernardino had persuaded them to
put it there and had urged them to use it on their palaces in place of
armorial bearings. It emphasizes once more how close were the church
and city government of Siena, as we shall see again in the council
chambers within. At the foot of the tower extending into the street
is an open votive chapel erected (1352–1376) in token of the city's
thanksgiving for the cessation of the Black Death.

One could hope that a visitor's first view of the Palazzo Pubblico
would be that dramatic one, framed by old palaces with bracketed
lanterns, from a steep slot-street leading down from the Via di Città.
Then the Mangia Tower (two hundred and eighty-four feet without
counting the lantern) 'soars and soars', as Henry James says, 'till it
has given notice of the city's greatness over the blue mountains . . . a
Declaration of Independence'.[31] Yet it was more than a symbol of
'pride and power and prodigious vitality': it housed at last the bells
that heretofore had hung in rented towers. Every morning at dawn
they had rung for an hour till every tired sleeper was awake. They had
called the councillors to their business, sounded the alarm when
danger threatened, summoned everyone to joyful celebrations. And
the man who had for years been ringing them, Giovanni di Duccio,

was out of a job, replaced by a wooden, later a bronze, contrivance. Over the wine tables in the *osterie* he had been nicknamed Mangiaguadigni—Mangia for short—and now this name was laughingly attached to the tower. The bells six centuries ago tolled him to his grave but still it is la Torre del Mangia.

One may climb the tower, if one has the energy, and look far across to the slopes of Monte Amiata. Most people, however, will prefer to go inside at once to explore the rooms upstairs in the Palazzo Pubblico where the *signori* used to hold their meetings and to see the exquisite little chapel there in honor of the Virgin. A beautiful wrought-iron gate gives entrance to it. Along its sides are carved and inlaid wooden choir stalls. Above these are Taddeo di Bartolo's frescoes of the apostles visiting the Virgin, of her death and funeral, and of her son welcoming her to heaven. Singing angels adorn the ceiling, and over the altar is a *Holy Family* by Sodoma.

The other rooms are decorated by frescoes both religious and secular by Sienese artists, Simone Martini, Ambrogio Lorenzetti, Guido da Siena, Il Vecchietta, Sodoma, and others. Two by Simone Martini in the main council chamber (Sala del Mappamondo) merit special attention. One, suitably, is his *Maesta*, the Virgin and child with angels offering flowers, and saints and apostles in attendance. Under a canopy she sits enthroned. The child stands on her lap, with one hand raised as if to bless the councillors; in the other he holds a scroll admonishing them to study justice. The Madonna is every inch a patrician, a mature and thoughtful woman. The child resembles her surprisingly, as if the same model had sat for both. The saints are grouped not in serried ranks, but with a degree of naturalness. The whole, though one of Martini's earlier paintings (1315), exemplifies his love of color and decoration. The throne is gilded. In the background are long Gothic mullioned windows of delicate tracery. The Madonna is robed magnificently in a bordered brocade with a jewel at her neck. The haloes round her head and that of her son are like golden dinner plates with rims embossed with leaves and flowers. If the councillors were ever to get bored in their deliberations they had but to look up at a lovely lady.

Across the room there is a fresco of *Guidoriccio da Fogliano* riding to the capture of Montemassi, one of Siena's subject *castelli* that had revolted. Simone Martini here shows both Guidoriccio and his charger in patterned coats of mail. On the hilltop ahead is the towered village etched against the sky, and in the background his camp and some of the engines of war.

In the Sala della Pace adjoining we come to the Lorenzetti allegories of *Good* and *Bad Government* with their attending virtues and vices. In the first, *Good Government*, an old man stands, and seated on a long divan are, on the right, magnanimity, temperance, and justice, on the left prudence, fortitude, and peace with their symbols. There are many other figures, citizens, prisoners, Romulus and Remus and the wolf, faith, hope, and charity. Peace, however, is set apart, a large feminine figure in a diaphanous white gown (giving somewhat the effect of sculpture), and with a crown of olive leaves. She is wistful and relaxed, half-reclining against a cushion, one arm supporting her head, a conception of peace, in these days, far from realistic. At the extreme left are other figures, a grandiose justice looking up toward wisdom, concord seated beneath.

His fresco of the *Effects of Good Government* is far different. In the background is Siena with its palaces and towers, even the *duomo* and the campanile at the left, and in the foreground the manifold activities of its citizens with their loaded donkeys, their dances, and their games.

In these rooms are other paintings worth noting, a Vecchietta of *St. Catherine*, the emaciated *San Bernardino* by Sano di Pietro, a *Madonna* by Guido da Siena, and three Sodomas in which one feels the liveliness of the Renaissance replacing the haunting beauty and color of the medieval Sienese.

As one leaves the Palazzo Pubblico on one's right is the Palazzo Sansedoni, of the same weathered red brick, the same curved façade, the same triple-light Gothic windows, though it was built much earlier, having been begun in 1216. At one time it had a tower but little lower than that of the town hall. The most beautiful palaces, in a city filled with them, are to be found, however, along the busy commercial streets just above Il Campo, Via Banchi di Sopra and Via di Città, and their tributary streets. One should therefore climb out of Il Campo beside the Loggia della Mercanzia, worth seeing for itself (statues by Il Vecchietta and Antonio Federighi, also high reliefs on the long marble bench, some of Romans by Federighi and some of the Virtues by Urbano da Cortona), and turn right to the Piazza Tolomei. There is San Cristofano, of no special distinction now, though once it was the meeting place of the Council of the Bell. It was here that the crowd first gathered before the battle of Montaperti. Directly across the street is the Palazzo Tolomei, supposedly the oldest private palace still existing in Siena. It was the home of one of Siena's greatest families. The two lower stories are a solid wall of stone pierced only by doors on the ground level and by two small shuttered windows on the second floor. This great expanse of wall gives it much the effect of a fortress, which it had to be in 1205, or thereabouts, when it was built, a Guelf palace in a city preponderantly Ghibelline. (Twice it was burned during political struggles.) Above, the third and fourth stories, divided from the lower part and from each other by decorative stringcourses, have each five twin-light rectangular windows. Over each of these is a Gothic tympanum enclosing three trefoils.

Only a block or two down the street on the opposite side is the Palazzo of the Salimbeni, sworn enemies of the Tolomei. Indeed, in the cloister of San Francesco there is a long flight of stairs leading to a sealed door. An inscription explains that this is the sepulchre of the Tolomei, eighteen of whom had been cut down at one time by an equal number of Salimbeni. The occasion, according to the legend, had been a banquet to which the Tolomei had been lured on a pretext of amnesty. There is also a more pleasant story. In 1260 just before the battle of Montaperti the German mercenaries demanded double pay for a month, and the councillors sitting in San Cristofano did not know where to turn for funds. Then Salimbene dei Salimbeni, head of the family, rose and somewhat diffidently offered to lend to the commune, without interest, the necessary one hundred and eighteen thousand gold florins. The offer was accepted. Thereupon Salimbene 'departed thence and got him to his palace to fetch the said money. And he set it upon a cart all covered with scarlet and decked with olive branches and conducted the said money with great ceremony to San Cristofano.'[49]

In this palace again we see the fortress-like wall and above, on the third floor, the characteristic triple-light pointed and mullioned windows under a Gothic, brick, bearing arch. The battlements, however, are carried by an arched corbel table. At either side are Renaissance palaces, that on the right the Spannochi Palace designed by Florentine architect, Giuliano da Maiano. All three are now occupied by the ancient and well-known Monte dei Paschi Bank of Siena.

Retracing one's steps to the Loggia della Mercanzia, one turns on the Via Banchi di Sotto, which angles downhill past, on the left, the University of Siena, an ancient and distinguished institution, and, on the right, the Renaissance Piccolomini Palace (1469), designed probably by Bernardo Rossellino. It greatly resembles the palaces of Florence of the same period. One should not overlook its wrought-iron brackets and the crescents of the Piccolomini crest. Today it contains the archives of the city, and a museum with many things of interest to an antiquarian, such as the will of Boccaccio, and especially a collection of the city's early account books, the '*Tavolette di Biccherna*', having on their covers miniature paintings done by some of Siena's greatest artists.

From there one may find one's way once more into Il Campo or go back to the Via Banchi di Sopra and thence south on its continuation, the Via di Città. Presently on the left one comes to another fine old palace, curving to the street, the Chigi-Saracini; in the thirteenth century it belonged to the Marescotti. Its tower then was much higher, and it was to its top that the drummer, Cerreto Ceccolini, is said to have gone on the morning of the battle of Montaperti to report the progress of the battle to the crowd beneath, mostly old men and boys —the women were in the churches praying. At intervals he beat his drum and shouted down: 'They mount the slopes of Monteselvoli; our line gives way, no, it is theirs'; and finally, 'their banners fall, they are broken, they are broken!'[49] At each announcement he added, 'Pray God for ours.'[36] Even today from the top of the Saracini Palace one can look far over the red and brown roofs of Siena to the green and purple hills to the east.

Count Guido Chigi-Saracini, an aesthete and a patron of the arts, has been the most recent owner. The courtyard into which one may freely walk is itself a lovely spot, with its wellhead, the sculptured faces on the high wall, the armorial bearings both Chigi and Saracini, the loggia high above, the figure of Pope Julius III guarding the entrance way. Upstairs there is a priceless art collection (open by request), largely inherited—Beccafumis, Sassetas, Sodomas, early Byzantine Madonnas, a Simone Martini, a Botticelli, a Lorenzo di Credi, a Neroccio di Landi, a Matteo di Giovanni, and many others. There, too, has been the Academia Musicale Chigiana, a summer school to which only musicians of proved merit are admitted. These study under distinguished artists. They have included such names as Fernando Germani, Alfred Cortot, Gaspar Casado, Pablo Casals, Yvonne Astruc, Artur Rubenstein. It is an international group of students and maestri and has done much since its inception in 1930 in developing concert musicians and musical research. From late November, also, to late May the concert hall of the palace has been used for benefit symphonies.

Almost across the street is another Renaissance Piccolomini Palace again of stone, designed by Bernardo Rossellino for the sister of Pius II. It is occupied by the Banco d'Italia. Inside in the courtyard an exquisite wrought-iron wellhead is set round with plants.

So along these streets one may go past one beautiful palace and another, each with its story or its particular architectural feature. The Buonsignori Palace, that of one of the leading merchant families of the thirteenth and fourteenth centuries, on the Via San Pietro is one of the most beautiful in its detail—its marble bench at street level, its delicate stringcourses, its arched corbel table supporting the battlements; on each crenellation is a quatrefoil within which is a bust. It now houses the local *pinacoteca*. On the Via del Capitano leading to the cathedral is the former Grottanelli, later the Palazzo del Capitano di Guistizia. It has a picturesque stairway in its courtyard and a cornice decorated with shields. Everywhere one sees sockets for banners or for torches, rings to which the knight tied his horse on dismounting, wrought-iron lanterns and family crests.

One may well believe that both personal and civic pride entered into the building of these palaces. The Sienese were like that; in 1398 the Council of the People passed something like a zoning law.

'You have,' their commission reported, 'your piazza of the Campo which is the most beautiful that exists, and you have had . . . the Strada dei Banchi . . . such that neither in Venice nor in Florence nor in any other town in this country was there a more beautiful street. Now it is spoilt; for shoemakers and tailors have returned to it, and it is spoilt. Let, therefore, our signori choose four citizens who shall have to embellish it, so that the bankers shall be together in one part of it, the drapers and goldsmiths in another, and that within these limits no other trades can be exercised. . . .'

Consequently, says Edmund Gardner, from whose story of Siena I have just quoted, '. . . there was a regular magistracy of three citizens elected annually to have the full authority of the General Council in all matters pertaining to the adorning of the city'.[17]

In nothing had the Sienese taken more pride than in their *duomo*. Sometime in the second quarter of the 1200's it was begun on the site of an earlier church dedicated to the Madonna. It was a communal undertaking, not of church dictation or direction. The popular assembly made the decision to build, determined the architect and supervisors, set their working hours and wages, and from time to time appropriated necessary funds. Marble was to be brought at public expense. Every citizen, however, with an ox or an ass was obligated to bring two loads a year from the quarries, and for each load the bishop was to give him a year's indulgence. Probably, too, a good part of the money brought in annually at the Feast of the Assumption (candles and wax were sold) was allocated to the building fund. Sometime in the early stages of the work the city fathers appointed a monk from Galgano as architect, first Fra Vernaccio, then Fra Melano.

The building grew slowly. By 1260 it was under cover; by 1270 the main structure was complete even to the cupola, and the magnificent pulpit had been finished. The work of decoration, however, had hardly begun. The façade was as yet a plain brick wall. Not until 1284 did Giovanni Pisano, Nicolo's son, begin work on it. Two years before the close of the century it was still unfinished. In the latter part of the thirteenth and in the early fourteenth century, however, Siena was experiencing an era of prosperity. The *duomo* began to look inadequate to her ambitious eyes, especially since Florence was building a great new edifice. Even the planned extension of the apse over the brow of the hill to accommodate a baptistry beneath was not enough. Sometime before, the idea had been suggested that a new cathedral be built incorporating the old as a transept. In 1339 the assembly voted this construction and a Sienese architect was recalled from Naples to take charge. Unfortunately a year later he died. After a temporary setback the work went on. The great new nave and aisles took shape, and a part was vaulted over.

Then in 1348 the Black Death struck. Two men would be talking together and one would drop dead. A man might lose all his sons, or a child be left with no father, mother, brother, or sister. No one knew the source of the contagion, only that 'the end of the world' had come. There was no time for graves or funerals. Great trenches were dug and bodies dumped in. 'And no bells rang and no man wept', wrote a chronicler of the time.[25] People were past grief. Each one thought that he was next. It was said that in Siena alone eighty thousand persons died. The once great city was but a town; in many a house and palace now no candle flickered. Then it was over. Those who were left embraced each other in the joy of being alive. There was a semblance of gaiety, and nobody had any zeal for work. Among some, as always, the occasion was one for drunkenness and wantonness. Many of the poor looted the homes of the rich, drank their wine, ate their food, and disported themselves in the gorgeous finery of those who had but recently, even as they, breathed the freshening air of morning.

There was no heart now, no money, no workers for any such ostentatious undertaking as the new cathedral. There may even have been a little of the spirit of an old Italian proverb, 'I care no longer for thee, Domine, now that the winter is past.'[56] Besides, it was found that some of the arches and vaulting were unsound. These were removed. But they left standing the skeleton, the bare bones of Siena's pride. There they stand today; and from the delicacy of a remaining portal, from the columns and walls one can dream of a magnificence that never was.

People call Siena's cathedral Gothic. Actually it is Romanesque. To be sure, the clerestory has Gothic windows. The façade, a modern reproduction of the original, is crowded with Gothic decoration, pointed gables, pointed niches, turrets, and pinnacles, all set round with twisted columns, statues, and fine stone embroidery till one does not know where to rest one's eye. Inside, the aisles are arched and vaulted but give no feeling of 'immaterial lightness' as in true Gothic. The multiple-columned pillars, too, would tend to lift one's eye but for their horizontal stripes. Sismondi in his *History of the Italian Republics in the Middle Ages* (p. 463) has well said:

'Italian Gothic . . . owes its sumptuous glory far more to glittering mosaic and precious marble than to purity of design. The Italian naturally inclined to the tranquillity of the long line, to shadow that required the small window, and to the cool spaciousness of the open dome; . . . The rich glories of color of Italian churches give the worshipper the feeling of heaven presented; there is little of aspiration.'[53]

So Gothic ornament was added to the bare wall of the façade; it had no structural function. Yet there is much both inside and out of the cathedral in which one may delight. Perhaps of a morning the façade may seem a glittering confusion, but if you come upon it first in a sunset light, you think it glorious. It glows; it is incomparably rich.

This is but an overall impression. One could spend days studying detail inside and out. He is fortunate who manages to see the cathedral in the weeks between the Feast of the Assumption and the middle of September, for then the pavement inside is uncovered. The designs were executed at many times, a few as early as 1369, others in the fifteenth and sixteenth centuries; by many different artists, Matteo di Giovanni, Pietro del Minella, Domenico di Nicolo, Urbana da Cortona, Beccafumi, Federighi, Neroccio di Landi, and others, and in different ways. In some the design was etched, as it were, in white marble and the lines filled with a black composition, hence the name *sgraffiti*. In other places the work is marble inlay in gray and white, black and white, or in soft reds and yellows. One need not identify the subjects. Any visitor will recognize Absalom hanging from a tree or Elijah taunting the prophets of Baal or other scenes from the Old Testament. Here, however, are ten sibyls of the ancient world, as well as Hermes. Socrates, Crates, and various philosophers appear in the allegories. There are also the seven ages of man and the symbols of various Italian cities. It is a unique pavement.

In 1266 Fra Melano had let the contract for the pulpit to Nicolo Pisano who had not long before finished that in the baptistry in Pisa.

Nicolo was allowed to bring along several assistants, among them Arnolfo di Cambio and his own son Giovanni. The plan of the pulpit differs little from that of the earlier one, though it is octagonal and is almost altogether of white Carrara marble. Here, too, the sibyls again appear, above the capitals of the supporting columns. The panels of the parapet are much the same in subject as those at Pisa, but here Nicolo (or perhaps one of his assistants) allowed himself to be somewhat more realistic.

Having looked at the pavement, the pulpit, Antonio Federighi's holy-water receptacles near the entrance, the exquisitely carved wooden choir stalls (fourteenth and sixteenth centuries) in the apse, the visitor might well suppose that he had already seen all that is significant within the *duomo*. Yet there is still much that he should not pass by, the Piccolomini altar with some of Michelangelo's early statues, the elegant baroque chapel of the Chigi (Cappella della Madonna del Voto), and in the Chapel of St. John the Baptist, the bronze statue of *The Baptist* by Donatello.

Most of all he will wish to see the Piccolomini Library (admittance by ticket), a great rectangular room, off the left aisle. For the ordinary person unversed in art it is a sheer heaven of color. It was built by Pius III to honor his uncle Pius II and ostensibly to house the latter's library. In cases around the walls are beautifully illuminated missals. Above them on the walls are frescoes by the Umbrian Pinturicchio assisted by his pupil Raphael. They show scenes from the life of Pius II: (1) as a young man on a white horse setting off to the Council at Basle (he was secretary to a cardinal. Raphael appears on one of the other horses); (2) as an envoy to the court of King James I of Scotland; (3) as poet laureate at Frankfort for the Emperor Frederick III; (4) as ambassador to Pope Eugenius IV; (5) as bishop of Siena outside Porta Camollia presenting the lovely Leonora of Portugal to Frederick III, to whom she is betrothed (in the distance are the *duomo* and campanile); (6) as bishop kneeling to receive the red hat of a cardinal; (7) as newly elected pope being carried in procession (1458); (8) at Mantua as promoter of a crusade against the Turks; (9) at Rome, as pontiff officiating at the canonization of Siena's own St. Catherine; (10) at Ancona as leader of the crusade preparing its departure. But all this history matters little. It is the people and the costumes and the color that matter, the far look through the arches of buildings, the glimpses of sea and sky and hills, of feathery green trees and dark cypresses, the glorious richness of the foreground fading into the limpid nothingness of the background. The same sort of thing is seen in many single Pinturicchio paintings elsewhere. Perhaps the greater impression that they make here comes from the fact that one is surrounded by many of identical quality. The sense of space is emphasized, the color as if heightened. Admitting that these frescoes are primarily decoration, as Bernard Berenson points out, not great art, one still must say, what decoration!

Outside, under the sky once again, is the entrance to the *duomo*'s museum built into the arches of the great cathedral's skeleton. It contains many things of interest, the *Three Graces*, for instance, once in the Piccolomini Library, Federighi's copy of a Roman work. There is also a famous Giacomo Cozzarelli statue in terra cotta of *St. John the Evangelist*. But one really goes to see Duccio's *Maesta*, previously mentioned.

Of course the visitor should go down the long flight of steps to the lower piazza. There the baptistry occupies as if the crypt of the cathedral. Inside it is a magnificent, vaulted, heavily frescoed room. In the center is the famous hexagonal marble font designed by Jacopo della Quercia. Around it in five bronze panels are bas-reliefs. Those of special distinction are that of *Zaccharius Driven from the Temple*, the work of Jacopo himself, *Christ's Baptism*, and the *Seizure of the Baptist*, both by Lorenzo Ghiberti, and *Herod's Banquet* by Donatello. From the center of the font rises an elaborate ciborium, also hexagonal, in the niches of which are five prophets all by della Quercia. At the very top on a column is a statue of *John the Baptist*. Though many artists had a share in the execution of this font, it is an outstanding example of Tuscan sculpture of the first half of the fifteenth century.

One cannot stop for everything. Yet there are churches to which one might well go, to San Francesco, for instance, on its hilltop, and to its neighboring oratory of San Bernardino filled with frescoes by Domenico Beccafumi, Sodoma, and Pacchia. To get into the oratory, however, is sometimes difficult, for one must ring for the *custode*, and 'peradventure he sleepeth'. San Agostino, too, is worth a visit for its Piccolomini chapel in which is a Sodoma *Epiphany* (Sodoma looks out

between two trees), a rare Martini triptych, and an Ambrogio Lorenzetti fresco uncovered not many years ago. In Santa Maria dei Servi
there are a *Massacre of the Innocents* by Pietro Lorenzetti and works by
Lippo Memmi. In the great church across the deep valley from the
duomo, San Domenico, are frescoes by Sodoma, his *Ecstasy of St.*
Catherine and her *Swoon*, also the supposed portrait of her by her contemporary and friend, Andrea Vanni. Besides, there is a beautiful
cloister and from a window of the main church a memorable view of
the city.

  Not far down the hill from San Domenico's towering walls St.
Catherine was born (1347) and lived, the twenty-fourth of twenty-
five children born to Giacomo (a dyer) and Lapa Benincasa (medieval
population explosion!). Even among so many she was never a child to
be ignored. She early began to think she was seeing visions, as later
she was often found in a trance before the altar. Sometime in her mid-
teens she chose the life of religion, never, however, becoming a nun
but associating herself with a Dominican lay order. She wore the
Dominican habit but lived as an ascetic at home, in a room she transformed into a cell, using a stone for a pillow. For three years only
she was a recluse. As a child she had spent much time on the little
Benincasa farm outside the city, and she was deeply sensitive to the
beauties of the world, to the violets and lilies, to the trees, birds, sky,
and 'the wind that bloweth where it listeth'. So in town as she began to
go about she became deeply conscious of her surroundings, of the
political shenanigans among rulers, of corruption in the church, of
strife among families, of pettiness, misery, and oppression everywhere.
She saw the church, if it could itself be cleansed, as a unifying element,
a deep well of peace. So she threw herself into the maelstrom. She
feared nothing apparently, held herself aloof from nobody. She nursed
the sick in time of pestilence, mixing them potions from the country
herbs she knew so well. She comforted a Perugian condemned to death
in Siena and held his head at the moment of execution. She wrote
letters to the King of France, to the Queen of Naples, and to others
in high places. Soon people began to seek her active participation in
their affairs. Montepulciano sent for her, as did Pisa and Lucca.
Florence, too, under an interdict from the pope asked her to go and
plead their cause with him at Avignon where the Papal See then had its

headquarters (1305-1378). She went, not only pleading their cause but that of the church, urging Gregory XI to move the papal throne back to Rome where it belonged. 'I beg of you,' she said, 'not to be a fearful child but a man.'[49] '. . . He who has no battle has no victory.'[35] She knew full well that the self-indulgent Curia, drunk with wine, fattened by gourmet-cooks, housed in palaces, would put every obstacle in the way of his moving to Rome. It is said that when she was first presented, after making suitable obeisance, she burst forth: 'To the honor of Almighty God I am not afraid to say that I smelled the stench of the sins committed in the Roman See more strongly in my native town than do the people in this very place who commit them here daily.'[37] It is thought that she had great influence with him. Some time later he did move to Rome, and there died. His successor not long afterwards summoned Catherine to Rome for her advice. There, at thirty-three, she died, and was buried. Her head, however, was carried back to Siena and is enshrined in a chapel of her native church.

Too often tourists shy away from art galleries thinking themselves untrained. But one can have fun in an art gallery if one approaches it with a certain gaiety and frankness of perception, not clouded by the comments of experts. It is fun indeed to go along with someone who sees it all a bit irreverently, who remarks on the 'overstuffed cherubs' or sizes up a situation: 'If only he'd had the story of Huck Finn to paint!'; whose interest is not half so much in Madonnas, however gorgeous with gold, jewels, and embroidery, as in the backgrounds and details and in the more realistic predellas—the latter usually show much more of the way of living and the temper of the period than do the paintings immediately above. Perhaps he spots a turkey in a painting dated earlier than any self-respecting turkey could ever have got to Europe. This is interesting. Anyhow before he leaves Siena, rather than at the beginning, every tourist should visit the *pinacoteca* in the Palazzo Buonsignori. There the impressions he has been getting all along of Sienese painting will be confirmed and amplified. He will see Madonna after Madonna, stiff in posture, ethereal in face and more or less expressionless; the detail and background rich in color and washed in gold. Here are all Siena's artists beginning with Duccio who set the style, both the Lorenzettis, Guido da Siena, Giovanni di Paolo,

Matteo di Giovanni (whom Berenson regards as one of the best of them), Sano di Pietro, Bartolo di Fredi and Taddeo di Bartolo, Neroccio di Landi, Beccafumi (see especially his *St. Catherine Receiving the Stigmata*), Sodoma, and others. These men were painting for the glory of God; their work was to be placed on the altars of churches. They were thinking not of earth but of the golden streets where, they had been told, saints and angels trod. There was very little effort at realistic human portrayal, very little dramatic quality or appreciation of the human form underneath the flowing robes. The feet of prophets and of saints, as Bernard Berenson points out, support only weightless bodies—as if they were in a space capsule. There are exceptions of course. Sodoma is one. He was a man of the earth, earthy. He loved animals, activity, especially horseracing. He had come from Vercelli and Milan, and in his youth had been greatly influenced by Leonardo da Vinci. One can easily see the difference in his strong but more muted colors, his more realistic showing of the human form (see *St. Catherine's Swoon*, in San Domenico, and his *Christ Bound to a Pillar* in this gallery). In Giovanni di Paolo's *Hell*, a detail of his *Last Judgment*, also one sees some of this interest, but in his *Paradise* the emphasis is once more on sheer beauty, on slim ethereal figures, on orange trees loaded with fruit, violets and lilies in the background—and strawberry trees such as the plant catalogues of today are advertising. Surely one need not be a connoisseur to enjoy an art gallery; one needs only to be able to see, and soon one will begin to recognize artists and schools of painting as one recognizes old familiar tunes.

Siena, like some others of the hill towns, is a place from which to make excursions. From there one can easily reach San Gimignano, Colle di Val d'Elsa, Volterra, Monteriggioni, yet there are two others one should not miss. One is the Abbey of Galgano, a ruin to be sure, but a national monument, and like Tintern Abbey on the Wye in England a place of dreams and 'the still, sad music of humanity'. The other is Monte Oliveto Maggiore, to the southeast. Each is eighteen to twenty miles away, for the most part over good asphalted roads.

The Abbey of Galgano lies to the southwest toward Massa Marittima. For several centuries the monastery of San Galgano, founded in the 1100's by Cistercian monks, presumably from France, was a center of learning throughout the whole Siena district. Among the monks were many physicians and surgeons trained at Montpelier and Salerno, architects, teachers, business men, and those whose work it was to clear the forests all about, to tend the vineyards and orchards, and sow the fields. Soon boys from all the country around flocked to San Galgano for instruction. In the early 1200's the monks decided to move down from their hill, Monte Siepi, where was the shrine of San Galgano and the little chapel, to the meadow. There they built living quarters for the order, a dormitory, refectory, rooms for a library and the various activities, barns, too. Then they began slowly to build an abbey church in Gothic style after the designs in northern lands, like those built by other Cistercians in Italy at Fossanova and Casamari. In the thirteenth century they became more prosperous, and their influence, too, began to reach farther. Siena, in particular, found their talents useful, sent for their architects for the *duomo*, for their business men to keep their money and account books. So it happens that Siena's *Tavolette* often bear the figure of a monk. But this prosperity was comparatively short-lived. The 'companies of adventure' came that way. Sir John Hawkwood, English mercenary in the employ of Florence, for a while made Galgano his headquarters. The abbey's influence and income declined. In 1503 the ruling pope gave the establishment to one of his cardinals who used it only for his personal aggrandizement. Then its doom was sealed. Finally there was only a caretaker left. Rain, wind, frost, and moss took over, and little animals made the abbey their home. One day the campanile fell. Then even the caretaker deserted. It became a lonely spot, and men began to carry away travertine for other buildings. In 1894, to save what was left, the government made it a national monument. Still standing are the Gothic arches, the clustered columns, the long pointed windows. Even in its bare outlines it is beautiful, one of the more beautiful churches of Italy.

Monte Oliveto Maggiore is in a highly eroded gypseous country, bleak and dreary, slightly resembling, though on a greatly reduced scale, the Bad Lands of the Dakotas. You approach along a ridge from which precipitous banks fall off at either side. Then all at once there is in front of you a gorge deep and green with stone pines climbing up its sides, their wide feathery tops glistening in the sunshine. A little way beyond and beneath, on what might geologically be called a bench, are the church and monastery of Monte Oliveto almost hidden among cypresses. Here it was to the family farm, in what was even then called the desert of Acona, that Bernardo Tolomei came one day in 1313 and built a cell and settled down. He had been in the University of Siena, a distinguished professor of law. Blindness struck him suddenly and though he soon recovered his sight, he accepted the temporary affliction as a warning and changed the whole pattern of his life. With him came two friends from other aristocratic Sienese families, and afterwards many of his students. There they planted vineyards and olive orchards, pears, apples, figs, almonds, ilex trees, and vegetable gardens, made walks outlined with roses, rosemary, and various herbs. They cleared out springs, made fishponds, places for bathing and for washing. Bernardo named it, probably with a double significance, Monte Oliveto. In time the group became the Olivetan order under the rule of St. Benedict. When in more recent years it with other monasteries was suppressed, the government nevertheless left a few monks in charge. One of them will take the visitor around to show him not only the buildings and grounds but the frescoes of Luca Signorelli and Sodoma illustrating the life of St. Benedict. It is for these especially that Monte Oliveto is maintained today as a museum. As one comes away and stands again at the top of the hill, looking now toward Monte Amiata, now toward the gypseous hills, then again at the glistening pines, one cannot help thinking that here it is not St. Benedict that lives again, but Bernardo Tolomei of Siena, in this green oasis in the desert where clouds and sky and trees are forever painting pictures.

7

The Island of Elba

'EH, MON ÎLE EST BIEN PETITE,' said Napoleon looking over the landscape from a hill above Portoferraio soon after his arrival in Elba in May 1814. A few days previously he had disembarked, ex-emperor of France, now emperor of Elba. There had been appropriate fanfare. On the way he had started his brief reign by designing a flag for the island, a white ground, a diagonal red stripe, and three bees. It had been immediately raised over Elba's fortifications and saluted by the British frigate and two ships of the French navy. Still on board, Napoleon had received many of the enthusiastic populace. Then in a uniform of a Chasseur of the Guard he disembarked. There was music, the firing of cannon, ships draped with flags, tapestries hanging from windows, many flowers, and the welcoming cries of the citizens. The clergy conducted him through lines of soldiers to the cathedral for a special service. Then everyone moved on to the town hall. Napoleon asked that the people be assured of his 'liveliest interest'. Seeing an old man whom he had once decorated with the Cross of the Legion of Honor, he sent for him, named him, greeted him with warmth. The festivities over, he retired to his temporary headquarters within the building. So began Napoleon's reign on Elba from May 5, 1814, to February 26, 1815.

He soon set about exploring his island, the fortifications, the iron mines, the granite and marble quarries, the salt ponds, the fisheries. He rode his horse everywhere over mountain trails to the farthest spots, often humming as he went. He visited Rio, Procchio, Marciana Marina, Campo, Marciana Alta, well up on Monte Capanne, Elba's highest mountain (over three thousand feet). He dreamed of what he would do, bringing water from the hills, building roads, developing the fisheries, the silk industry, the quarries, the mines. Elba of course reminded him of his native Corsica. It had the same rugged terrain, the same mild climate, much the same vegetation, and many of the same fruits. The hills were covered with beech, chestnuts, ilex, and pines. There were olives and grapes, figs, pomegranates, plums, almonds, prickly pears, lemons, oranges, and grain. The hillsides bloomed with poppies, morning glories, rosemary, broom, lavender, heather, agaves. There were many ferns, green and cool and moist. The woods and fields were full of hares, of birds of various sorts, quail and partridge, canaries, pigeons, blackbirds, sparrows for shooting. Little lizards basked in the sunshine on the tops of stone walls and went scurrying into crevices. The harbor was deep, sickle-shaped, and beautiful.

It was a garden spot where he could take a holiday enjoying his ease, holding court, gathering around him artists, men of learning, of affairs. It was a place which he could transform and develop—if only he had money. They had granted him an annual stipend of only two million francs. He was forty-five, and he longed to do things.

He began first of all to arrange for himself comfortable quarters in town, a house on the hillside where he could look out to sea. Two old windmills he transformed into a single stone house, with a library for his books, a main salon, reception rooms, bedrooms, a garden behind on a high point where he could mount a telescope and scan the sea for sails. There was a small theater, too. He would have liked also a stable for one hundred and fifty horses. He decided to have a country villa as well, a few kilometers out at San Martino on the slopes of a hill. There, too, through the fertile valley in the foreground he could look out to sea. It was not a large place, but had a studio and a kitchen, a room upstairs frescoed by Ravelli in Egyptian style to remind him of his Egyptian campaign, a bedroom or two, his own of course (his bed there is still shown), with a bath down a long flight of steps. Here, too, was a garden at the back and sides. He hoped that Marie Louise would come from Austria, but she never came. Only his Italian mother came to Elba and stayed, and for two tempestuous days Mme Walewski. His favorite sister, Pauline Borghese, came too,

Poggio

amusing herself by putting on theatricals at the town house in Portoferraio. There was another small place high in the hills near Marciana
Alta with a mineral spring, only two rooms where he went sometimes
to rest and have dinner outdoors. It was cooler there in summer, and
he could see Corsica when the weather was right.

At first he used to ask Sir Neil Campbell to dine with him, apparently
enjoying his company or thinking that some company was better
than none. Sir Neil was the English resident assigned to Elba to protect
Napoleon 'from insult and attack'. The emperor looked in vain,
however, for approaching visitors. He had his French guard of four
hundred men, but they showed little friendliness. The initial enthusiasm
of the people of Elba seemed likewise to dwindle. He was very much
alone. At night he often played cards with his mother. And when the
clock chimed ten he went to the piano and struck a few notes as a bed-
time signal. He was rotting here, without friends, without money,
without real activity, without anything to feed his ego. The island
indeed was small, only twenty-seven kilometers at its longest, only
eighteen at its widest.

So the months wore on in beautiful Elba. The winter came, with its
chill winds and fogs. Napoleon read the news from France; it was often
insulting. Louis XVIII and his ministers evidently had no fear of him;
they had not troubled to send even a French frigate or two to guard
against his possible escape. That was the cruelest cut of all. He could
take it no longer. In late February, with a carefully prepared plan,
he took off for France, to win back for himself the plaudits of the
multitudes, and after one hundred days to go down to final defeat.

The Napoleonic story is but a short bit of Elba's turbulent history.
The island was settled in the sixth century B.C. by Etruscans from
Populonia on the mainland of Italy, near the present Piombino. They
were seeking what men still chiefly seek there, iron ore and copper for
their foundries. Two centuries later the Greeks came from Syracuse;
still later the Romans colonized the island, and used the ore for the
making of their weapons of war. Virgil in the tenth book of the *Aeneid*
(Conington translation) refers to

> '. . . Ilva [Elba] . . .
> Rich island-home of Chalyb ore'

meaning copper. Throughout its later history the island was passed from hand to hand. The Pisans held it in the eleventh century and again in the early fourteenth. The Genoese had it for a while and ceded it to Lucca. In 1399 the Milanese took over, in 1437 the Florentines. Cosimo I dei Medici in the sixteenth century purchased Portoferraio, and built two fortresses, one at Marciana on the sea. For a while later the French held the island, and the Spanish. In the end it became a part of Tuscany.

It had from early days been subject to raids. The Carthaginians had ravaged it. Later there were Barbarossa of Algiers in the sixteenth century, and the corsairs. Not until in the seventeenth century was Elba freed of Barbary pirates, at last attaining some peace. It was no wonder that Elbans had early taken to the heights of Monte Capanne and established villages there at Marciana Alta and Poggio. The church had pioneered in this. When the Lombards had swept over Tuscany from the north, Bishop Cerbone had fled to Elba (probably in the 560's) and set up a hermitage on the mountain. There is a small oratory in his honor and in the village of Marciana Alta a small ancient church, San Nicolo.

Today all Elba seems a sweet and pleasant land. Villas cling to ledges along the rocky coast, dripping with bougainvillea and other vines, shaded by semi-tropical trees. Roads wind along much of the shore line, with magnificent views of mountains, sea, and forest, and through occasional valleys where vineyards, orchards, and fields are being tended. There are bathing beaches at Marciana Marina and at Campo di Marina. There, too, are harbors full of colorful fishing boats bringing in many kinds of fish and shellfish, even crayfish. Procchio has an artists' colony, for Elba offers much that tempts painters. At Poggio there are narrow stairways, old stone houses, secluded patios filled with plants. From high on the mountain at evening there are glorious sunsets, and after dark the lights glimmer far down along the shore. There are festivals on occasion, that of the flowers in May, of the fish in August, of the grapes in autumn, and the blessing of the sea in midsummer. There is much fruit, fine table grapes, and two good local wines, the white Moscato, the red Aleatico. And there are fresh winds off the sea. One need not be conscious of the cement works or industrial activities of Portoferraio, of the iron mines still feeding ore into the refineries at Piombino and elsewhere, of the granite quarries near Seccheto. Today the only corsair one is likely to meet is a friendly man leading his donkey into town with a load of grapes covered with leaves. Perhaps one may beg him to stop a moment to let one smell of their sweetness.

Elba is a vacation spot. It is a place in which to linger, and be lazy, to read and to dream, and perhaps, like Napoleon in his happier moments, to hum a little tune.

8

Arezzo

IT IS no mean thing to be able to say: Here lived a friend of the Emperor Augustus, a friend of Horace and Virgil; here was born Petrarch; here were found the great Etruscan bronzes of the *Chimera* and the *Minerva*; here were made the unique coralline vases; here lived and worked for years one of the greatest, if not the greatest, of the Renaissance painters of central Italy, Piero della Francesca, known also as Pietro dei Franceschi. To all this and more Arezzo proudly lays claim. Its street names are almost a roster of the great men it has given to Italy or sheltered for a time within its walls.

In its churches are frescoes and paintings by Cimabue, Luca Signorelli, Pietro Lorenzetti, Margaritone, Aretino Spinello, Bartolomeo della Gatta, Lorenzo di Bicci, and by many another. Ammannati, Bernardo Rossellino, Sansovino, Antonio Sangallo, Benedetto da Maiano, all had a share as architects in designing or beautifying its buildings. Andrea della Robbia left there, as in so many towns, evidence of his genius both in marble and in terra cotta.

Guido Monaco—Arezzo has named both a piazza and a street for him—in his youth taught music in his native town, then in Rome. Later a Benedictine at the abbey-monastery of Pomposa in the Po delta, he instructed his fellow monks in music. It was at Pomposa, there in the lagoons where the sea and river mingle and one is always conscious of the rhythm of the waters, that he worked out the principle, though not in final form, of the stave and the F and C clefs. For this he won lasting recognition. Fra Guittone, and Pietro Aretino, and Margaritone came from Arezzo, as did Redi, poet and naturalist, Andrea Cesalpino, physician and botanist, and Fossombrone, engineer.

Of course to most travellers Arezzo means the church of San Francesco and the frescoes there of Piero della Francesca. Yet to a few it is also the city of Giorgio Vasari, architect, painter, and writer of the sixteenth century. He was an indifferent painter though he left many works, in Florence, Rome, Venice, Camaldoli, Arezzo, and elsewhere. His home at 55 Via Venti Settembre, a house he bought and renovated, is decorated very largely with his own frescoes. As an architect he was more gifted. In Florence he built the Uffizi with its colonnades and the corridor along the top of the Ponte Vecchio that connects the Uffizi and the Pitti. In Arezzo his great work was the Palazzo delle Logge, extending from the Via dei Pileati to the Piazza Grande.

It is, however, on Vasari as the author of the *Lives of the Painters* that one prefers to dwell. To be sure, as history, the *Lives* are not accurate; they have been severely criticized and edited by scholars. Yet they are full of contemporary art criticism, of local color, and are often as flavorsome as a spice cake. Through a long life he had many opportunities to know artists, architects, and sculptors, and to gather the gossip about them, and he had made it his business to keep notes. As a youth, for instance, he had known Michelangelo well in Florence. In the *Lives* he tells of Paolo Uccello and how suddenly painting in San Miniato Paolo abandoned his work without a word. Finally, pressed persistently by the monks, he explained that the abbot had allowed him only cheese to eat, every day only cheese, and he was not going to take it. Laughing, the monks reported back; the abbot relented, and Uccello resumed the work. Paolo, too, was very poor, yet he loved animals, longed to keep them in his house as pets. Unable to afford to feed them, he filled his house instead, not with live animals but with paintings of them, dogs, cats, particularly birds; hence his name Paolo of the birds (*uccelli*). Sodoma, Vasari relates, had a whole menagerie in his home.

In the *Lives* one gets almost first hand the story of Luca Signorelli and how he comforted himself in the death of his son (see chapter on Cortona), of how Benedetto da Maiano turned to sculpture from the making of fine inlay woodwork. There one reads in detail the marvellous story of Brunelleschi and the building of the dome of the Florence cathedral. For years Brunelleschi had been preparing himself for just

Monte San Savino

this task, the like of which no contemporary architect had attempted. He had gone to Rome to study ancient methods; he had built himself a secret model to prove how it could be done—by building a dome within a dome. One learns with what cunning he finally competed for the job, of the details of the project itself, of the jealousy of Ghiberti, appointed by the city fathers as his assistant, and of how he handled this by absenting himself from the job, pretending to be ill, thus showing up the incompetence of Ghiberti. Vasari tells of the careful arrangements Brunelleschi made for his workmen, setting up eating places and taverns in the high scaffolding of the dome so that during the day they would not have to go down to the street at all; he had the wine, however, diluted with water to prevent them from falling off the roof. To one who has read Vasari, the building of that dome no longer seems just an architectural feat but a great human enterprise.

Arezzo, however, is not just a town where distinguished men were born and lived. It has its own distinction. Along with Cortona and Perugia it was one of the major cities of the Etruscan federation. Yet little remains from that era. The best of the bronzes—they were some of the best found anywhere—long since found their place in the Archaeological Museum in Florence. The *Chimera* belonged to the fifth or fourth century B.C. Two of its legs, however, are of the sixteenth century, restored by Benvenuto Cellini. In the local archaeological museum there is, to be sure, much of both Roman and Etruscan workmanship. One finds the usual urns, domestic utensils, decorative objects, votive figures, but also some specimens of the well-known *bucchero*, a glossy black pottery made even in earlier times by primitive people but greatly refined by the Etruscans (see Chiusi).

In this museum there is pottery also peculiarly of Arezzo, the coralline vases. They were manufactured roughly in the period from 200 B.C. to A.D. 100 during the Roman occupation of the city. The potters bore Roman names, but they employed great numbers of slaves, artists, and artisans; it may well have been that Etruscan workmanship found an outlet also in these. The vases are, it is said, of kneaded clay, fired under intense heat, and whether by an admixture of dye or some other means given a distinctive coral color. They are relatively small, and heavily embossed, in designs of fruit or flowers or sometimes of human figures. The clay may well have been that of the barren gypseous hills between Arezzo and Siena. The red clay of Siena has of course long been known.

During the Dark Ages the story of Tuscan hill towns varies little from that of Florence. Invasions from the north all took their toll. Arezzo in the eleventh century became a commune with its own consuls. For several centuries, however, it was really ruled by a succession of warrior bishops, by Guglielmo Ubertini, later by Guido Tarlati, greatest of them all, and at his death in 1327, by another Tarlati, Pietro Saccone. At one time or another it dominated many of the smaller towns about, Lucignano, Monte San Savino, Castel Fiorentino (then known by a different name), Borgo Sansepolcro, and various others. It was almost constantly at war with Perugia, Florence, Cortona, occasionally even with Siena, for possession of these minor towns. Arezzo was normally Ghibelline; Perugia and Florence were strongly Guelf. When Arezzo was defeated in battle, its Ghibelline leaders were exiled, their homes despoiled and burned, and the Guelfs moved into town and established their government. When the Guelfs in turn were worsted, their homes were burned, they were exiled, and the Ghibellines moved back from wherever they had taken refuge. These were bloody occasions. There was no mercy. Prisoners were usually tortured in process of being killed. To celebrate a victory there were always races before the gates or around the walls, often horseraces, sometimes an entirely different kind of *palio*. Once when Perugia had defeated Arezzo, the victors camped for five days outside the walls, had masses said by a rival bishop in the cathedral (at that time outside the walls). Then before the gates they held a *palio* of harlots who ran 'with their garments raised even to their girdles'.[24] And afterwards, 'the prostitutes which had run the *palio* at Arezzo returned [to Perugia], and they came all clad in rosy red, both they and their horses'. Such a race was no uncommon thing in the Middle Ages. Finally, toward the end of the fourteenth century Arezzo yielded its independence to Florence.

In Arezzo the Tarlati have never been forgotten. In the cathedral the visitor may be interested in seeing, close to the sacristy door, the grandiose marble tomb of the Bishop Guido Tarlati. The design of the tomb is said to be Giotto's, the execution that of two Sienese sculptors, Agostino di Giovanni and Angiolo di Ventura. The bas-reliefs depict the story of his life from his anointing and election as lord of Arezzo to his death, showing especially the sorry plight of the city before his ascendancy, its happier state thereafter, and the various villages in all the surrounding district that he took over.

There is much else worth a brief look in the cathedral; the sixteenth-century stained-glass windows of William di Marcillat of France; the fresco in the sacristy of St. Jerome by Bartolomeo della Gatta; the several terra cottas by Andrea della Robbia in the chapel of Our Lady of Comfort; the *Arch of San Donato* on the high altar. The latter is of white marble enriched with pinnacles and statues and many bas-reliefs depicting not only the life of the saint but scenes also from the life of Mary and of Christ. It is the work of two Florentine sculptors, Giovanni and Betto di Francesco. San Donato, whose reliquary it is, was the patron saint of Arezzo, martyred in A.D. 362.

The work of greatest importance in the cathedral is the fresco of *Mary Magdalene* by Piero della Francesca, beside the entrance to the sacristy. Here against a richly ornamented Renaissance background stands a heavily robed, flabby-faced woman. In one hand she carries a cruse for ointment; with the other, the broad coarse hand of a peasant woman, she tightly clasps her robe. The light and shadow, the colors, most of all the characterization, make this a memorable fresco.

The *duomo* itself, begun late in the thirteenth century, and not completed till toward the end of the fifteenth, is Italian Gothic, but in no way impressive. The hexagonal campanile is of the middle nineteenth century. At the far end of the park at the side of the *duomo* is what was once the *fortezza* built by Cosimo I dei Medici. From there, the highest point in town, there are excellent views across the city and to the mountains in the background.

From the *duomo* one may well walk down the rather steep Via dei Pileati, past Petrarch's birthplace (the present house is new, though reconstructed on the old plan; the original house was destroyed in the last war), and the Palazzo Pretorio, a picturesque building largely covered by the armorial bearings of the many lords and governors of Arezzo.

Even from the top of the street the campanile (a hundred and ninety feet), with its 'hundred holes' (windows), of Santa Maria della Pieve dominates the landscape. When one comes closer it is the façade of the church that rivets one's attention. With its eaves overhanging the heavy upper wall, its three tiers of loggias, its Romanesque arches on the ground floor, it seems much more like a great *palazzo* than like a church. At once one sees here Pisan influence in the four blind arches, two on each side of the central portal, and in the loggias. The lowest of these has thirteen round arches, and twelve columns. The middle one has twenty-five round arches, spaced more closely, and twenty-four columns. The topmost, spaced still more closely, has thirty-two columns supporting the wall above. In studying these columns and their capitals, however, one soon sees that these are not just Pisan; here is strong Lombard influence. The columns are of many sorts, some spiral, some plain, some carved in various designs; one seems to have a snake twisted around it, another on the topmost tier seems to be a human figure. The variation in the capitals is even greater. These are not Corinthian, Doric, or Ionic. They are crudely carved as by a people with no settled artistic tradition but rather with an untrained and unhampered imagination, characteristic of the more uncouth invaders from the north. Sometimes the Lombards did carve plant forms, but they gloried most in depicting creatures of the wild, birds, or beasts, or even men.

Lombard also are the bas-reliefs in the intrados (undersides of the arch) of the central portal. In each of four compartments the symbols of three months of the year are shown. For January there is the ancient Janus, or two-faced man, and a small kettle on the fire. For February there is the pruning hook (grapes doubtless and probably also olives were pruned in February). For March a bearded man is shown blowing a trumpet, an age-old reference no doubt to the winds of early spring. In the compartment to the lower right, April appears with flowers. For May there is a warrior on horseback. June is the month of reaping. In July the grain is threshed. In August the casks are being made ready, under a fig tree. September is grape-picking time. October is the month for seeding. In November men gather in the turnips. In December there is the butchering of a pig. War in these days was as much a routine activity, one notes, as seeding or picking grapes.

One need not linger long inside. This is in the general form of a basilica with a nave and side aisles divided by pillars and columns. One sees at once the raised presbytery with stairways leading to it. Below is the crypt, which contains a gilded silver reliquary of San Donato, the work of two Aretine goldsmiths of the fourteenth century. One notes also the pointed and Romanesque arches in the main body of the church, the blind loggias, the cupola, the carving of heads on the capital of one of the pillars supporting the cupola. Over the high altar is a polyptych by Pietro Lorenzetti, with his signature.

To see the apse from the outside—it is worth seeing—one should pass through the narrow Via Seteria (street of silk manufacture) to the well-named Piazza Grande. It is one of the memorable spots of Arezzo, a fitting backdrop for the 'Joust of the Saracen', the revival of a medieval tournament held here annually in early September. The piazza is on a hillside and irregular in shape, not a square, not a rectangle. The buildings to the north and south climb up the hill each some steps above the one below. The pavement, in herringbone design of brick, is divided into sections by strips of travertine, leading to a more or less central circle. To the west and south are ancient towers and dwellings, many with picturesque wooden balconies. In the lowest corner, not far from the Via Borgunto, is the old *pozzo* with its modern, though highly decorative, wooden roof. To the east is Vasari's Loggia, under the arches of which were the shops. Turning to the north again one sees to its best advantage the campanile of the Pieve and the apse.

Next to this but on a considerably higher level is the eighteenth-century Palazzo Tribunale (Justice) approached by a wide semicircular flight of steps. Beside it is the Palazzo della Fraternita dei Laici (palace of a layman's brotherhood, established in 1262). It is a strange edifice, having been built in various centuries, by various architects, and in various styles. It is like a layer cake. The lower part built by Florentine architects in the fourteenth century has a high portal and Gothic single-light windows at either side. Then Bernardo Rossellino in 1434 took over; his style was that of the early Renaissance and he introduced statues of the *Madonna della Misericordia* and of *San Donato* and *San Gregorio*. In 1460 still other architects added their bit, this time a loggia under the broad eaves and a balustrade adorned with a frieze of amphorae. As a *palazzo* it was complete. Then Vasari came along and he put on the belfry, which fools many persons into thinking that this is a church. The clock, however, by a still different hand, belies the thought; it is a thoroughly mundane object, recording the hours, the days, the movements of the sun, the phases of the moon. The whole effect of the building, nevertheless, is not unbeautiful.

There are many other things to see in Arezzo. If one wishes to get the flavor of the town, one should explore, as everywhere, the narrow side streets where many of the artisans and workers of today are living. The streets to the south and east and west of Piazza Grande comprise such a region, of old houses, palaces, and little churches. It was beside the church of San Lorenzo that the Etruscan *Minerva* was found. San Bartolomeo was built on top of a bit of Etruscan wall. In that district, too, was the old Roman theater (as distinct from the Roman amphitheater across from the archaeological museum). One should note especially the Vicolo Appuntellato to the right off Via dei Pescioni.

If one wishes to see the modern town, one should go all the way down the hill. There on the flat are the hotels and banks and modern shops; and outside the walls, the railroad station, the psychopathic hospital, and industry of one kind or another. It is outside the walls, too, along the Viale Mecenate, that one goes to see Santa Maria delle Grazie with its delicate portico built by Benedetto da Maiano. Inside the church one should see the Andrea della Robbia tabernacle of marble and terra cotta. It frames a fresco of the *Madonna* by Parri di Spinello.

If one is an enthusiast, one should go to San Domenico to see the Cimabue *Crucifixion,* to Santissima Annunziata to see the stained glass by Marcillat (sixteenth century), to the Church of the Badia for the carved and gilded door of the tabernacle by Benedetto da Maiano, to Santa Maria in Gradi for the *Madonna del Soccorso* by Andrea della Robbia, and of course to the *pinacoteca* in the Palazzo del Dogana. There are to be seen in this gallery not only the famous primitive of *St. Francis* by Margaritone, but works by Bartolomeo della Gatta, Luca Signorelli, Spinello Aretino, Parri di Spinello, Neri di Bicci, and many others. There is even a Salvator Rosa and a Grechetto. Besides these there are three rooms of majolicas (thirteenth–eighteenth centuries) from Gubbio, Deruta, Urbino, Durante, Faenza, Montelupo, Città di Castello, which, if one has not seen such majolicas elsewhere, are worth seeing. Incidentally, one can see an excellent collection of these in the South Kensington Museum in London.

All this, however, is really an aside, for most people who come to

Arezzo take off at once to the Church of San Francesco, to see the frescoes by Piero della Francesca on the walls of the presbytery.

Piero della Francesca (1405?–1492), born in Borgo Sansepolcro in Tuscany near the border of Umbria, early found his way to Florence. There he became a pupil of Paolo Uccello, who was already studying the principles of perspective. With an aptitude for mathematics, Piero, in time, developed skill in the application of these principles to a much greater degree than ever had his master, even writing a treatise on the subject. His composition, as Mr. Bernard Berenson points out, is not that of an arrangement of persons and objects on a simple flat surface, as had been the practice of artists of an earlier period, but the placing of them in space as well. His paintings, consequently, had depth, were three-dimensional.

Piero had studied persistently also Masaccio's and Masolino's frescoes in the Carmine church in Florence, had been an apprentice of Domenico Veneziano who was painting at San Egidio in Florence and Santa Maria Nuova. It was from Veneziano, Mr. Berenson says, that Piero learned much of the art of characterization. This was indeed when art was becoming more down-to-earth, when saints and sinners were not being idealized quite as they had been, but shown as simple natural persons who felt and moved and stood upon their feet, types the populace knew and met upon the streets. It was but a step from this more human presentation of Biblical scenes to that of historical painting, and another step to actual portraits (as Piero's portraits of the Duke and Duchess of Urbino in the Uffizi).

Mr. Berenson stresses the point that Piero's paintings are always 'impersonal' and 'impassive', a point that one does not fully understand until one has the chance to see several of his paintings. Piero, Mr. Berenson says, 'avoids' even trying to reproduce his own feeling. He presents a significant type, a factual scene or landscape. There is no sentimentalizing of either scene or character. They are there, simply, before one. And seeing them thus objectively presented, the observer is able 'to react' to them 'as he reacted'. For feelings cannot be exactly duplicated in another person, but the facts that create the feelings, light, color, movement, and form, are a language in themselves and speak directly to the person who sees them. Mr. Berenson refers also to Piero as 'perhaps the first to use effects of light for their direct

tonic effects or subduing and soothing qualities'.[4] These points one
should keep in mind in viewing Piero's paintings.

Lorenzo di Bicci had first been commissioned to paint the frescoes
in San Francesco; it was only at his death that Piero took over. Bicci
at that time had completed only those on the great arch and its under-
side. It was for Piero to paint the famous series on the walls of the choir,
that representing 'the invention and exaltation of the Holy Cross'.
This was a small part of the *Golden Legend of the Saints*, stories collected
and retold in the thirteenth century by Jacopo da Voragine, archbishop
of Genoa. In the latter part of the fourteenth century this work had
become, so to speak, a best seller; edition had followed edition, in
the original Latin and in nearly all the languages of the common
people throughout Europe. This then became for Piero, in a sense
though not in fact, a kind of historical painting, one of the first
examples of its kind.

In the story Adam is dying. He implores his son, Seth, to seek from
the 'Angel of the Terrestrial Paradise' the 'oil of mercy' with which to
anoint his sick body. The angel refuses but sends him back instead
with a twig from the tree of good and evil. On his arrival, finding his
father dead, Seth places the twig in Adam's mouth. There it sprouts.
At length it becomes a great tree. It is still standing when Solomon
begins to build his temple but it is considered ill-adapted for use in
that edifice. It is cut down and made into a bridge. When the Queen
of Sheba arrives to make a state visit, she kneels down at the bridge
and worships, for she knows that from this wood the cross will eventually be made. So she tells King Solomon, saying also that when the
crucifixion occurs, 'the realm of the Jews shall be defaced and cease'.[10]
Thereat Solomon has the bridge torn down and the wood buried.
(One wonders why Solomon in all his wisdom did not burn it.) Yet
as destiny ordains men build a pool above the spot where it is hid.
The time comes for Christ's crucifixion. The wood of the tree rises to
the surface of the pool, and men make from it the cross. Thereafter it
is buried again. Many years later it happens that Constantine, the
emperor, is awaiting on the banks of the Danube (Tiber in the picture)
Massenzio with his hostile army. That night in his tent, guarded by
two sentinels and his chamberlain, he dreams that a brilliant light shines
on him and his tent. The light comes from a small cross, on which,

in letters of gold, is written: 'In this sign thou shalt overcome the battle.' In the morning Constantine has a cross put upon his standard and carries it before him into battle. The enemy is defeated and driven into the river. Then Constantine inquires the meaning of the cross, and, learning, he is baptized. Later the empress Helena is sent for to come and find the holy cross in Jerusalem. Only one man, Judas by name, knows where it is hidden. She has him let down into a well for six days until he reveals the secret. The three crosses of Calvary are unearthed, yet no one yet knows which is the true cross. Only when one of the three touches the body of a dead man and he revives is the fact revealed. (The city in the background is not Jerusalem but Arezzo.) Helena carries a part of the cross back to Constantinople, and leaves the rest in Jerusalem. With the eighth picture the scene changes. Cosdroe, king of Persia, has pillaged Jerusalem and has carried away the part of the true cross left there. He has set himself up on a throne and is causing himself to be reverenced as a god. Thereupon he is set upon by Heracles and killed, and the true cross is carried back to Jerusalem. The final picture is the *Annunciation*. Such roughly is the story as depicted in the frescoes, though these show variations in places from *The Legend* itself. The frescoes are disposed upon the walls somewhat irregularly. Yet if one is familiar with the story one can follow the different incidents.

Of course San Francesco contains some other paintings, an *Annunciation* by Spinello Aretino, another by Luca Signorelli in the Tarlati chapel to the left of the choir. There, too, is a painting by Neri di Bicci. One should notice also the rose window by Marcillat.

Arezzo, with its good hotel, is a place from which one may make various excursions. Monte San Savino, some miles to the west, is a sleepy, little, walled hill town. From it Sansovino, the architect, came. It has buildings of his, others by Sangallo, a fourteenth-century church, Santa Chiara, with some good terra cottas and enamels, old walls and gates, Roman remains, and two or three small churches of minor interest. The town claims, rightly or wrongly, an Etruscan background. It is high, with far views over the countryside, to Cortona, to Lucignano, and other hilltops.

From Arezzo, too, one may go to Gropina, where there is a church probably of the twelfth century. Its plain sandstone façade with blind rose window has little to recommend it, but the rounded sandstone apse outside with its blind arches and its loggias, all framed by trees, is beautiful. Inside it is very dark; there are a few slit windows on the side like those of a fortress; the only real light comes from the window in the apse. It is a small basilica, a nave and two aisles, divided by seven arches at each side, columns, and one pilaster. The capitals are very crude, undoubtedly Lombard, carved with heavy leaves, with animals, and faces. The pulpit, too, is beautifully, if crudely, carved with wolf heads and eagles, and other creatures, all bound together by designs which look Byzantine. It was a Sunday morning when we were there; the padre was preaching, and the church was full of people, most of them young men. In a dark corner by the entrance on the floor sat two men and their dogs.

Gropina is up a hill just beyond Loro Ciuffenna. This picturesque town, said to be Etruscan, lies along the gorge of the Torrente Ciuffenna, which one crosses on a camelback bridge.

There is one pilgrimage, however, that any visitor to Arezzo will wish to make, to see two great paintings of Piero, one at Monterchi, the other at Sansepolcro. We set out on a misty morning and were soon climbing the first range to the east, winding among hills clothed with spruces and with hardwoods just turning from green to yellow and to red. The dampness made the coloration seem more intense; one might have thought oneself among the Pennsylvania hills. Up the valley of the Torrente Cerfone we finally saw on our right, on the crest of a steep hill, the village of Monterchi. We were not bound there, though it looked inviting, but rather to its *campo santo* (cemetery) a little farther on and up a long lane to the left. There close beside a farmhouse is a tiny chapel, to which the farmer's wife gives admittance. The whole air was redolent of the new wine in her cellar and while we were there two teams of white oxen came down the hill bringing more grapes from the vineyards above.

Now here was the painting, occupying the whole back wall of this tiny chapel, the *Madonna del Parto* or *Madonna Gravida* (The Pregnant Madonna). Clothed in a bright blue robe, parted slightly in the middle to show how far gone she is in pregnancy, she stands under a canopy, held back at either side by an angel. She is not the expectant mother tremulous with excitement at the thought of her first-born, not the adoring mother-to-be. She is a simple peasant girl, not even beautiful. She is utterly human and natural, very solemn, and somewhat worried, facing the world straight on, clearly unconscious of the ministering angels. It seems almost as if she knew instinctively that she carried within her him who would take on himself the burden of mankind's sin, as if she already saw in the far distance Gethsemane and the cross.

We backed down the long lane, for the oxen and the carts took all the turning space, retraced our way to the main road, crossed another low range of hills, and came into the wide valley of the upper Tiber. Beyond at the foot of the next range of hills was the walled town of Sansepolcro. Here is the *palazzo* where Piero lived and here in the Palazzo Communale, the local art gallery, with his *Resurrection*.

The time is early morning, at that moment when the world is not yet light but bathed in a kind of transparency. The wisps of cloud above the far hills are just slightly tinged. Deep shadows lie on the nearer hills. In the foreground at either side are trees. In the center is Christ. Across his left shoulder, hanging down, is thrown a great scarf, the color of a cloud at dawn touched by the sun. The spear cut in his side and the nail prints in his hands and feet are clearly visible. His face shows great suffering. Yet he is fit. Holding in his right hand the banner of the cross, he dominates the world. One foot is up on the stone coping of the tomb as if he were just then stepping out from its dark depths. In the extreme foreground, sprawled on the ground in postures of complete abandon, are the four guards sound asleep. There is no sentimentality here, just a great event happening in silence at early dawn without spectators. Aldous Huxley has called it 'the best picture in the world'. One cannot but agree.

9

Cortona

SIDE by side in Cortona are the alley of the night (Vicolo della Notte) and the alley of the dawn (Vicolo dell' Aurora). A Tuscan umbrella opened on either one would scratch its sides. They are stairways really leading nowhere in particular. They are dirty, hung with washings, and the walls of their houses are plastered with a variety of signs, an announcement of a movie perhaps, or a *Vota Communista* placard. Yet I never think of Cortona, perched high (two thousand one hundred feet) on a shoulder of Monte Egidio (three thousand four hundred feet) but I remember those two small streets. In how many places in this town, where one street is often almost at the level of the rooftops of the one below it, one could in fact watch the dawn over the Apennines to the east or in the evening look far out over the valley of the Chiana and the western hills, seeing perhaps the towers of Lucignano against the round red orb of the sinking sun. Or one could watch the mists over Lake Trasimeno, or the shadows creeping toward one up the long steep hillside while the light still lingered on the mountain-tops in the east.

But then remembering Cortona one thinks of many things, of views, yes of history, and legends, too, that cluster round it as pigeons round scattered corn, of simple parish churches from whose ogival towers the bells ring out across the roofs, of persons occupied with homely everyday activities who stop one on the street to talk a moment, of men and women, 'saints and sinners' who have called Cortona home and given it distinction, of colorful paintings, of bronzes cast by people who left few records of any kind save in their tombs, of great uncemented prehistoric walls.

First, perhaps, looking out from the hilltop over Lake Trasimeno, set with villages, one thinks of Hannibal, the Carthaginian, who, bent on conquering Rome, had driven his elephants across the Alps, had in early 217 B.C. followed through the flooded valley of the Arno till he had reached Fiesole and then had turned south burning and pillaging all the way in this rich Tuscan countryside. Meantime two Roman armies waited for him, one in the mountains to the east, one under the proud and arrogant Flaminius at Arezzo. The Roman general let the bold Carthaginian pass Arezzo, skirt the hill below Cortona, and go on to the more open ground beyond, where he camped for the night. Hannibal, however, had scouted well; he knew the narrow defile through which the Roman troops must pass in pursuing him, knew their numbers and character, and the reckless temper of Flaminius. Under cover of night he deployed some of his best troops on the hills above the narrow road, and his cavalry he placed just out of sight to guard the exit to the defile. The morning mists rising from Trasimeno, as he had known they would, hid them all successfully. The next day, early, Flaminius, thinking his enemy would already have headed down the road toward Perugia and Rome, hurried his troops along. As they got well into the defile, the Africans fell upon them from above. In front, escape was barred by cavalry. The mists that hemmed them in but added to their panic. That day fifteen thousand of the Roman army were slaughtered. Many not at first cut down ran for the lake and there, pursued to the end by Hannibal's cavalry, were drowned. Flaminius himself was killed. Yet of the troops of the Carthaginian only twenty-five hundred, Livy says, were lost. For days the buzzards must have circled round above that battlefield, as in later days after other battles by Trasimeno's lake.

Etruscans lived in Cortona then, had lived there no one knows how long, and probably before them the Umbri, and yet earlier possibly the Pelasgi, whoever they may have been. Parts of the great walls of these early peoples still stand in various places along the hilltop, used as foundations for later medieval walls. You can find them outside the Porta Colonia, circling to the left, or at Porta Montanina near San Cristoforo. On some of the hillslopes nearby, too, there are several Etruscan tombs; and in the museum (Palazzo Pretorio) a famous bronze candelabra—as well as bits and pieces from the tombs—dating

Cortona

to the end of the fifth century B.C. It is well worth seeing. There are sixteen oil cups fed from a central bowl. Around and between them are various mythological figures. Underneath, for this lamp was evidently intended to be hung from a ceiling, maybe in a tomb, is a large Medusa's head, surrounded by animals fighting one another, by dolphins playing in the waves, and by sixteen other figures, variously identified. Every other one of these sixteen is playing a double flute, the instrument so often seen in Etruscan paintings and sculpture. The candelabra is one of Cortona's proudest possessions. Many of their Etruscan findings have been lost to other museums; this they have kept. It is unique.

Cortona has other treasures. The paintings, for instance, of the white-robed Fra Angelico. For four years he lived there in the Dominican convent by San Domenico. The lunette above the door of the church is his. Several other of his paintings are to be found in the Diocesan Museum, the old Chiesa del Gesu, across from the cathedral. The greatest is his *Annunciation*. It is as beautiful as anything you will ever see of his. The spirit of Angelico was not confined to any cell; the whole vault of heaven was his, and the everlasting beauty of the earth. Here, as in others, there are a garden gay with flowers and the familiar columned portico into which the angel is entering and where the Virgin is sitting, just interrupted in her reading. With great solemnity the angel points a finger at her. His other hand, too, is raised, a finger upstretched as if warning her to keep silent. The placid Virgin showing more by her hands than by her face her bewilderment accepts him nevertheless as if the visit of an angel were an everyday occurrence. She seems indeed no more amazed than we were—when suddenly as if from nowhere a rat appeared on the top of the gilded frame, stopped a moment to look us over, and then went on. This was surely an earthy touch, yet probably it would not have shocked Fra Angelico half as much in his day as it did us.

At Cortona one thinks also of Luca Signorelli, its most distinguished citizen, born here in 1441. The town is full of his paintings, in the Diocesan Museum and in the churches. He was very much a family man, had three sons and two daughters. His mother had been Elisabetta Vasari, a great- (or great-great-?) aunt of Giorgio Vasari's, and Luca often went to Arezzo to visit his kinfolk there. Back in Cortona he was an influential citizen, a member of the Rotary club, probably. Time and again he served a term as one of the *priori*, one of the town council, so to speak, was sent once to Gubbio, and more than once to Florence, on municipal business, once as a member of a delegation to welcome the Medicis back to Florence. (Cortona was playing politics just then.) Luca's business, of course, was painting. Apparently he made it pay, for from all accounts he lived in no penurious way, loved clothes, and dressed himself 'handsomely'. Down in Orvieto's cathedral in a corner of one of his great frescoes, he painted himself—along with Fra Angelico. He is wearing a natty fur hat, mode of the day, and from under it his long wavy locks hang loosely to his shoulders; one could believe they had been freshly waved. He has a kindly face, and his eyes look out half-humorously on the world. That he was a kindly soul we have other evidence. Once visiting the Vasaris in Arezzo, he found the boy Giorgio with a serious case of nosebleed; it seemed that he suffered often from it and was in consequence weak. Luca came through with the best preventive that he knew, a jasper charm to hang around the boy's neck. Learning, too, that the boy, only eight at the time, liked to draw, he urged the father to have him taught 'because . . . to know how to draw cannot but be a source of honour and enjoyment, if not of utility, to him, as to every honourable man'.[13]

In the course of a long lifetime (he died in 1523) he went himself to many places painting, to Arezzo, to Volterra, to Città di Castello (where he was made an honorary citizen), to Loreto, Siena and Monte Oliveto, to Orvieto, Rome, Urbino, Perugia, Umbertide, Foiano. Lorenzo dei Medici was his friend and patron and for him he painted a Pan with attendants. After such a life, he finally came back home to stay, determined for his remaining years to paint only what gave him personal pleasure. One of these paintings was for San Nicolo away up toward the top of the hill, an altarpiece, a *Dead Christ among Angels*, one of whom is supporting him, and saints, and on the other side a *Madonna with St. Peter and St. Paul*. You feel almost as if you were entering a private garden when you come upon this small walled-in grass plot and at its end the simple low fourteenth-century church. There is a homely look about it all. All along the front and the left side of the building stretches a colonnade like a porch. Vines on that side hang down over the wall and flower pots are set around on the pavement.

During the last years, too, he painted for the Franciscan brotherhood of San Girolamo of Arezzo an elaborate altarpiece, the *Virgin and Child with Angels, Saints, and Prophets* (in the gallery at Arezzo). When they heard it was finished the monks came to Cortona and carried it back to Arezzo on their shoulders. Luca, old as he was, feeling no doubt as if he were losing a child to a new home, went along to see it suitably installed. When the ceremony was over he went again to his relatives to rest and to visit. When he started back, however, the monks came again and kept him company for a great distance on his way. It is a rather touching story.

There is another, however, more moving. It may well be a family legend only, yet Vasari tells it. One day one of his sons, the apple of his eye, beautiful in face, beautiful in body, was killed. Luca had him carried home and stripped of his clothes. Then, never shedding a tear, but sitting down beside him in his studio, he painted the son's nude body. So he preserved for himself the beauty that 'nature had given him but which an adverse fortune had taken away',[60] every rounded muscle and hardened sinew, every shapely feature.

For Luca Signorelli belonged to the Renaissance. He had studied nature and the classics, but most of all delighted in the human form. He had been a pupil of Piero della Francesca, had seen much of Donatello's statues, and probably had worked also with Antonio Pollaiuolo. He had learned much from them. But he had gone beyond them in his understanding of anatomy and in the depiction of movement. Even Michelangelo is supposed to have owed much to him. Signorelli's angels have the figures of athletes with powerful wings that fitted them for the space flights they were forever taking. The Virgin is always a stalwart and queenly person, and the Christ child, always in the nude, usually seems about to jump off his mother's lap. The men in Luca's pictures have steel-like muscles, and even the blessed just rising from their graves, in an Orvieto fresco, look as if for months already they had been out chopping wood.

I remember, too, at Cortona, Santa Margharita and her little dog. Her church on the very top of the hill, though first built in the 1200's, has been modernized and is now very ugly. Santa Margharita herself, however, was young and very pretty, the daughter of a farmer at Laviano, somewhere near Chiusi and about halfway between Montepulciano and Cortona. Just as in a fairy tale she had a cruel stepmother. A young man from Montepulciano, of good family, out hunting, saw her and was fascinated. Presently she succumbed to his blandishments and went away with him. For nine years she remained his mistress, bearing a child by him. Then one day when he had been gone long, and she was watching and waiting, his little dog came to her, caught at her dress and led her out the door. Apprehensive, she followed, and found her lover under a bush, stabbed to the heart and bathed in blood, victim of an assassin. In tears, realizing her sin and the vanity of earthly things, she went back to her father's home. Driven away from there, with her child she set out to Cortona and entered a Franciscan convent. Until her death in 1297 she subjected herself to its rigorous rule, suffering every hardship and privation, living the life of a penitent. She was full of good works, also, founding the Casa di Santa Maria della Misericordia, now Cortona's hospital. Her tomb is in the church, and her mummy on view to any who wish to see it. I didn't, but the Franciscan *frate* showing us around was a truly zealous soul. He got a stepladder, helped me to the top of the high altar, pushed back a lid, and there she was. He was determined evidently to make a convert, as for half an hour thereafter he filled my ears with stories of her miracles both before and after death, all vouched for by the bishop. He exhibited also a piece of the 'true cross' nearly as long as a fence rail, 'brought from Constantinople'.

She is Cortona's much beloved saint. The steep grassy slope below the church, set with cypresses, is a memory garden of Santa Margharita's favorite plants and herbs. What lovelier place for a memory garden, and what lovelier view!

Cortona is a place of simple people and simple human values. To be sure, it has its art, its history, its museums, a few important churches, Santa Maria Nuova, for instance, and that of the Madonna del Calcinaio, its town hall approached by high wide steps, its Palazzo Pretorio covered with the escutcheons of its great governors. Yet sitting in the park by San Domenico one Saturday afternoon, we looked up the hill, roof rising above roof, and counted from this one spot five ogival bell towers. They seemed a symbol of the town, for they spoke not of monumental structures but of small neighborhood churches where for hundreds of years simple human beings had been seeking comfort and strength for daily living; and I thought of the tiny piazza we had come upon that day, high up on the hill near San Nicolo, and not far from San Cristoforo. It had been almost closed in by small houses. Children were playing there. A few flowers bloomed in a corner. Smoke was rising from a fire of sticks, and two women sat there in the autumn sun. The older one was mending; the younger was picking feathers from a chicken, getting it ready for the pot and Sunday dinner. Probably it was one of her own chickens housed close by, though maybe she had bought it at the market in the morning, carrying it home live under her arm, along with some onions, fruit, and a long loaf of bread. And I thought again of the Vicolo dell' Aurora and the Vicolo della Notte and of a people whose joy was often in a flaming sunset or a dawn among the mountains.

10

Chiusi—Montepulciano—Pienza

THE Etruscans chose well when in the seventh century B.C., or earlier, they took possession of the ridge we now call Chiusi. It is in the softly undulating country of southern Tuscany, a land of green and growing things. Olives and grapevines are contoured along the hillsides. On lower ground there is grain and food for man and beast. Even in September it has an air of early spring; things are still sprouting from the earth. To the north and east is a small lake. Toward the west across a narrow valley a lone pine on a hilltop marks the site of an Etruscan temple long since disappeared. Its wooden roof and superstructure were probably destroyed by fire and there was left only a stone foundation and a heap of terra cotta.

In the sixth and fifth centuries B.C. Chiusi—the Romans called it Clusium—was probably at its height. At least that was when the Tarquin kings driven out of Rome by the leaders of the new republic appealed to Lars Porsena of Clusium for help. Porsena accepted the challenge. He established himself on the Janiculum and was on the point of crossing the Tiber into Rome when Horatio, as every schoolboy used to know, took over singlehanded and held the Etruscan army at bay until the bridge was cut from under him. Even the Etruscans could hardly keep from cheering Horatio's exploit, as Livy tells the story, for they and especially Lars Porsena admired valor wherever it was found. Livy adds other probably apocryphal details. The Etruscans covering all the riverbank and the country around had reduced the Romans to a state of siege.

Thereupon with the consent of the Senate Gaius Mucius, a young Roman, concealing a dagger under his cloak, slipped across the Tiber into the enemy's camp, mistakenly killing not the Etruscan chief but another. Seized, Mucius freely confessed his intention, hinted darkly at other plots against Porsena's life. To make him reveal these he was put to the ordeal by fire. He held his arm in the flame, never flinching, never telling what he knew. Amazed at his bravery Lars Porsena let him go, but sent an embassy after him to Rome offering terms of peace. In the compromise arranged, the Romans sent hostages to the Etruscan camp, among them a group of young women. With their leader, Cloelia, however, they eluded the guards and under a rain of Etruscan darts swam the river back to Rome. Porsena demanded that the Romans under the treaty return the hostages. This they did. But Porsena, again marveling at the bravery shown, sent Cloelia back with half the others. Though Livy in relating these details aimed at highlighting Roman valor, he also aroused in future readers admiration for Lars Porsena, who had, it would seem, a certain quality of greatness.

In its museum, skylighted and built for the purpose, Chiusi still possesses much that belonged to its Etruscan period. There are sarcophagi, the lids of which carry the sculptured likenesses of the deceased, with bas-reliefs along the sides; cinerary urns, many of individual artistry, though showing the usual sacrificial and battle scenes, stories, too, from the *Iliad* and the *Odyssey*, as of Penelope welcoming Ulysses on his return. One shows a man being crushed by a python while two other men are trying to save him. In some one sees clearly Egyptian influence and motifs, once at least the double-edged Mycenaean axe. Occasionally there is a frieze of birds, almost life-size, along the rim of a lid, on another a border of small human figures and the heads of some wicked-looking, open-mouthed creature, possibly a horned viper. Some few are in color. Some are canopic urns of bronze or terra cotta. The lids of these usually represent the head, occasionally only the helmet, of the deceased; the urn itself is his bust, and his arms form the handles. This urn rests inside a larger receptacle.

In the museum, too, are amphorae and vases in imitation of the Greek, and an especially good display of *bucchero*. This black pottery was a specialty of the Etruscans of Chiusi, though its use and manufacture spread to other Etruscan towns. The method was based on that of primitive man who burned his clay, before kilns had been invented,

Montepulciano

slowly in an open fire. The smoke impregnating the pores of the still-soft pottery turned it a shiny black. The earlier Etruscans doubtless used this same method, adding perhaps some manganese or possibly even charcoal to the mixture. Their artistic impulse appears in the embossing of figures of animals and men on the vases, bowls, and cups.

Outside the town on hillsides several Etruscan tombs have been excavated. (The museum furnishes guides to visitors.) The Tomba della Granduca of the third to the second century B.C. is built like a small arched stone house. Its doorway shows evidence of the use of hinges. Its heavy walls are fitted together without mortar. On benches along three sides the cinerary urns were placed. The Tomba della Scimmia (monkey) is of the fifth or fourth century B.C., consists of several rooms, and its benches are arranged for sarcophagi or embalmed bodies. Here between an upper and a lower decorative frieze are wall paintings in reds, blues, and greens. The deceased, a woman, is presiding over her own obsequies, which take the form of various games. She is seated on some sort of couch with her feet on a stool. She is grasping what appears to be an umbrella or parasol open above her head. A master of ceremonies directs activities, which include wrestling, boxing, swimming, the riding of spirited horses by both men and a woman. One man plays the characteristic double flute; for among the Etruscans nearly all occasions from the kneading of dough to the burial of the dead were accompanied by music. A dog is present, too, his tail up, presumably wagging. The startling picture is that of a monkey chained to a tree. The Etruscans often painted animals not native to Italy. After all they were a sea-faring people, traded with the Near East and Egypt—Egypt traded in turn with Nubia —and possibly with Gibraltar. It is not unlikely that an occasional sailor may have brought a monkey home.

From Chiusi it is only a few kilometers to Chianciano Terme, a surprising town out in the country yet beset with hotels, shops, and people—there to take the baths, drink the waters, and have a vacation. These waters were undoubtedly the Fontes Clusini known to the Romans and doubtless to the Etruscans as well. Whether or not one uses this town as a base for exploring the district, it is only a few miles over the hill from there to Montepulciano and to Pienza beyond. Città della Pieve, birthplace of Perugino, is close as well.

Montepulciano was also an Etruscan town though there is little left today to show its origin. In the ground-floor walls of the Renaissance Palazzo Bucelli, however, along the main street, three tiers of Etruscan cinerary urns filled with cement were used in place of building stone. Though for a while it existed as an independent commune, Montepulciano through much of the Middle Ages was thrown about almost like a football between the rival forces of Siena and Florence. The town hall, built in the fourteenth century, a small imitation of the Palazzo Vecchio of Florence, is the most significant relic of this period. Most of the palaces of the town and at least one of the major churches belong rather to the Renaissance and had as architects, Vignola, Antonio Sangallo, the elder, Michelozzo, Ippolito Scalza of Orvieto, Peruzzi of Siena. As one climbs the main street up the long hill to the piazza (almost two thousand feet at the top), one recognizes the classical features: massive walls, columns or half-columns, the arched or triangular pediments of the windows. Perhaps the most beautiful of these palaces, the Tarugi, is attributed to Vignola. It is across the piazza from the Palazzo Communale. The Contucci Palace across from the *duomo*, begun by Antonio Sangallo, the elder, was completed in the baroque style by Peruzzi. Other buildings which one should note in passing are the Palazzo Cervini, designed by Sangallo, near the foot of the street to the left, and the façade of San Agostino by Michelozzo at the lower end of town.

Ippolito Scalza designed the *duomo* with its bleak, unfinished façade. Within are the scattered pieces of a once great tomb, that of the bishop Bartolomeo Aragazzi. It had been executed by Michelozzo and Donatello. Fragments may still be seen incorporated in the high altar and on various pilasters. There is also at the high altar a triptych, an *Assumption*, by Bartolo of Siena.

Well below the walls, as one approaches Montepulciano from Chianciano Terme, at the end of a long drive of cypresses, rises San Biagio of yellow travertine. It, too, was designed by Sangallo, the elder, a Greek cross crowned by a cupola, with two free-standing campaniles—one was never finished. Like Santa Maria della Conolazione at Todi it is on a level piazza, though of grass. To the amateur eye its detailing, inside and out, is not so satisfying as that of the church at Todi. There is a patterned pavement inside and beautiful **carving** just below the drum. But niches for statues have been left unfilled, and around the high altar frescoes and gilded decorations give an almost tawdry effect.

For generations on the fifteenth of August citizens of Montepulciano and the surrounding countryside have been gathering for the annual Bruscello Poliziano. The festival takes place at night on the high piazza floodlit for the occasion. It is a play or pageant based on some story or legend of Montepulciano's past. The neighboring *contadini* have leading parts. There is singing, dancing, a local choir, and local orchestra. Costumes, however, are brought from Florence. One of the actors always carries a tree. The Bruscello is much simpler than the festivals of some hill towns, but for that reason is perhaps truer to the life of the people.

Some say it was named partly at least in honor of the town's most famous son, Poliziano, born Angelo Ambrogini, in 1454. When he was only a young boy, he got to Florence, was something of an infant prodigy, and became a favorite of the Medici to whose inner circle he belonged. He was an Italian poet and a Latin and Greek scholar of reputation. Among his well-known works was *Orfeo*, 'the first Italian attempt at secular theater' (1471).[37]

Eight or nine miles west of Montepulciano is Pienza, a small hill village distinguished not so much because it was the birthplace of Eneo (Aeneas) Sylvio Piccolomini in 1405 as because of what he did to it. Its piazza with its patterned pavement of brick and travertine, its palaces, cathedral, and well, is a study in Renaissance architecture. Soon after his accession as Pope Pius II Aeneas had called in from Florence Bernardo Rossellino, and in three years had transformed the village of Corsignano, given it a new name, and an air of elegance. It was his own memorial. Aeneas Piccolomini came of an aristocratic family of Siena. His father, Sylvio, had estates at Corsignano and retired there after the nobles of Siena had been deprived of their power in the government. Aeneas was one of eighteen children, only three of whom lived to grow up. They were people of education.

Aeneas went of course to the University of Siena, studied poetry, oratory, history, but took his examination in civil law. All his life he had that large curiosity that made him one of the most alert and knowing men in the Europe of his time. In his youth he wrote much poetry, later an occasional poem or hymn. He was an historian, a biographer, geographer, wrote a history of Bohemia, a life of Frederick III of Germany, sketches of many personalities, a work on Asia, and one on Europe. These latter were said to have inspired many young explorers to go out and see the world for themselves. He wrote a comedy in Latin, a love story, treatises on political science, on horses and their care, on family life and conduct. He was an advocate of sports, boxing, swimming, racing. He interested himself in the founding of the University of Rome, in that also of Ingolstadt, Nantes, Basel. He urged that young women be brought up on Cicero, Seneca, Plato, and other Greek and Roman writers, felt that only educated daughters were truly fitted to bring up right-thinking and right-acting families. Of course he approved for them also the more practical and aesthetic arts, music, dancing, embroidery.

Aeneas travelled widely. As a youth, secretary to a cardinal, he had gone to a council of the church in Basel, thence on political errands to Cologne, Aix, Liége, Louvain, Arras, and on a still different mission to Scotland. Walking barefoot for ten miles in Scotland, in fulfilment of a vow, he frosted his feet which all his life thereafter gave him trouble. All in all he did not think much of Scotland which was 'rude, uncultivated, and unvisited by the winter sun'.[19] Moreover he could find no wine, except a little he begged from a monastery—no one evidently thought to offer him any Gaelic *usquebaugh* (whisky) which might at least have warmed his frosted feet. Later he spent several years in Germany in the employ of Frederick III, some time also in Austria. During all this period he had been learning his way around in ecclesiastical circles. He had served as secretary for a brief period even for an Anti-Pope. Frederick, too, had sent him to Rome on business.

He had already turned forty before he took orders. Till then he had not felt the urge for or seen ahead the opportunities in a career within the church. A few short years later be became bishop of Siena; in 1458 he was crowned Pope. Watching the factional intrigues in the College of Cardinals, he was almost surprised at his own election, though not unwilling. Putting on the white tunic, he was asked what name he would assume in his new office. Remembering his Virgil, *Sum pius Aeneas* (I am the dedicated Aeneas), he answered, 'Pius.' He had always been a student of the classics and was ever mindful of the name he bore. Thereafter he was Pius II.

At once he set about promoting a crusade against the Turks, a project which, though unsuccessful, was always close to his heart. He summoned all the princes of Europe and all the cardinals and important churchmen to a Congress at Mantua. Many of them never came. Most of the others were cold to his spellbinding speeches. He went home a disappointed man. He had travelled slowly to Mantua, by Terni, Narni, Assisi, Perugia, Corsignano, Siena, Florence, Bologna, Ferrara, stopping at many of these places for a few days or weeks. He went back by much the same route, staying longer at Siena, and from there proceeding to Rome by a more western route. Not till six years later did he seem to be on the verge of success in his project. Ill as he was, and lacking in adequate support, he had arranged to lead the crusade himself. The ships were ready at Ancona when he arrived, but he never boarded them. Instead he died (1464).

Pius made many short trips, too. He was afflicted with gout and other ailments, and frequented the baths of Macereto near Siena and of Petriolo. In these places he lived much outdoors, sitting on the grass by the riverbank while he received embassies and conducted affairs of state. The peasant women strewed flowers in his path as he walked or was carried about in a sedan chair, and they knelt to kiss his feet. He went also to Viterbo, famous for its springs. In his *Memoirs* he talks of these places, of the beauty of the Valley of Spoleto, of Orvieto and its cathedral, Montefiascone, Radicofani, Aquapendente, Bolsena, and Capodimonte by the lake where he discussed 'political matters with the cardinals'[19] while he watched the boat races out of the corner of his eye. He never missed an opportunity to see races, whether of horses, mules, men, or boats—while he was doing papal business of course. During the heat of the summer he used to go to the high slopes of Monte Amiata, to Abbadia 'protected by precipitous crags'[19] on one side, 'by a wall and moat kept full by running streams' on the other.

He loved the country around Rome and knew the stories attaching to each town; Nemi, its blue lake, its orchards, its sunken galleys, Albano, too. He went to Palestrina, to Tivoli where he admired the waterfalls and the Temple of Vesta. He visited the Benedictine monastery at Subiaco, wrote with affectionate regard of the twenty old monks there, of the buildings 'clinging' to the cliffs like 'nests of swallows'.[19] There he picnicked beside 'a bubbling crystal spring'.[19] For the crowd that had gathered around him in a field he had food sent out.

In his *Memoirs*, which anyone interested in Italy of the fifteenth century would do well to read, he grows almost lyrical about the green fields, the crops, the ilex-, oak-, beech-, and chestnut-covered hills, the singing birds, the yellow broom in flower, the blue of 'blossoming flax'.[19] He used, it is said, sometimes to get up at dawn and go into the country to enjoy its freshness.

He was a man of the Renaissance, a man of great awareness of many things, screech owls, leaky roofs, rats in the monasteries, the conflicts that were racking Europe, the jealousies, and the political intrigues. He knew who was who, was inclined to sift the evidence of what he read in books, to regard even some miracles—except those of Holy Writ—with some mistrust. He must at times have been slightly uneasy in St. Peter's seat. He deplored, and quite sincerely, the luxurious living of many prelates of the church, particularly of the Curia, riding, as they were accused of doing, 'the fattest mules and the most spirited horses',[19] of walking 'the streets with puffed-out cheeks under red hats and full hoods'.[19] He himself tried to live with relative simplicity; he picnicked, he sat on the grass. Yet he knew where the 'small white eels'[19] were finest, where there were cherries and wild strawberries, where the trout were 'the most flavorsome',[19] where the beef cattle had been fed 'on thyme and other fragrant herbs',[19] where the cheese was best.

As he went about, the towns through which he passed made his coming an occasion, twined the bridges with ivy, spread carpets on the streets, hung tapestries from the windows. The boys and girls crowned themselves with laurel. The clergy put out statues and paintings before the churches and said prayers for his welfare. There was always music. He moved in a kind of triumphal procession. He complained that of the money Florence had appropriated for his reception much had been diverted to other uses. The fête provided for him as he started home from Mantua was much more to his liking. The river was already crowded with skiffs decked with waving flags as he boarded the boat on the Po. On the banks boys and girls were singing. There was the blare of trumpets. Many came playing musical instruments. Impersonations, too, had been arranged in his honor, of gods and various allegorical figures.

Yet Pius had a sense of humor, sometimes a wry one. Perhaps he would have called it rather a sense of righteousness. Sigismondo Malatesta of Rimini, though a man of parts and a patron of the arts, was a despot considered by Pius the basest of all men; there was no crime of which Pius—any many others—felt he had not been guilty, 'robberies, arson, massacres, debauchery, adultery, incest, murders, sacrilege, betrayals, treason, and heresy'.[19] Pius had been urged to canonize three godly women, among them Catherine of Siena. This he could gladly do. Yet if he 'had the power to declare that they had been received into the heavenly city',[19] had he not equal power to consign to eternal damnation one whose crimes were so patent? He need not wait for Malatesta's death. He would do so now, leaving it to a cardinal to try him formally before a church court. The cardinal conducted the trial. Then Pius called a consistory. By a unanimous vote Malatesta was condemned. In front of St. Peter's they erected a pyre on which they burned his effigy.

Pius indeed had as many sides to his nature as his new palace in Pienza had rooms. It had everything, a colonnaded courtyard, wide flights of steps, hanging gardens, a great hall, summer dining rooms and winter dining rooms, three great loggias one above the other looking toward Monte Amiata, a great kitchen outside the main house, a reservoir on the roof from which water was piped through gravel into cisterns below, fir panelling in the master's bedroom, gold leaf on beams, fireplaces everywhere. Even the chimneys on the roof were painted in colors. Much must have taken place there in the two years left to Pius after it was built, many conferences with his cardinals, much bargaining with secular princes at war with one another. One can only imagine the dinners there under glowing candelabra, the whispered comments under the stars in the loggias, cardinals in their red hats, ambassadors courting who most needed courting, with an eye to the future and an ear to the underground.

Next to the palace Pius had Rossellino build a *duomo* modelled, it was said, on a church Pius had known in Austria. For its adornment within Pius ordered paintings by Sienese artists, by Sano di Pietro, Matteo di

Giovanni, Il Vecchietta. The church was built on two levels on the hillside; the lower was used as a baptistry. There was trouble finding a solid foundation, though the builders dug down more than one hundred feet. Besides, sulphur fumes kept coming up—but for the fact that Malatesta had not yet died, one might have supposed that he was blowing sulphur rings down underneath. Finally, however, they threw arches across from rock to rock, and so built above. Yet today the church leans like the tower of Pisa, and engineers have explored new ways to shore it up.

Pius was not satisfied with just a palace and a church. Across from his own residence he had built also a bishop's palace, and across from the *duomo* he had the existing houses torn down and a Palazzo Municipale erected. After that he left building to others and others came and built. So Pienza became and is a museum of the fifteenth century, and the Pope who made it so is a true representative of the Renaissance, loving the classics and all learning, loving nature and all beauty.

The Marches

11

Urbino

I F Duke Federigo Montefeltro of Urbino had lived in our day, he'd
have had after his name a string of L.H.D.'s as long as a kite tail. He
had prestige. He had money and was generous with it. Every college
looking to its own best interests would have hung a hood around his
neck. Federigo would have deserved them all. His citation would have
begun something like this: A *condottiere* winning many battles, a friend
of popes, a great humanitarian, a dispenser of justice, a collector of
books and manuscripts from far places, a lover of the beautiful. . . .

Condottiere was the name given to a war lord who gathered around
him an army of trained men, and hired himself and them out to whatever prince or potentate had a war to fight and was willing to pay.
Federigo (1422–1482) was one of the best of these. He was sent for
all over Italy. He had studied the tactics of war and had a band of loyal
mountain troops. He did not rush in fast, but by every means sought
to discover the weakest spot in the enemy lines, and there he hit the
hardest. The contract was for a definite period, and the pay was settled
in advance. If the time ran out before the war was finished, or if
remittances fell behind, the *condottiere* was free to stop or even to change
sides. There were certain appurtenances as well. If a wealthy prisoner
fell into his hands, any ransom accrued to the war lord. Apparently it
was a lucrative business, even when one paid one's soldiers well.
Alfonso of Naples, for instance, paid Federigo a monthly stipend of
three thousand ducats while he fought for him, and for years thereafter
an annual pension of six thousand ducats. At the end of his life Federigo
is said to have been receiving from his various accounts one hundred
and sixty-five thousand ducats annually, of which forty-five thousand

were his alone. That must have been a tidy sum, however one figures the purchasing power of the ducat. His soldiers he always treated as his friends; he knew them individually, was solicitous for their welfare, and saw to it that when sick or wounded they were cared for. It must be remembered that war in the fifteenth and sixteenth centuries was a respectable but rough trade. However considerate any war lord may have been to his men, he was often equally cruel to his enemies. That was the code of the age.

Federigo had holdings throughout much of the northern Marches, a palace at Urbino, one at Castel Durante on the banks of the Metauro, and at Gubbio. Under his lordship he claimed seven cities ranking as bishoprics, many smaller towns, and villages. Until 1474 when he married off his daughter Giovanna to a della Rovere, nephew of the pope, he and his forbears had been counts. Friederich Barbarossa had conferred that title on the family in 1160. Then Sixtus IV, meeting him —he was accompanied by two thousand horsemen—at the great door of St. Peter's awarded him the dukedom of Urbino. In that same year Edward IV of England conferred on him the Order of the Garter. He wore also the Ermine of Naples.

His rule was paternalistic. He sent out scouts over his domain to find out what people were doing, how they were faring, what were their specific needs; to the convents and monasteries, too, to see that they were adequately supplied. When he found a bright boy, son of a poor father, he often undertook to educate him. If someone was building a house and badly needed a loan he gave it to him, or even offered suggestions for the improvement of the house. If he found a man with many daughters yet lacking dowry with which to marry them off, he helped out. Once during a heavy winter the monks of San Bernardino rang their bells for help. Federigo himself led the rescue party through the snowdrifts to take them food. In the morning for a while he went into the garden and held open house; he was always accessible to everyone with problems or complaints. When he found anyone trying to get a corner on wheat or something of the sort, he made sure that that person was thwarted, for he truly sought the common good. In his own palace he carried out the same principles. He was kindly but strict. There could be no swearing and no gambling. He insisted on cleanliness.

Urbino

When he was away on military errands, the administration of the province was in the hands of his wife, Battista Sforza, who had come from Pesaro. She was able. When the occasion called for a public speech in welcoming visiting dignitaries, she made it graciously and well. In Rome her fluency in Latin was a matter of remark. She was also an accomplished needlewoman. At fourteen she had borne Federigo his first of eight daughters. She produced, however, no heir, and this failure preyed on her. She besought the saints for a son even though he were to cost her her life. Particularly she called on San Ubaldo whose shrine was on the top of Monte Ingino at Gubbio. Ubaldo was the special protector of the Montefeltri. People all over the province joined in her petitions. When her time came, she bore at last a son. They called him Guido Paolo Ubaldo, shortened to Guidobaldo. But she had had a dream and she had for it her own interpretation. After the baptism of his son, Federigo went off again to the wars. Soon after his triumph a messenger reached him. Battista was very ill. Urging his horse across the mountains night and day, he reached Gubbio just in time to see her die. He was bereft. Of course there was a great funeral. Hundreds of prelates in their robes marched in the procession to San Bernardino outside Urbino's walls, thirty-eight envoys from other provinces and a great host of citizens from all the towns within the Montefeltro district. Unfortunately she never lived to be a duchess.

Yet maybe her sacrifice was worth it, for Guidobaldo was a true son of his parents, able, just, learned, generous, a model ruler when the duchy fell to him. Then the Borgias took over and he had to flee to the north. Eventually, he was able to return to Urbino and live out his life. He had no son, however, and the dukedom descended to the della Roveres. The glory of Urbino was in the past.

To Federigo's other qualities he added that of an inquiring mind, missed no opportunities for learning. He loved mathematics and music —the organ was his favorite instrument. He knew Greek and Latin, read Aristotle. He delved into architecture, knew more about it than many builders. Though he took a horseback ride before breakfast, during the meal itself he had Latin historians read to him, Caesar, Livy, Tacitus, and others. (He couldn't have had the continental breakfast or he would have got nowhere with his reading.) During Lent he turned instead to theology, St. Thomas Aquinas perhaps, or Duns Scotus. Often he went over to one of the monasteries nearby to discuss theology with some of the friars. He was devoutly religious. The palace was always full of visiting poets, artists, scientists, philosophers, musicians. At one time or another, too, some of the sons of Italy's first families, Orsini or Colonna, for instance, were members of his household, entrusted to his strict but beneficent tutelage to be trained in the art of warfare.

Federigo's special pride was his library. In this he sought eventually to have every book on every subject, medicine, architecture, physics, philosophy, theology, history, the poets, the Greek and Latin classics, and every manuscript in vellum, complete and illuminated. The books he bound in crimson with silver trimmings. Two large rooms at either side of the main entrance to the central courtyard were set aside for these, one for manuscripts, one for books. Besides, he had made, one above the other, two large closets, one fitted with table, chairs, a lectern, carrells, as it were, for private study and for consultation. He had some thirty transcribers of manuscripts in Florence and elsewhere, others scouting far and wide for whatever they could find. Vespasiano, his librarian, with perhaps undue but surely pardonable pride, claimed that Federigo's library surpassed that in Florence, that of the Vatican, or even that of Oxford University. After Federigo's death, Guido-baldo carried on the good work, and to some extent so did the first of the della Roveres. Eventually, however, the library went to the Vatican with the exception of some valuable works lost in the sixteenth century.

In the building of his palace at Urbino, Federigo surpassed himself. It is to this day magnificent and beautiful, worth for any tourist the trip to Urbino. For it he employed a Dalmatian architect, Luziana Laurana. The special limestone used in many of its parts was also brought from the coast of Dalmatia. To be sure, other architects had a hand in it, notably Baccio Pontelli of Florence, who took over after Laurana's death. Many artists of one kind or another were brought in, Francesco di Giorgio Martini, Ambrogio Barocci of Milan, Francesco di Simone Ferrucci, Domenico Rosselli of Florence, tapestry workers from Belgium, the local Timoteo della Viti. Even Botticelli designed drawings on which certain of the intarsia works were based.

The palace stands on two great rocks, which, so to speak, it welds

together. It has two façades. The one, and the far more impressive, you
see from the valley below or from the opposite hill, its slim twin
circular towers, the succession of loggias between, one above another,
the massive walls. The other façade faces on the piazza above, next to
the cathedral and across from San Domenico (see the Luca della Robbia
over San Domenico's door). On that side one studies rather the richly
ornamented doors and windows, each different. A door leads into a
central courtyard, arcaded. From a corner there the grand staircase
leads up. Above the first landing are the arms of the Montefeltri. In a
niche farther up is a statue of Federigo added in a later century. Upstairs there is room upon room, most of them now used as background
for the National Gallery of the Marches. Every room is in itself a
museum piece, for its sculptured doorways, its inlaid doors, its magnificent ceilings. Around one door will be carved the implements of
war, around another fruit and flowers, or birds; another will be of
arabesques. The lintel of one is carved with figures of children riding
pigs, no doubt a carnival scene. The chimney piece in another room
is of dancing angels in gold and blue and white. So with the inlay of
the wooden doors themselves; there are arabesques, fruit, and flowers,
but more often whole scenes in perspective, a view perhaps down a
street between buildings, towers, and balconies. The duke's private
room is completely panelled in intarsia. There is, for instance, a squirrel,
'wide-eyed and bushy-tailed', and a basket of flowers in the foreground.
Beyond there are arcades through which one looks into the distance.
From this room Federigo could readily step onto the loggia between
the towers to rest his eyes on the view of the city and the surrounding
hills. Elsewhere in the palace was a courtyard with a roof garden,
doubtless the special pride of Battista.

In the towers, now floodlit at night, there were spiral staircases.
One of these led down directly to the stables, which Federigo made a
point of inspecting from time to time. He had there three hundred
horses, a room for shoeing them, another for the repair of harness
and saddles, quarters for a head groomsman, holes for dropping hay
from a loft above, water piped in for flushing off the floors.

The art gallery in the palace merits special attention. There is Raphael's
Portrait of a Lady on a special easel, for Urbino was the home town of
Raphael Santi. There is Piero della Francesca's *Flagellation*. There

are paintings by Timoteo della Viti, by Cola dell' Amatrice, by Paolo Uccello, Carlo Crivelli, by Giovanni Santi, Raphael's father, by Federico Barocci, another of Urbino's native artists, and by many others. Incidentally, there is a portrait of Duke Federigo wearing the Garter and the Ermine. His young son Guidobaldo is shown with him. The best portrait of the duke, however, is that in the Uffizi, with Battista. It is by Piero della Francesca, and is in profile as always. In his early life, in an accident, he had lost one eye and had broken the arch of his nose.

There is one view of the palace no visitor should miss, from the other hill. One follows the signs through the main piazza and to the left on the Via Barocci to the oratory of San Giovanni. At its end, again to the left, one looks down the steps of a steep stair-street, across tile rooftops to the twin towers of the palace. In a terrace-garden in the foreground there are trees and on the walls red geraniums blooming. One should make a point of going at the time of day when San Giovanni is open, for inside are frescoes worth seeing, a *Crucifixion* on the end wall, scenes from the life of St. John the Baptist on the side walls. They were painted in the fifteenth century by the Salimbeni brothers, artists of San Severino in the Marches. Nearby, too, is the oratory of San Guiseppe in which there is a life-size crèche, kneeling cows and all, by a sixteenth-century Urbino artist. Though in clay it has through centuries attained the hardness and brilliance of polished stone. It is realistic and beautiful. In the background are depicted hill villages.

On the steep main street, Via Raffaelo, of this other hill is Raphael's birthplace. The plaque on the wall outside reminds one, as one is so often reminded, that great genius often originates in small places. Inside one sees a house, upstairs and down, kitchen, patio, bedrooms, workrooms, and a drawing or two. Raphael's father died when the boy was in his eleventh year. He is said to have stayed in Urbino until he was nearly seventeen, when his two uncles, guardians, sent him off to Perugino's studio. Though from the Marches, his paintings are therefore notable for their Umbrian backgrounds. On the high piazza at the head of the street there is a monument to the painter. There are also wide views of the countryside.

If you are a Montefeltro enthusiast, however, before you leave the town, you will drive over, about a mile, to the church and monastery of San Bernardino on a hill to the east. There are the imposing black marble tombs of the dukes of Montefeltro. Truly princes in their time, they were worthy and greatly loved, and neither Urbino nor Italy will ever entirely forget them.

There is another inscription there on a wall that one should see. It is dated the fifth of July, 1855. It reads—though in Italian:

> 'V Years   VI Months   VIII Days
> I was Giocannina Viviani
> First-born of Fulvio
> And Teresa Amalia della Massa
> Now I am a little angel
> Flown to heaven
> To pray for them'

Then, as in an antiphonal chorus, the parents speak:

> 'Goodbye Dearest
> With such grace of spirit and body
> You were not meant for the earth'

One has no idea who Giocannina was nor who were her parents. Yet the citation they wrote for her is one of Urbino's treasures. One often discovers the great in Italian hill towns, but sometimes one may find also the memory of a lovely little girl.

12

Ascoli Piceno

' . . . .
. . . on Tops
Of craggy Rocks so many Towns uprear'd;
And Rivers gliding under antient Walls.'

VIRGIL, *Georgics*
Translation by Joseph Trapp (1755)

BETWEEN Ascoli and its Adriatic port is a green and fertile country-side. Oleanders bloom along the road; in places hedges are of topiary work like those around some Tudor country house in England. Along this lower coastal plain of the Marches, sometimes narrow where the Apennines approach the sea and break off sharply, sometimes fifteen or twenty miles wide as here, the fields are all well tended. Much oil is made from olives in this region. Grapes of the Marches provide some of the fine wines of Italy, the Piceno Rosso of the southern district, the Verdicchio in the north. There are peaches, apples, pears, though not in such abundance as in the valley of the Po and its tributaries. Wheat is grown, and hemp, and mulberry trees for the feeding of the silkworms. In the fall trucks carrying sugar beets to refineries retard the normal traffic on the north–south Adriatic highway.

Along the shore are many old towns and villages. Some of them harbor fishing fleets; some are resorts with bathing beaches, crowded all through Italy's hot summers with gay umbrellas and lazy vacationers resting on the sands. There are seaside restaurants with menus of fish familiar and unfamiliar and sauces equally unknown to visitors from outside Italy, yet usually delicious. Whenever one looks out to sea there is always somewhere a sail, sometimes white, often brightly colored.

Of the little towns around in this district of the Marches bordering the Abruzzi, many have their specialties. Some, where the clay is right, fashion ceramics, some turn hemp into rope. In other places accordions are built. The women of Offida make lace. Ascoli itself seems something of a business and industrial center with its three- and four-story office buildings, its department stores, one of which, the Gabrielli, bears a name dating at least from Dante's day. Across the valley to the south the saws in the travertine quarries work day and night. Partly for this reason a visitor's first impression may be disappointing. Even topographically Ascoli may not seem a hill town. Yet it is in a special way. Here the Castellano flows into the Tronto, and each has cut a gorge, the one to the south and east, the other to the north. Except to the west high bridges control the approaches to the town. There a spur of hill reaches down, and the town has climbed up on it. Possibly on this hill the first village was founded.

Though this is Roman town, once called Aesculum Picenum, it was, before the Romans came, held by the Picenes, one of the early tribes of this part of Italy. Little is known about them, though it is fairly safe to say that the first of them go back to the neolithic age. Later, weapons of their bronze age suggest some Bosnian influence, and still later, about the sixth century B.C., the pottery of the district shows geometric designs. Doubtless the natives traded with Greek colonists farther down along the eastern coast of what we now call Apulia and copied their designs. There were, of course, some Etruscans, too, on this side of the Apennines. The most significant fact about these people of Aesculum was that they were valiant warriors. They long held out against the Romans, and even when they had been subjugated about 268 B.C. still kept their tribal loyalties and insisted on their rights. In 90 B.C. in the Social War they rebelled, killing the Roman proconsul and the Roman residents. The next year, however, Gnaius Pompeius Strabo laid siege to the town and finally conquered it, in turn putting their leaders to death and exiling many others. In the local archaeological museum one will see acornlike slingstones, used, it is thought, in this war.

All through the town are many evidences of Rome's domination.

Ascoli Piceno

In the west there are the remains of a Roman amphitheater, part of a Roman wall, a double gate, the Porta Gemina. Even churches have been built over Roman temples, as San Gregorio, where several Corinthian columns are embedded in the walls, where nearly one whole side is of honeycomb brickwork, the *opus reticulatum* of the Romans, such as one sees at Hadrian's villa near Tivoli. Sant' Annunziata, too, is supposed to rest on a Roman substructure.

A narrow street, too, in Ascoli often is a *rua*, not a *via* or a *vicolo*. The word, as also the French *rue*, of course, is derived from the Latin *ruga* meaning crease or wrinkle. It is easy to see the picture; these once-dirt alleys between houses were worn into deep ruts by the feet of men and animals and the washing of storms. Even after generations, and the later levelling and paving, they kept their original designations.

Of course the Romans built bridges across the rivers. Of these one over the Castellano, near the medieval fortress of the Malatestas, was blown up in the last Great War; only some buttresses remain. Another, of the Augustan age, however, still stands, the Ponte Solestà, spanning the Tronto by a high round arch sixty feet at least above the river.

There is no better place than on this bridge to begin one's acquaintance with Ascoli. There one sees to advantage the hills in the background, the newer suburbs to the north, the gorge of the river with its steep green banks, the houses and towers nearby of a once-flourishing medieval town. To be sure, only a few of these fortress-towers are left of the two hundred that used to rise above the roofs. The Porta Tufilla a few blocks downstream is of the sixteenth century. Above, it has a triple-arched loggia; below there are embrasures. Close by are the church and campanile of Santa Maria inter Vineas, originally of the ninth or tenth century, though recently restored. It was built into the walls of the town and fortified, to serve the military as well as the religious interests of the community. It takes its name, however, from a huge statue of the Virgin found reputedly somewhere out among the vineyards in the fifth century.

Nearby, too, is the church of the Saints Vincenzo and Anastasio. Its entire façade is in square panels of travertine. Its doorway, too, commands attention, with its grooved and twisted columns, its denticulated friezes, its round, elaborately carved architrave, its stylized lions in profile. The statues in the tympanum of the arch are dated 1036, but the church itself is without much question of a later date. Inside, the crypt represents a time when Christianity was still young in Ascoli. There had been a German priest, Emygdius (Emidio), who had found his way to Rome. Thence he was sent as a missionary to the district of Ancona on the Adriatic. He became a bishop and the patron saint of Ascoli, where along with three others he was put to death in the last days of the emperor Diocletian. One of his sins undoubtedly was the conversion of Polisia, daughter of the resident Roman prefect. Presumably he had gathered together a group of Christians who after his martyrdom, if not before, sought perhaps a secret place to worship. This little room may have been that place. To reach it today you go down several steps from the floor of the main church, feeling your way with a candle, for it is very dark in that low vaulted room. The columns there have crude capitals, and at one side, down another step or two, is a well dedicated to San Silvestro. The waters were supposed to have had miraculous powers in the curing of the scab.

A few blocks farther uptown facing into the narrow Via Malta is one of Ascoli's major churches, San Francesco, almost as large as the cathedral. It is as if the designer, whoever he may have been—and on this point historians seem to differ—had been conscious of St. Francis's self-abnegation that he so placed the church. There its magnificent central doorway and those flanking it seem almost lost, yet on them the architect let his imagination go, remembering perhaps that, after all, St. Francis was a joyous soul. They are Gothic in the high sharp point above the central arch and in the pinnacles, Byzantine in much of their ornament. The main portal is enclosed by an ornamental band, the characteristic Byzantine trailing vine woven around flat flowers. There is a column, too, at either side with a lion perched on its top. The clustered columns of the recessed doorway are some spiral, some of geometric design. Even from the Piazza del Popolo, of which its one side occupies the whole north end and more, San Francesco fails to show itself to advantage. There one is aware of several Gothic windows, a polygonal apse, twin hexagonal bell towers, and a cupola, but not of its length or breadth. Over the large side door, in a niche, a statue of Pope Julius II presides. On the far side there is a large cloister, one-time haunt of brown-robed monks walking sedately in the shadows of the arches, reading from their books of prayer or the writings of the church fathers. Today here are other men calling their wares, weighing out fish and other food stuffs, haggling over prices.

The cathedral, dedicated to the martyred bishop Emidio and fronting on the Piazza Arringo, is much more striking. It was built according to tradition on the site of a temple to Hercules, and part of it, the presbytery and crypt, may go back to the eighth or ninth century. The façade, severely straight across the top though finished with a balustrade, is the sixteenth-century work of Cola from Amatrice, a village to the southwest deep in the mountains. One sees much to admire in his building and painting in Ascoli. The Renaissance door, too, at the side of the cathedral is particularly beautiful, framed by fluted columns reaching to the cornice of the building and garlanded with leaves and fruit. Over and over again in Ascoli this motif appears in the bas-reliefs over doors and in Renaissance paintings. It is almost as if these artists had taken a leaf from the della Robbia book, a pale leaf by comparison but a lovely one.

Within the cathedral one is at first startled. The roof is blue dotted with golden stars as if someone had thought to bring heaven inside. Here one passes in review many kinds and periods of the art of Ascoli: nineteenth-century frescoing, woodcarving of the fifteenth century in the choir stalls and of the seventeenth century in the pulpit, in the Cappella del Sacramento a *polittico* by Carlo Crivelli (1473), and in the crypt an eighteenth-century marble statue by Lazzaro Giosafatti of *San Emidio Baptizing Santa Polisia*. Almost beside the cathedral is the baptistry, square at the base, octagonal above. It is dated variously from the sixth to the twelfth century.

Ascoli has two municipal buildings, the old one belonging to the period of the commune on the arcaded Piazza del Popolo, and the present structure, built in the seventeenth century on the Piazza Arringo.

The old one built in the thirteenth century and modified by Cola dell' Amatrice in the sixteenth is the more impressive, with its great clock, its rather unusual fenestration, the running eyebrow, so to speak, over the windows of the top floor. Here again in a niche above the main door a pope looks out on the goings and comings of the populace. That popes should so seem to dominate the city from their high seats is no accident, for from 1564 on, Ascoli and its surrounding district lived under papal rule. Within, upstairs of course, is the archaeological museum containing many things dug up in the vicinity: flints, bronzes, Etruscan mirrors and figurines, pots, vases, goldwork, even breast-holders (Etruscan brassières). There is, too, a fine piece of Roman pavement.

The present municipal building houses a remarkably good art gallery for so small a town, as well as the municipal offices. As in the churches of the city here are works by Cola, by Carlo Crivelli, Pietro Alemanno. There is a Titian, too, a Guido Reni, an Antonio van Dyck, and works of course by many lesser persons including those of the nineteenth and twentieth centuries. The great hall itself in which the paintings are displayed is beautiful, and from it one looks down into a green courtyard full of palms. The building can be largely credited to the Giosafatti, first Giuseppe, then Lazzaro and Lorenzo. They were a family of architects. The first, one Antonio, also a sculptor, came from Venice. So indeed also did the Crivellis, of whose painting one sees so much in Ascoli. Venice has never been far from the port of Ascoli. Even today many a sail on the Adriatic nearby flaunts the red and tawny canvases of Venice.

In the end, however, the things one comes upon unexpectedly in rounding a corner or opening the door of some ancient church are those which make one remember Ascoli long afterwards. As one wanders through the city, along Via Soderini, for instance, Via delle Donne, the Piazza Ventidio Basso, the Via dei Longobardi (Palazzo Longobardo), the Via delle Torri, and many other streets, one discovers perhaps an old Roman column or other Roman fragment embedded in a wall; or around a window a frieze as delicate as some piece of hemstitching, a wedgelike architrave, some faded frescoes in a church dating possibly to the ninth or tenth century.

The doorways especially often make one wonder who once lived within, what their stories were. Some are elaborate, some simple; many carry inscriptions in vulgar Latin or in the dialect of the age and region. Some are serious: 'He who fears death is unworthy of life' (translation). Some suggest that the owner looked out upon the world with a jaundiced or maybe a merry eye. There is one, for instance (Via Antonio Orsini), with a snail carved above the door, and an inscription that seems to say, 'Don't be in any hurry.' It is dated in the sixteenth century. Was the man who ordered that inscription lazy, or satirical, or just wise? Only his closest friends would know. Then there is the obviously cynical one: 'He who knows what should be done is too lazy to do it; he who is willing to work lacks the ability; he who is smart, loafs; he who is diligent is stupid. And so the world goes from bad to worse.' (Rua Lunga, again of the sixteenth century.) Another reads: *Fac bonum et non timeas*, do good and fear not (Via Curzio Rufa). It is in a way the equivalent of the Scottish 'Do weel and doot not' or of an inscription over a firehouse in an Austrian village, 'Honor God but watch your step.' (Translation again of course.)

Two palaces in Ascoli stand out not only because of their architectural interest but because of their associations, the Palazzetto Bonaparte on the street of that name, and the Palazzo Malaspina, far out on the Corso Mazzini in the direction of the Castellano River.

On each side of the heavy doorway of the Bonaparte Palace there are fluted columns and between these and the doorway a band carved in relief with military symbols, a helmet, a spear, a scabbard, for instance. On the double lintel above are carved, as it were, two scrolls, which on closer inspection one finds to be rather the undulating tails of mythological creatures. Above these again is the rounded arch with a sunburst in the center, and at either side an angel. Above the windows, too, are other carvings. The Bonaparte family was active in Ascoli in the thirteenth and fourteenth centuries in both civic and military affairs. Whether there is any truth in the inevitable tradition that Napoleon's forbears came from here is very doubtful. Most historians say they came rather from Tuscany or even from Sarzana in Liguria. It is interesting, however, that Napoleon at St. Helena is quoted as once having regretted that he had never seen Ascoli.

The most imposing palace in the city is that of the Malaspinas, dating from the sixteenth century. It has three tiers of windows, each row of a different design. At the top under the eaves is a wide loggia. Its stone columns simulate the trunks of trees from which the branches have been lopped off leaving knotty stubs. At street level two large portals lead through corridors to a gardened courtyard. In one corner of this, in a niche in the palace wall, is an ancient and very beautiful fountain. In its general feeling it seems to carry out the motif above the two main portals. Immediately above each of these doors is, of course, a crest. Resting on this, almost a part of it, is a wolf's head flanked by wide-mouthed heads of monsters, or possibly of men, for they strongly resemble tragic masks.

Malaspina is an old Italian name. The branch in Ascoli, tradition says, dates to the eighth century, though historians using city records cannot definitely place it earlier than the 1300's. Then Federico Malaspina had a home almost on the site of the present palace. The other Malaspinas lived in the Lunigiana, that part of Liguria back of the coast and the present towns of Sarzano and La Spezia. It was there that Dante is supposed to have stayed for a while after his exile from Florence. One of this Ligurian family, too, went to Spain, became a well-known sea captain, and was sent on a voyage of exploration to the Americas. He turned up eventually at Acapulco. Thence he was ordered to go to Alaska. On his way back he explored the coast of northern California including San Francisco Bay and Monterey.

Ascoli is in back country, though it was once probably the richest town between Rimini and Rome. The Romans early built the Via Salaria as far as Ascoli on its way to the Adriatic; and of course the sea lanes to Venice and the south were always open. A high mountain barrier, however, shut the city off from most of Umbria and Tuscany; this town did not look to Florence for its cultural and artistic influences but rather to Rome and Venice. The Byzantines had left their traces all up and down the coast. The Lombards, too, during the Dark Ages had swept in from the north. In fact, a Lombard necropolis has been found not many miles from the city. This is a different Italy. Even the names of architects and artists here are comparatively unfamiliar to the average tourist—Carlo and Vittore Crivelli, the Giosafatti, Cola dell' Amatrice, Antonio Vipari, Lazzaro Morelli, Pietro da Carona. Here, in general, one might say art came to a somewhat later flourishing. People with a different heritage lived here.

Topographically it is very different. Though near to the sea it is not far from some of Italy's highest mountains, the Gran Sasso group in the near Abruzzi, the Sibilline mountains to the west along the back road to Norcia. Among these is Monte Vettore, second highest peak of the Apennines. Through all this country there are occasional resorts and in some places thermal establishments. To reach it one may come from the north along the Adriatic through a fruitful landscape, or one may cross the Apennines from several directions, see high bleak villages still reached mainly by donkey trails, see snow-capped peaks in winter, travel roads sometimes winding through narrow gorges. Ascoli is an excellent introduction to those who would explore Italy's hinterland.

Umbria

13

Gubbio

GUBBIO is a country town. In the fall along the roads in the surroundings, one finds the houses draped with strings of yellow corn.
Even the great barn near the Roman amphitheater may be heavily
hung with it. Not all of this goes to the pigs; much of it is later ground
and made into polenta. As one walks around one discovers a bank of
some pretension for so small a place, but almost no stores selling the
necessities of life. In a far corner there are one or two antique shops
with old furniture, and up on the hill where tourists penetrate many
places where ceramics of various kinds are on display. At a public
faucet on the street near the *bargello* women gather to fill their copper
jugs with water, and then carry them home on their heads. If one
arrives on a Saturday afternoon, one will find the great piazza at the
foot of the mountain surprisingly deserted. On Monday morning,
however, the whole piazza is alive. The market has come to town.
Everything is there and everybody. There are bedsteads, mattresses,
jewelry, copperware, potties, clothes, thread, *scaldini*, toys, baskets,
hardware, lingerie. Truly this is a rural community.

It seems, in fact, remote, though actually only twenty-nine kilometers from Umbertide and forty-five from Perugia. The town lies
at the base of and along the rather barren slopes of Monte Ingino
crowned by the ancient shrine of San Ubaldo, the patron saint of
Gubbio. Part of the rocky path up the steep hillside is marked by

> ' . . . cypresses rising and falling
> Along the hill lines like an old forgotten
> Musical notation. . . . '*

* Russell, A. W., *An Excellent Moment.* By permission of the author and *The Times*
(London) *Literary Supplement.*

Though there is many a *festa* on that hilltop, Gubbio still retains a kind of somberness, a flavor of the medieval past. It is not hard to picture St. Francis here for a while in his travellings through Umbria. He felt at home in Gubbio.

It was in the thirteenth century, of course, and these desolate hills around were probably full of wolves. Yet usually the wolves had stayed their distance, and only occasionally had given cause for grave alarm. But this time there was one lone wolf seriously molesting the countryside, killing animals and men. Doubtless it was an old wolf, replaced by a younger in the leadership of the pack, and so, alone and discredited, it had grown vicious, as animals do under such circumstances. Anyhow the people of Gubbio were terrorized, and St. Francis offered to do something about the situation.

He had a way with animals as everyone knows; they were his brothers in God's world; and they obviously sensed the gentleness of his spirit. He once preached to the birds and they gathered about, as everyone has heard. One does not discount the story, yet it would have been just like the kindly saint to have had some grain along to scatter around, and of course the birds would stay expecting more. Saint that he was, he was doubtless absent-minded, and might never have thought of the grain when he recounted the tale.

The wolf was bigger game. However, it, too, was God's creature and St. Francis's brother; yet it had done grievous wrong. So, though the people of the town tried to dissuade him, St. Francis set out to reason with the wolf. Now wolves are intelligent animals—though one doubts whether this one understood vulgar Italian or even Latin. Yet he knew when someone was not afraid, when someone approached him with a kindly word, reaching out a hand. All the time St. Francis was talking to the wolf in the gentlest of tones, though solemnly and firmly. No one, not even a wolf, had been so friendly for a long, long time. The wild creature was as if hypnotized; this was something new in his experience. Just as any good dog, he knew that here was some-one he could trust, and so he came a step nearer, then another step. Before long St. Francis was rubbing him behind the ears—though the story does not specifically make note of this fact. Anyone who has ever known and loved a good German shepherd dog knows what happened next. The wolf sat down, then licked St. Francis's hand and

Gubbio

lifted up a paw to him. Things just as strange as this have happened many times between animals and men. St. Francis held that paw and interpreted the wolf's action as an agreement to the compact he had been proposing: the wolf would thenceforth do no harm to the people of Gubbio or to their animals, and in return they would supply him with the food he needed. Everything seemed understood between the two. Yet like a marriage this compact must be witnessed before all the people and confirmed by them. So he asked the wolf to come with him into town; and he came, trotting meekly beside his friend. The people then came out from their houses in amazement. St. Francis told them what had happened and of their responsibility for feeding the wolf thereafter. They agreed. Then once more the wolf sat down and held up his paw, and St. Francis once more took it. Thereafter Gubbio was a peaceful town. The wolf went in and out, even entering houses, and did no harm to anyone or any creature, but became the mascot of the town; and the people fed him as agreed. Two years went on thus. Then the wolf died, and I can well believe that many a man and child shed a tear that day. There is a little church at the corner of the Via Maestro Giorgio and Via Savelli. Within it is preserved the stone on which St. Francis is supposed to have stood when he made the compact, and outside over the door is a bas-relief of the wolf with his paw in St. Francis's hand. Some years back, it is said, men digging beside one of the churches found the skull of a wolf. It is a medieval legend in a medieval background, yet it makes of Gubbio a living place, of warmth and understanding.

Gubbio has other distinctions. Its Palazzo dei Consoli, tall and graceful, towering far above the town, is one of the more beautiful of hill-town buildings. From almost any spot on the flat one sees its profile cutting the skyline, symbol of strength and government. Its massive walls supported on the downhill side on high, narrow arches have nevertheless lightness. This effect is emphasized by a loggia near the top running all along the side. At the corner, above cornice and battlements, facing both the town below and the Piazza Signoria on which the building stands, is a high, slim bell tower. Seen from this piazza in front, the *palazzo* has greater width, windows that add grace and beauty, a wide flight of steps fanning out at the base in a welcoming gesture and ending above at the recessed door in a balcony. This door, the windows at either side, and the stairway may have been the work of Angelo da Orvieto, but the building itself is attributed to Matteo Gattapone da Gubbio, an architect of considerable distinction at that period, fourteenth century. Before turning away, a visitor should notice high up on one wall an iron cage, something one sees in various places. In it prisoners in the medieval period were displayed to the populace.

The Palazzo dei Consoli is, however, no longer the town hall but houses the museum. The vaulted room at the top of the stairway, built for popular assemblies, contains fragments of various periods, particularly of the Roman era. In a smaller room, once a chapel, is Gubbio's real treasure, the seven bronze Eugubine tablets, believed to be of the second or third century before Christ. They were found in 1444 under the Roman amphitheater, and were for long a mystery. Latterly, however, scholars have determined that the lengthy inscriptions, on both sides of some of the tablets, describe certain priestly rituals practised among the Umbri. These were tribesmen living in various parts of northern Italy even before the Etruscans had appeared. For those interested in coins, there is, too, a collection, Roman and Gubbian.

On the floor above, up a steep stairway, where the council used to meet, is the art gallery. Here have been gathered various works of Gubbio's greatest artists, of Oderisi, a thirteenth-century miniaturist of sufficient repute to have been mentioned by Dante in his *Purgatorio* (Canto XI); of Palmeruccio, and Ottaviano Nelli. There is also a carved chest by Antonio Maffei of Gubbio, whose work of the sixteenth century in the choir stalls of San Fortunato at Todi we shall see later.

Across the square is the present town hall, the Palazzo Pretorio, possibly also designed by Gattapone, though lacking in the beauty or distinction of the other. It is full of offices, and of stored archives going back to the early days of the commune. There is a library and choral books painted in miniature. From the parapet between the two buildings is a view that stretches far across the landscape to the south.

To reach the cathedral you climb still higher. It is not striking, yet the inside is surprisingly satisfying. A succession of Gothic arches supports the roof of the basilica (no aisles) and their shape is repeated in the window of the apse. One gets a sense of depth, if not of height. We wished especially to see *Il Tesoro*, yet there was no one about to whom to apply for the privilege. Eventually, however, we found the right bell, outside the cathedral, on a house to the right. A woman leaned out of a high window and directed us down the alley to a large door and a wide stone stairway up which one could easily have ridden a horse. She met us at the top, led us through room after room, finally unlocking a door into the sanctum itself. There was the sixteenth-century Flemish cope, presented to the cathedral by a one-time bishop of Gubbio when he became pope. It is embroidered in gold, red, blue, green, and pink, picturing scenes from the Passion, truly a treasure.

Across from the cathedral is the ducal palace, built by Federigo Montefeltro, and improved later by his son Guidobaldo. (Here it was that Battista had given birth to that son.) It is in every way a much simpler palace than that at Urbino, though it has a stately courtyard, simply carved windows, doors, and fireplaces. From the garden there is another lovely view over the town.

As one walks back down the hill from the ducal palace toward the Piazza Signoria one may well stop in at some of the ceramic workshops to watch men and boys turning out on a potter's wheel the modern *bucchero*, as they call it quite mistakenly, of course. It is an imitation of the old Etruscan ware, in shape and in general coloring. These pieces are painted, however, in black usually, and occasionally are slightly etched. Gubbio has a tradition of ceramics. In the sixteenth century Maestro Giorgio Andreoli, better known as Maestro Giorgio, came to town, and in return for establishing an industry in majolica was granted citizenship. His brothers assisted him. There is now little left of his ware in Gubbio. One can see it better elsewhere, in the museum and art gallery at Pesaro, for instance. It is a lustre ware, of a ruby-red and gold, on an oyster-white background. This district of the Marches—for Gubbio at one time was in the Marches—became famous for fine majolica. Those pieces made in Urbino, Pesaro, Castel Durante, Faenza, and Gubbio all differed slightly from one another. They came in many forms, plates, vases, bowls of various shapes, and these were much used as gifts. Today little shops along the uptown streets, near the Palazzo dei Consoli and the *bargello*, are full of majolica, but of a different sort, in blues especially. They are not the old lustre, have little resemblance really to the old designs, but here and there one finds a few in muted colors that are rather beautiful.

There are many other things in Gubbio, of course, to remind one of its past. Not least is the piazza of the forty martyrs down on the flat. It was named in honor of the forty men and women killed in the last war in revenge for partisan activities in the mountains not far off. Gubbio itself was threatened by German guns mounted on the top of Monte Ingino. Farther out, just beyond the edge of town, is the Roman amphitheater, not remarkable in any way, but evidencing the period when Gubbio was allied with Rome and her people Roman citizens. It was restored in the Augustan era. Today the town is using it again for occasional performances in the summer. Bordering the great market piazza is a strange relic of medieval days, the Tiratoio, once a place for fulling wool, now referred to as the weavers' gallery. Along various streets there are modest palaces. In more recent centuries many of their openings have been walled up, but if one looks closely one will still see doors and windows, and cornices that have beauty. There is especially the thirteenth-century *bargello* near the foot of the Via dei Consoli where the street widens into a piazza with a fountain in the center.

Toward the far end of the Via Venti Settembre you will find the church of Santa Maria Nuova in which the *Madonna del Belvedere* still sits enthroned. It was painted in 1403 by Ottaviano Nelli, probably his greatest work. She is robed in a beautifully flowered brocade, and surrounded by angels, four of whom are playing musical instruments. At either side is a veteran and a bearded saint, and below in profile two of the smug donors of the painting. The coloring is beautiful. The Virgin herself is a simple but rather lovely young woman, and the child on her lap, holding out one hand in blessing, is almost dancing. It is one of those rare gay moments in the life of Christ and his mother that one finds in medieval painting. At old San Agostino there are other frescoes by Nelli and his pupils but nothing so refreshing as the *Madonna del Belvedere*. No other churches particularly command attention, though at each there is something of interest: in San Giovanni, for instance, the door; at San Francesco on the great square downtown, the triple apse.

Gubbio keeps fresh the memory of its history and its legends. There is the Ceri festival, for instance, celebrated each year on the fifteenth of May. It is in honor of San Ubaldo, once bishop, regarded as special protector of the town. Three groups of men participate, the masons, the business men (*commercianti*), and the countrymen (*contadini*). Three candles (*ceri*), so called, though made of wood, are fastened on three platforms, and each platform is carried by twelve men. At the top of each candle is a statue, one of San Ubaldo, one of St. George, one of St. Anthony. The festivities begin in the early morning. There are rituals at various places in town, processions, horsemen, banners, gay costumes. Finally in the late afternoon the bearers take off with their loads and race to San Ubaldo's church at the top of Monte Ingino (three thousand eight hundred feet). There statues are unloaded, and *ceri* remain until the following May. What the exact origin of the festival is no one seems to know. It may go back to some Umbrian rite; it is probably medieval. Here in this small country town the narrow streets, the towering Palazzo dei Consoli, the bonfires lit on occasion high up on Monte Ingino, and perhaps in addition the costumes of a bygone day, give almost any festival a flavor, a medieval flavor, even now.

Bas-relief at Gubbio

14

Spoleto

I N 1958 Spoleto was for the first time host to the Festival of Two
Worlds, under the general direction of Gian Carlo Menotti. Assist-
ing him were artists in the dance, music, the drama, the fine arts,
John Butler, Thomas Schippers, José Quintero, Giovanni Urbani, as
well as a group of advisers. There was something here for everyone
responsive at all to music and the moods of the human spirit. There was
opera; there were ballets graceful as fallen leaves caught up in a gust
of wind; there were young voices, clear and eager and smooth. In its
first season Verdi's *Macbeth* was the major attraction. There was much
else of a different sort, a light and tuneful comedy, for instance, *Lo
Frate Inamorato*; the ballet, *Afternoon of a Faun*, and various others;
Daudet's *L'Arlésienne* with music by Bizet, and *The Glory Folk*
featuring folk music and costumes. There were singers from the
Metropolitan in New York, an Italian group from Lake Como, the
Trieste Philharmonic Orchestra, and many others. Among the performances were several world premières as there have continued to
be from year to year. There were concerts, intrumental and vocal,
exhibits of painting and sculpture, movies, too. The Festival has now
become an annual June-to-July event, sometimes beginning early in
the month, sometimes late, and drawing to this hilltop people from
Italy, Rome especially, all Europe, and from America. Once a new
production of *La Bohème* was given, directed by Menotti himself;
once Thomas Schippers directed Richard Strauss's *Salome*. Ballets
have come from the Soviet Union, Belgium, the United States. Once
a company from Spoleto was used. There are informal noon concerts,
and sometimes chamber music. Brahms' *Deutsches Requiem* was
given in an outdoor setting.

Spoleto itself has known many worlds and many kinds of people since first prehistoric man, possibly Pelasgian, fitted together there the huge polygonal rocks to make his walls. It has known Romans, Goths, Lombards, Carolingians, the French as late as the early nineteenth century, Hannibal, possibly Constantine the Great, the Byzantine general Belisarius, Totila, the yellow-haired and red-bearded Barbarossa, St. Isaac of Syria, St. Francis preaching to the birds in the Valley of Spoleto, San Bernardino of Siena, and in the last days of the fifteenth century even Lucrezia Borgia clad in red and gold and riding a white mule through the narrow streets to the Fortezza on the high rock above. A girl not yet twenty though three times married, she had been sent by her father, Pope Alexander VI, to take possession as governor. She was accompanied by a great band of retainers and was welcomed by an apparently jubilant citizenry. For at this time Spoleto and all Umbria had been for a long while a Papal State.

No town in Italy can claim a more varied history than Spoleto or represent more truly the accumulation that has made Italy, layer upon layer. The prehistoric walls below the Fortezza, for instance, back of San Nicolo, were a basis upon which Romans and medieval peoples laid up portions of their walls. Spoleto was from 241 B.C. until the decline of the empire a Roman colony, sometimes flourishing, sometimes impoverished. In 90 B.C. she won her place as a Roman *civitas*. The present market place, full of color and the goings and comings of people, was then the Roman forum where much weightier matters were argued than the price of a hen or of a bunch of carrots. The level of the piazza now, however, is considerably higher than in the Roman period. Close by is the arch of Drusus built in A.D. 21 to celebrate his victory over barbarians. Under San Ansano in the same neighborhood one can clearly see the outlines of a Roman temple, and under the Palazzo Communale is a Roman house, presumably that of the emperor Vespasian's mother. The rooms are easily identifiable: the atrium or main *sala* with its rain-basin in the center, the sleeping rooms, the dining place, the bath, the garden court. Some of the mosaic pavements, too, remain. High in the city at one side of the Piazza della Libertà is what was once a magnificent Roman theater nearly four hundred feet in diameter, and downtown near the Piazza Garibaldi are the remains of an oval amphitheater converted into a fortress and

Spoleto

citadel by Totila, the Goth, when in 546 he ravaged Spoleto. Just in front of the gate through which one usually enters the town from the north is now a subterranean Roman bridge, the Ponte Sanguinaria, so named from the blood of Christians martyred in the amphitheater just upstream.

The Porta della Fuga, a medieval gate along the west wall, supposedly marks the spot from which Hannibal in 217 B.C. was turned away. He had been on his way to Rome, exultant after his victory at Trasimeno, and he expected everyone now to cower before him. The Spoletans, however, rose as one man and drove him off. Fearing to go on immediately in the shadow of defeat, Hannibal took off instead to the north and east through what we now call the Marches as far as the port of Adria and thence down the fertile coast, fattening his army on the countryside. So Livy records.

To the Roman period the Dark Ages succeeded. There was chaos as the western empire fell apart and the eastern rose in Constantinople. Ostrogoths, Visigoths, Vandals, Huns fought with each other and the natives across the fields and mountains of Italy, laying waste, though sometimes seeking to fortify and restore and even beautify as in the time of Theodoric in the fifth century, and of Justinian and his general Belisarius in the early sixth. Then in the late sixth century the Lombards swept south, establishing themselves on Spoleto's hilltop beside the old Flaminian Way, making it the capital of a district, the Duchy of Spoleto, settling there a resident duke.

In the fourth century, despite destruction and desolation all about, Constantine the Great, himself at least a half-hearted Christian, had made possible a new freedom of worship. Churches consequently began to rise. San Salvatore, Spoleto's oldest existing church, was one of these. It is outside the walls by the present cypress-studded *campo santo*, near what had been the local Christian catacomb. It has of course been much changed through the centuries. Earthquake, possibly fire, took their toll. There were renovations and the addition of a dome and a chapel at either side of the presbytery. It is nevertheless still beautiful within and sheds a kind of radiance on all who enter. Though small, it has great dignity in height and depth, great simplicity, a kind of clean other-worldliness. This atmosphere is enhanced when, passing under the triumphal arch at the end of the nave, one sees the high fluted columns giving entrance to the chapels. These columns are fragmentary, probably brought here and pieced together at a later date from the ruins of Roman buildings. Their heavy entablature carries the triglyph design. It is usual to say that this church was built over a Roman temple, but investigations do not bear out this claim. It was planned rather, one may suppose, by those whose eyes had rested on classic architecture and who knew nothing else. In this familiar atmosphere they could worship God and find peace for their souls. Santa Eufemia just around the corner from the cathedral, though built in the tenth century, gives one much the same feeling.

San Giuliano on another hill outside of town, though of the twelfth century, has in its façade fragments of a sixth-century church which preceded it. The *duomo* of today replaced an early seventh-century church destroyed by Friederich Barbarossa in 1155. The crypt of San Ansano is supposed to date from the seventh century. It was during these Dark Ages, too, that the ilex-covered slopes of Monteluco across from the high Rocca first became the home of hermits. They had fled from the Near East and established themselves in shelters on this mountainside, which then became known as a sacred grove. On its top later, monasteries were set up. It was at about this time that monasticism was taking hold in Italy, that St. Benedict went to live in a cell on the mountain by Subiaco, south of Tivoli, where he was to found the first monastery of his order. To Monteluco both St. Francis and San Bernardino of Siena were later visitors.

On a high bench at the foot of this mountain outside the town stands San Pietro, first built, supposedly, in the fifth century. The bas-reliefs of the façade, now its oldest part, were, according to authorities, executed by various hands between the years 1000 and 1200. These give the church its distinction. Some of them must have been carved by Lombard sculptors or their descendants; they bear the Lombard impress, for here on the façade is a zoological garden in stone. Of this peculiarity in style Charles A. Cummings in his *History of Architecture in Italy* has written:

'... in all the greater towns there were doubtless to be found either Italian or Greek workmen whose hand and eye had been trained to more or less of artistic perception and execution. Often, no doubt, the Lombard builder was fain to avail himself of the knowledge and capacity of the Byzantine craftsman. . . . The Lombard found no delight in the contemplation of saints and angels, of prophets and martyrs. . . . His imagery was of a fiercer sort, savage beasts and birds of prey, fighting and destroying, . . . men and beasts struggling with each other, —all sorts of mythical and impossible creatures,—centaurs, griffins, dragons, chimeras, and the like, either in action or not. . . .'

Earlier in the same volume he said:

'For the action of the Lombards on Italy and of Italy on the Lombards was reciprocal. . . . Their savageness was tamed, their rudeness was smoothed; they took from Italy as much as they gave her, and the style of architecture which began with them was continued by their descendants and successors, at first with similar rudeness, then with less, but always with vigor and individuality. . . .' (Vol. 1, pp. 178–9 and p. 94)[14]

Here in the smaller panels beside the door jambs one sees the peacock plucking at a fruit, the deer attacking a snake, a team of oxen at work; and in the larger panels of the outer frame of the central doorway, to the left, three scenes of a man's struggle with a lion; to the right, a fox playing dead ready to grab the curious hens; a wolf and a ram; and a lion attacking some mythological creature. In at least two scenes the lion's tail ends in a serpent's head, a detail characteristic of Lombard sculpture. Above the door are eagles quietly alert.

Yet there are religious scenes here too, in the top two large panels at either side. These may have been by a different hand. Around the jambs of the door is the meandering Byzantine design and also around the small panels; there are, too, four intricately carved small colonnades each in a small panel. In the horseshoe arch above the main door and at either side of this in the small interlacing circles is the familiar mosaic work of the Cosmati. Above the left door is a relief of *St. Michael Slaying the Dragon*, and high up on the façade are two angels and two bulls. The church itself is next to a farmyard and sometimes geese from there stray out across St. Peter's lawn, weeding their way to heaven.

The *duomo*, consecrated in 1198 by Pope Innocent III, has a unique position. One approaches it from above down a long ramp broken by occasional steps. This fans out beside the curving walls of an old palace into the level piazza below. The *duomo* is Gothic in its conception, with a pointed gable, pointed decorative arches in the upper of the three horizontal divisions of the façade, and, a most unusual feature in Italy, modified flying buttresses instead of the usual heavy abutments. These buttresses one sees only as one looks down on the rear of the *duomo* from the park above. Unusual, too, is the battery of rose windows small and large. The three in the top section are arranged as if in a point around the central mosaic and so accentuate the pointed arches and the gable. The mosaic, 1207, though recently restored, the work of a Spoletan, Solsterno, shows *Christ between the Virgin and San Giovanni.* The portico at the base, of five round arches, a frieze, and balustrade, is a later Renaissance addition of the end of the fifteenth century. Underneath this is an unusual portal with a flat lintel but a high, sharply pointed, and carved architrave. The square campanile was built from the travertine of Roman buildings destroyed in the chaos of preceding centuries.

Within, in the Eroli Chapel are Pinturicchio frescoes; in the Chapel of the Santissimo Icone, a much reverenced Byzantine *Madonna* presumably from Constantinople. In the apse are the frescoes by Fra Filippo Lippi, scenes from the life of the Virgin, the *Annunciation*, the *Nativity*, her *Death*, and her *Coronation*, and in the right transept the artist's tomb. These frescoes in Spoleto were his last, for he died there and his assistant and pupil, Fra Diamante, finished them. Actually one sees his work to better advantage in Prato or in the galleries of Florence than in Spoleto. Some years after his death and burial in the cathedral, Lorenzo dei Medici, remembering with affection Lippi and his work in Florence, asked Spoleto to return his body to his native city. The magistrates refused. Thereupon Lorenzo sent the artist's son, Filippino Lippi, to erect a monument to him in Spoleto's cathedral and instructed Poliziano to write for it a Latin inscription.

Fra Filippo (1406?-1469) was one of those joyous, unpredictable souls who was the pride and despair of those who knew him best. Browning made him famous in his poem *Fra Lippo Lippi*, yet he would have been famous anyhow, for he could paint. He loved bright colors,

the clothing of his figures in heavy draperies, the detail of Renaissance
buildings, landscapes in the distance. He drew people as he had seen
them, in monastery and on the street. His Madonnas were beautiful,
his monks realistic but not always saintlike. Even his angels sometimes
look around a corner and smile. He was eminently human, not an
'Angelico' surely, more perhaps of a *diabolo*.

Son of a Florentine butcher, Filippo had been orphaned early. The
aunt who undertook to bring him up found him difficult; besides he
was a mouth to feed, and she was poor. Browning pictures the boy as
living

> 'On fig-skins, melon-parings, rinds and shucks,
> Refuse and rubbish. . . .'

It was probable that he hovered around the markets, eating what he
could find, perhaps occasionally helping himself to a chestnut or two
or maybe an egg when nobody was looking. He would have loved
the markets anyhow, for people were there, animals, other boys, and
excitement. At length his aunt gave up, led him, at eight, to the door
of the Carmelite monastery. 'Here, take the boy,' she said, 'and bring
him up.' They did. Yet they, too, found him something of a handful.
He did not wish to work; he did not wish to study. He drew pictures
on his copybooks, on walls, and doors, rough outlines of fat-bellied
monks, or women whispering into the grating of a confessional.
The prior, seeing that it would be wise to encourage the boy's natural
bent, put him to study art with Lorenzo Monaco, it is thought, a
miniaturist. At fifteen he took the vows of a monk, put on

> 'The warm serge and the rope that goes all round.'

But the vows to him were ritual, not life; life was people, activity,
and art. He was sensitive to many things:

> 'The beauty and the wonder and the power,
> The shapes of things, their colours, lights and shades,
> Changes, surprises—and God made them all!'

When in 1423 Masolino, then Masaccio began their frescoes in the Brancacci Chapel of the Carmine, Filippo stood watching many an hour and many a day. He learned much from them.

Before long he was taking commissions, mingling with other artists, people of all sorts, yet the prior still thought it best to let him go his way. In time Cosimo dei Medici found him out and brought him to the palace. Yet Filippo's interest too often wandered from the work in hand. One day, consequently, Cosimo shut him in his room and kept him there while the artist painted

> '. . . saints and saints
> And saints again. . . .'

He could have painted a halo in his sleep. One night a gay company passed under his window, singing, laughing, joking with one another. It was spring. Filippo looked out for only a moment, to get a breath of air. Then he tore sheets and coverlets from his bed, shredded them and tied them together, and slid to the street, a cowled and tonsured monk, to join the company. There was much explaining to do to the watchmen on the street and later to Cosimo, but the latter forgave him, and shut him up no longer lest he should come to grief in one of his escapades and a great painter be lost to the world.

Cosimo at a later time got him out of the financial straits in which he was always finding himself, by securing for him a post as abbot and rector at Legnaia near Florence. For some years after this all went well. But 'dogs that have licked cinders cannot be trusted with flour',[56] as goes an Italian proverb. Anyhow, according to the legend, once more Filippo fell in debt, this time to one of his assistants, and forged a receipt. This act, after much painful ado, cost him his position. Besides, he had become the talk of all Florence.

Sometime earlier he had begun work on frescoes for the cathedral at Prato. Now he moved there and got himself a house near the convent of Santa Margharita. He was to be the chaplain of the convent. The abbess asked him to paint for them a Madonna as altarpiece. He set to work. Among the novices, however, he had already discovered a beautiful young girl, Lucrezia Buti. He requested that she be allowed to pose as model for the painting. This, however, was only the

beginning. At a May festival when as chaplain he accompanied the nuns
to the cathedral he managed somehow to slip away to his home with
Lucrezia. He was much in love, and she, a young girl irked with life in
a convent, was nothing loath. From that time on she sat for many of
his Madonnas. If you look closely you can see this sweet young face,
sometimes shy, sometimes adoring, in several of his pictures. In time
the pope was persuaded to absolve them both from their vows, yet to
the end Filippo signed himself Frater Filippus. They had two children,
Filippino, a great artist like his father, and a daughter Alessandra.

According to Vasari, the municipal authorities of Spoleto gave
as reason for their unwillingness to return Filippo's body to Florence
that 'they were but poorly provided with ornaments, above all with
distinguished men; they consequently begged permission as a favor
to retain them' (the remains of Fra Filippo).[60] In a sense they spoke
truly. To be sure, they possessed the blessed icon from Constantinople,
but little else that seemed permanent. Theirs had been a history of
destruction and change. Romans succeeded prehistoric man. Goths,
Vandals, and Huns destroyed what was Roman. Lombard dukes came
and went. The Franks established their own duchy. Spoleto was
declared a Papal State. Barbarossa came representing the Hohen-
stauffens of Swabia and the Holy Roman Empire. The Spoletans
resisted, and their city was destroyed. Later the Papal States once more
obtained the mastery—Romans had taken over the ancient citadel on
top of the hill. The stones of Roman buildings had been used to build
Christian campaniles. Corinthian columns broken to bits had been
pieced together to ornament Christian churches. Totila had destroyed
an amphitheater to make a fortress. Twelfth-century churches now
occupied the sites of those built in the fifth and sixth and seventh
centuries. And in the middle fourteenth century Cardinal Albornoz,
Papal legate, had dragged the stones of Totila's citadel up the hill to
build a Rocca at the top.

This Rocca with its six towers and heavy walls was half-fortress,
and half-residence for the papal governors. Various popes stayed there
for a period of time, among them Julius II in whose honor Lo Spagna
executed several frescoes now in the *pinacoteca*. It was built largely by
Gattapone of Gubbio, though begun by another architect. Though it is
no longer open to the public, there is a garden and a walk all the way

around from which one may look down on the town, on the Valley of Spoleto, and to the north sometimes as far as Assisi. To the east an aqueduct, probably also built by Gattapone in the fourteenth century and still in use, bridges the gorge of the Tessino. The bridge is over seven hundred feet long and stands more than two hundred and fifty feet above the stream. It is carried by ten slightly pointed arches, based, it is thought, on an earlier structure going back at least to the sixth century.

Spoleto is truly a place of the many worlds that have made Italy, a background for those who would explore the little towns around in Umbria. There is Trevi climbing up the hillside among the olive trees. From the forests on the hills behind the Romans are said to have harvested much timber for their buildings. Everywhere as one wanders through the town one finds bits of interest, shrines over arches, doorways. The streets, if they could be, are even narrower than some of those in Spoleto. Here indeed, Adimari, if he had come riding his horse from Florence, might have polished his shoes well, wiping them as was his wont as he went along, against the clothes of pedestrians flattened against the walls at either side. Nor is Trevi without some art. In the Madonna delle Lacrime there is a notable Perugino executed when he was seventy-six, and in the *pinacoteca* a Lo Spagna.

There is Narni, too, a place of wonderful views. Here one looks down a cliff to the Nera far below over which are broken arches of a bridge of Augustus. There are many Roman fragments in town, medieval towers and buildings, and in the *duomo* a chapel with a façade of square panels that reminds one of that of San Vincenzo and Anastasio in Ascoli.

There is Montefalco to the northwest whose church of San Francesco is a national museum because of its Benozzo Gozzoli frescoes of the life of St. Francis. Among these is one of his instituting at Greccio (near Rieti in the mountains) the Christmas custom of the crèche. There are frescoes of his also of other saints, particularly St. Jerome. There is a Perugino to the left of the main door.

Still nearer beside the road to Foligno are the fountains of Clitumnus (Clitunno), known since the days of Virgil and Propertius. Pliny the Younger wrote[42] of the Roman villas in the neighborhood, of the 'little hill covered with venerable cypress trees', of the spring that 'bursting forth forms a broad pool so clear and glassy that you may count the shining pebbles', of the reflections of ash and poplar trees in the water—which is, he said, 'cold as snow'. There was in the Roman era a temple there to the river god Clitumnus. Today there is instead a primitive Christian church as beautiful as a pagan temple.

To the north and east of Spoleto toward Norcia lie high Apennines. At dusk on a winter day, driving down the long mountain road from that direction, one may sometimes get a view of snow-capped peaks crimson in the sunset while down below at Spoleto all is already dark. It is a symphony of light and shade and color that is unforgettable.

15

Todi

TODI is an old, old town. Men have probably lived on its windy hilltop overlooking the Tiber valley for at least three thousand years, possibly longer. Spearheads, axes, and daggers of polished stone have been found on the hillsides around. Legend says that a tribe of Umbri once occupied the highest spot, where the Rocca and the city park are now. Then came the Etruscans, settled on the next and lower hilltop where now is the Palazzo Popolo. Between the two hills ran a little stream. In the deep dark one night the Etruscans fell upon their neighbors and massacred a large number of them. Thereafter the Umbri who survived became for the Etruscans the hewers of wood and drawers of water. In time, so the legend goes, the stream that separated them was re-routed, its channel filled, and it all became one town, Tuter.

The Etruscans who lived there were artists of no mean ability, bronzefounders, potters, goldsmiths. The necropoli found just outside the walls and on a neighboring hilltop have yielded treasures, the famous bronze statue of *Mars* now in the Vatican Etruscan collection; fine goldwork, ear-rings, and necklaces from Todi are in the Villa Giulia in Rome and in Florence. Three circuits of walls have at various times been built around the town, the innermost Etruscan, the middle Roman, the outer medieval.

Of the Roman and medieval periods there is little to record. The Romans built their temples, theaters, basilicas, and forums. These have all but disappeared. The story of the medieval period is that of other hill towns. As a commune it sided now with one neighbor, now with another, often with Perugia, in the perennial struggles of Guelf

and Ghibelline. Two towns it took under its own protection, Terni
to the southeast, Amelia, another old, old hill town, to the south.
These proud conquests it took pains to record on its coat of arms;
the great fierce eagle of Todi, with its wings outspread, carries two
small eagles. Through a major part of its history from the medieval
period on Todi was under papal jurisdiction.

Todi is not a place of great paintings though there are a few worth
seeing. Its central piazza, however, is one of the loveliest to be found
in Italian hill towns. It has also one of the most beautiful of Renaissance
churches. Even to this day the town has an air of wellbeing. One feels
as one walks through the streets, observes its shops and what they offer,
that people of some background, education, and sophistication live here.
To be sure, it has almost a comic-opera name, but the town provides
all the makings of grand opera, the setting, the backdrop, and one of
the most distinguished and romantic personalities of medieval Italy.

As one approaches halfway up the hill, one comes first to Santa
Maria della Consolazione. It is outside the walls, standing alone, a great
white church, beyond which one looks upon the green hills of Umbria.
It was begun in 1508 by Cola da Caprarola, possibly after a design by
Bramante. It is what St. Peter's, begun two years earlier on Bramante's
design, might have been had it not been altered later and enlarged by
first one architect and then another. To a lay eye it is in its simplicity
far more beautiful than the magnificent St. Peter's with its dome by
Michelangelo and all its fulsome decoration. It is beautiful, not over-
powering, a place apart, and in its bareness invites contemplation.

It is a Greek cross standing one hundred and forty-six feet to the
top of the lantern of its dome. Around the main cupola are the four
half-domes, each seventy-seven feet high, representing the four equal
arms of the cross. On the outside the half-domes abut on a great
square mass of stone with corners reaching to the ground, and at the
level of the apex of these domes a balustraded gallery surrounds the
drum of the main cupola. In these corners are stairways entered from
inside, leading to the gallery. On the outside on the corners one observes
the eagle of Todi. The windows of the edifice are high and are capped
alternately by triangular and curved pediments. On the inside the
pattern of the Greek cross is more clearly evident. Of the four apses,
crowned with their half-domes, one, of course, is occupied by the high

Todi

altar designed by Andrea Polinori of Todi, whose work one finds in various churches of the town. The intrados (undersides of the arches) are carved in the rose design. In the pendentives (triangular spaces at the intersection of the arches) are figures of the four evangelists, and in the twelve niches statues of the twelve apostles.

Santa Maria della Consolazione was one of the early examples of the Renaissance conception of church architecture in Italy. This conception had been developed by Bramante, Alberti, Vignola, and others in the late fifteenth and early sixteenth centuries. Santa Maria delle Carceri had already been built at Prato by Giuliano da Sangallo, San Sebastian at Mantua designed by Alberti.

In the early days the basilica church had served many purposes. It was a place of worship but also one of social fellowship, even a place of business at times and public discussion. Near the high altar men and women might be listening to a sermon or kneeling while the priest intoned the mass. Near the outside doors they might be discussing crops or babies or the latest threat of war from a neighboring town. Whatever sense of awe they were led to feel for the ruler of the heavens and earth came from the ritual, the incense, the flickering candles, from the richness of the decorations, the frescoes, or the gorgeous mosaics on the walls. The saints, God himself in all his awful majesty, looked down on man and his insignificance. Not at once did architecture itself become a means and symbol of worship. In time transepts were added, and the basilica became a Latin cross. Through the Middle Ages there had been little change in general conception, though aisles were sometimes added, and chapels, and as Gothic influences from the north penetrated deeply, there were other modifications, vaulted roofs sometimes, or pointed windows and portals.

As the Renaissance harked back to classical styles, however, and architects increasingly betook themselves to Rome to study ancient buildings, there developed a new emphasis; they began to think of churches as a reflection rather of God's greatness, of the perfection of his planning as shown in the ordering of the sky and stars, even in the simple roundness of fruits. They thought now of purity of form, of geometrical proportion, of the relation of the square to the circle, of harmony. So instead of the Latin cross, symbol of Calvary, there came the Greek cross, symbol of God's perfection, four equal arms and at the center a great dome like the sky. The church, Alberti argued, should be set apart on a great piazza, not crowded in among other buildings. If possible it should stand on a platform, for all men should go up to approach God. Windows should be high, cutting off from within all contact with the world. The whole edifice should be white and pure inside and out. Even the pavement should, if possible, be laid in geometric design to inspire one with a sense of order. Statuary as having greater purity was to be preferred to painting of any kind. The building itself and every part of it should incite reverence for God.

With these ideas in mind, Santa Maria della Consolazione was designed. It took ninety-nine years to build. In 1607 it was finally completed when the cross carried in procession from the *duomo* was affixed to the apex of the lantern. Caprarola had died a few years after beginning the work. The construction was carried on by architects, Ambrogio di Milano, Francesca da Vita, and others, and consultants were called in at various times, Baldassare Peruzzi, Antonio Sangallo, Vignola, Ippolito Scalza, Alessi.

Let's hope it is market day when you reach the main piazza, really two adjacent piazzas, and that the arcades beneath the communal palace are full of vegetables and flowers and fruit. It is these markets more than anything else that supply color to gray Italian towns. There has never been much room on walled hilltops, cluttered as they are with buildings, for grass and trees and flowers. On the way up, to be sure, modern parkways are usually lined with trees and bushes, and nowadays, as in Todi, there has often been a park made high up where an ancient fortress has crumbled away. To those parks one should make a point of going, for they almost always offer views one should not miss. In Todi, especially, one should go there to get the view down through trees on Santa Maria della Consolazione. It is but a short way uphill from San Fortunato.

Yet before inspecting the piazza there is another closer place where one may wish to go to rest one's eyes on the flowing Umbrian hills. If so, there is a little *ristorante* to be reached beyond the market under the arcade. There on a terrace, in the open season of the year one may sit under an old grapevine and sip the wine of the region or a glass of the local mineral water, Vasciano, and taste perhaps the white figs of Amelia. If one is really hungry, of course, there is always a *pasta* of some kind, *gnocchi*, for instance, or *tagliatelle*. At the south end of the piazza is the old Palazzo dei Priori, begun in 1293, completed between 1334 and 1337. It has a massive tower and square battlements. High up on the face of the wall is the bronze eagle of Todi. This palace was the residence of the *podestà*, later the home of the papal governors, rectors, and vicars. It held also the council chambers of the *priori*.

The communal palace on the east is much more beautiful. It is really two buildings. The older, the Palazzo del Popolo (1213, 1228–1233), protrudes into the piazza. Beside it and now joined to it is the Palazzo del Capitano (1290–1296). An outside stairway of fine proportions (1267) leads from the piazza to a wide landing from which there are entrances to both buildings. The older building has forked battlements, and handsome, three-light, round-arched windows. The Palazzo del Capitano's windows are strikingly different. Those on the first floor (*piano nobile*) are Gothic, three-light windows under a rose and bearing arch. Over each there is an ornate gable, crocketed (leaves bent and curved) and a finial in a kind of lily design. On the top floor the windows again have round bearing arches.

The two buildings house the city offices, communal archives, and a collection of documents and photographs relating to Jacopone, Todi's most famous son. There is as usual a *pinacoteca*, which contains a Lo Spagna of the *Coronation of the Virgin*, what remains of a Bicci di Lorenzo triptych, a few Etruscan and Greek ceramics, as well as medieval chalices and paraphernalia of the church. There is nothing here, however, on which one needs to spend much time.

The cathedral approached by a wide and dignified flight of steps stands at the far end of the piazza. The squared-off façade is of the thirteenth century, and resembles that of many of the churches of the Abruzzi. The rose window above the central portal is noteworthy as is the portal with its vine and floral design. The building itself is of the twelfth century. The striking fresco on the inside wall is of the *Last Judgment* by Ferrau da Faenza, one of several artists from the north who had a hand in work at Todi. The carved and inlaid stalls (1530) of the choir are especially to be noted, the work of Antonio and Sebastiano Bencivenni da Mercatello of the Marches. The apse on the outside is particularly beautiful. One notes the double row of columns, one literally on top of the other, the variation in their design and in their

capitals, the delicacy of the workmanship on the cornice just above, the short suspended columns underneath, the leaves and animal heads.

Before going to San Fortunato, one may well explore some of the back streets of the town, to the west of the *duomo*, for instance, the Via Paolo Rolli and Via del Monte from which one has not only lovely views but where one may see portions of the old walls. Returning to the main piazza one may follow down the street to the right of the *duomo*, turning right into Via San Prassede and again right on the Via Cesia until one comes to the fine old Fonte Scarnabecco, built by order of a *podestà* from Bologna of that name in the middle thirteenth century. The crude capitals of its seven columns suggest a Lombard carver. Nowadays it is a public fountain where women do their washing, but in the Middle Ages it was primarily for horses. Records do not tell exactly how many horses were housed in Todi at that time, but in the middle fourteenth century the number is given as nearly one thousand. When the owning of a horse was a badge of aristocracy, it is easy to gather what a community Todi must have been at that time. A little way beyond the Fonte is the church of San Ilario (formerly San Carlo) near which Jacopone is supposed to have had his home. To the left of the church the Via del Mercato Vecchio leads up to the piazza of the same name. There are five large niches, Roman, possibly of the Augustan age. This was undoubtedly a part of an ancient Roman building. From the old market place one may go on to the Etruscan Porta Marzia. From here the Via San Fortunato leads through a district of medieval houses to the Via Lorenzo Leoni. Turning right and then left one arrives at the Piazza della Repubblica.

Here is San Fortunato, titular church of one of Todi's saints. It is high inside and light, with Gothic arches and vaulting. Its carved choir stalls again are by a northern workman, Maffei da Gubbio. And here in the fourth chapel to the right is Todi's most distinguished painting, a fresco of the *Madonna and Child and Two Angels* by Masolino da Panicale. In the crypt is the tomb of Fra Jacopone. The façade of the church was never completed, but its recessed triple doors give it distinction. The central portal is particularly lovely with its carved and twisted columns, its elaborate carvings of leaves and vines and faces. In the niches at either side are statues of *Gabriel* and the *Virgin*.

San Fortunato stands on a little hill high above the street. A broad stairway, of several tiers, leads up to its triple portals. At the foot to the left, draped with ivy and in the shadow of a deodar, is the bronze statue of *Fra Jacomo dei Benedetti*, known to all as Jacopone. He it is who is the real romance and the real saint of Todi, so regarded by many of the simple common people among his contemporaries, though never accorded that distinction by the church. Nor would he, probably, have been happy at the thought of sainthood; he had refused to become a priest; he preferred his humble role, to be rather 'a fool for Christ's sake'.

Born in 1228 or 1230, he started life quite otherwise, as did St. Francis. His father, a notary of Todi, was probably of the lesser Umbrian nobility, had position in the town, and outside the walls a small estate. Of his mother, Jacopone's few brief references are all we have. The usual solicitous mother, she waked often at night to gaze down, lantern in hand, at her young child to see that all was well. The boy, eldest of three sons, was strong and self-willed, eager to pick a fight with other boys. He often probably earned the thrashings his stern father administered. As he grew older he was still more of a worry. He was extravagant; he gambled; he indulged in feasting and fine clothes; he loved to lie abed in the morning and live a life of ease. His father had other ideas, and sent the young man off to the university, probably Bologna.

Though it specialized in law, the University of Bologna was at that time a center of culture, of ideas. Men came there from everywhere, were discussing everything. Many of its students lived in the families of professors. Just to be in such an atmosphere was something of an education, yet no doubt in addition to the law Jacopone was exposed to other liberal studies, philosophy and rhetoric, music and poetry, for instance. Nearly everybody in that day with any pretension at education dabbled in poetry, not just verses composed in Latin, the literary language and the language of the church, but poetry in the vulgar tongue of the Provençal and Sicilian schools. Though even at the university Jacopone continued to be a gay young blade and waster of his father's substance, he must have had some taste for education, for in the course of time he was accredited as an attorney. As was the custom on such occasions, gowned in red and on horseback, he paraded through the streets accompanied by trumpeters. That ceremony must have fed the already fattened ego of Jacopone.

Then he went back to Todi to practise. Every attorney was something of a personage in the thirteenth century; he was not supposed to go out on the piazza save as he was accompanied by clients—a not too subtle form of advertising, and perhaps slightly inconvenient if one suddenly decided to go and get a haircut. However that may be, Jacopone settled into his profession, determined to support himself in the manner to which he was accustomed; and apparently he did. At thirty-eight or-nine he married a girl of suitable background, Vanna, of the Umbrian aristocracy, young, beautiful, rich, amiable. She followed her husband's lead with never a sharp word. She was also a simple soul and deeply religious. Jacopone loved her dearly, loved to dress her in clothes of the finest, to heap jewels upon her. He wanted her to cut a swath in Todi. She often talked to him of the values of religion, but made no impression. Finally she yielded and allowed herself to be dressed as his fancy dictated.

It happened one day a year after their marriage that Vanna was sitting with other women of the local aristocracy on a platform at a public festival. Suddenly the platform gave way. Vanna was mortally injured. Her husband arriving quickly at the scene carried her aside, tore away her clothes to ascertain her injuries. To his horror he found that underneath her gorgeous raiment next her white skin she wore a coarse hair shirt. Then in his hands she died.

He could not be comforted. He was like a madman. From that moment dated his conversion. All his luxurious living, all his pride of position rose up to haunt him. He got rid of his house, gave his wealth to the poor, cut himself off from relatives and friends. He went about the streets of Todi like a scarecrow, dressed in rags. At the wedding of a niece he appeared, to be sure, but covered with feathers. Sometimes he crawled on all fours, followed by a crowd of jeering boys. He sought at once to join the Brothers Minor, an order established at Todi by St. Francis himself. They would not have him; his conversion was still too new; his behavior was rather that of a mountebank than of a pious monk. He did, however, take the vows of a Tertiary, a lay order of those who not only preached but undertook charitable works such as nursing. For the next ten years, dressed in the hood and rough tunic of the order, observing their rule of continence and poverty, he wandered over the hills of Umbria and the Marches, preaching, and singing, studying holy writings, and in every way living a life of self-abnegation.

> 'Famished and weak I fasted many a day;
> Dried up by heat and punished by cold I lay;
> I was a pilgrim on a weary way,
> Or so it seemed, in sunshine or in rain.'[59]

> (Lauda 28, p. 385)

It is said that he had a gift for fervent preaching, that he drew both laughter and tears from his hearers, as he sought to bring them to a new and more sober understanding of life. He knew, however, the value of brevity.

> 'To be longwinded, I confess,
> For those who hear is weariness;

The skilled abbreviator's art
Will make the listener glad of heart:
So will I shorten all I say,
Compress my writings as I may,
And who attends to what I tell
Within his mind may store it well.'[59]

(Lauda 71, p. 84)

He used proverbs much, sometimes putting them into a couplet:

'Who hath never been a fool,
Wisdom's scholar cannot be.'[59]

(Lauda 84, p. 283)

He excoriated the evils of his time, the life of the senses, the frivolities of women, such as the wearing of false hair. He spoke with personal conviction; he was himself a penitent. No doubt his earlier experience as a lawyer had served him well; he knew the tricks of emotional appeal.

At the end of ten years he applied again to the Brothers Minor at the Convent of St. Fortunato and they admitted him. Of the order there were two branches. Jacopone chose the more strict, the Brothers Spiritual. He wished to punish his body, believing that in doing so he was glorifying God and making atonement for his own sins. Rising before dawn for prayer, he ate a breakfast of bread and water, went hungry, thirsty, cold, even dirty, put wormwood in his food to make it repugnant, sought to be assigned the most menial of tasks.

Now in his brown habit, the rope dangling from his waist, he was going once again back and forth across the familiar Umbrian hills from the convent in Todi. He was still preaching, still composing lyrics, religious songs that went to the heart of the common people, for they were in the dialect of the Umbrian hills. Some were autobiographical, some philosophic. Some were satires, and some brief sermons, perhaps on old age or the passing of personal beauty:

'Lo! beauty, fair of face,
Hath no abiding place;

> At dawn the flower is gay;
> At dusk it fades away!'[59]
>
> (Lauda 22, p. 88)

Here was no admonition to enjoy life while one can—'Gather ye
rosebuds while ye may'—but rather one on the vanity of earthly beauty
in contrast to heaven's abiding glory. He was not like St. Francis, or
even Albert Schweizer, filled with joy in God's creation and with appreciation of all the little creatures of the world. Sometimes, only,
one sees evidence of an awareness of such things:

> 'Here dwell the birds and sing all day,
> Here sweetly through the winter rest;
> From envious eyes within the spray
> Safely they hide the secret nest.'[59]
>
> (Lauda 88, p. 224)

The thought of sin had laid too heavy a shadow across Jacopone's soul.
Sometimes he wrote Christmas carols:

> 'Come, come with me!
> Folk why so tardily?
> Eternal life to see
> In swaddling clothes.'[59]
>
> (Lauda 2, p. 147)

Sometimes he wrote poems for other festivals of the church, the
Assumption, the Resurrection, the Passion, or even for the celebration
of saints' days. In some of these Christ and other characters were given
speaking parts—and as these were acted out later by peasants before
the churches, they became the first simple examples of medieval
religious drama in Italy. In all he wrote two hundred and eleven poems.
Frederic Ozanam in his *Franciscan Poets in Italy of the Thirteenth
Century* (p. 188) calls him 'The most popular and the most inspired
of the poets of the Franciscan Order.'

The composing and singing of the *laude* was no new thing. St. Francis
had gone singing across the hills and had encouraged such activity
among his brethren. Since the late twelfth century the *laudesi* had been

organized to meet together at stated times and places, to sing in the streets and piazzas, a kind of remote ancestor of the Salvation Army. As Evelyn Underhill has aptly said in her life of Jacopone, these *laude* had the informality of and served much the same purpose as the spirituals in the southern United States. They comforted the people in much the same way.

Frederic Ozanam says:

'The people have never had greater benefactors than the men who taught them to bless their fate, who rendered the spade light on the shoulder of the labourer and made hope gleam in the weaver's cottage. More than once without doubt, at sunset, when the good people of Todi were returning from work in the fields and wending their way up the hill, the men goading their cattle, the women carrying on their backs their dark-haired babies, behind them some Franciscan monks, their feet covered with dust, they were to be heard singing the song of Jacopone, which mingled with the tinkling of the Angelus bell:

O tender love of poverty, how deeply should we love thee!
Poverty, my little one, whose sister is Humility: one bowl for
    eating and drinking sufficeth thee.
Poverty requires nought beside bread and water and a few herbs.
    If a guest visits her she adds a pinch of salt.
Poverty walks without fear; she has no enemies; she has no
    dread lest thieves shall molest her.
Poverty knocks at the door; she has neither purse nor store;
    She carries nought with her excepting bread. . . .
Poverty dies in peace; she makes no will; there is no need
    for parents and relatives to quarrel over her riches.

. . . .
. . . .
. . . .
. . . .
. . . .
. . . .

Gracious poverty, ever generous and joyful! Who can say that
    it is a base thing ever to love poverty?'[38]

In due course, however, Jacopone fell on unhappy days. He had been outspoken about evils within the church. He had in all probability lived in Rome a while, possibly as secretary to a cardinal from Todi, and had seen and heard too much of ecclesiastical intrigue to remain tongue-tied. When Boniface VIII, hard, unscrupulous politician, became pope, Jacopone allowed himself to sign as a witness a manifesto protesting Boniface's election. He and others were at once excommunicated. Jacopone had known Boniface, who had been a frequent visitor in Todi and had a permanent stall in its cathedral. Now the friar blasted forth:

> 'Blasphemous tongue, that has poisoned the world,
> There is no kind of ugly sin
> In which you have not become infamous . . .'[61]

and much more. He was thrown into a dungeon in Palestrina near Rome. There, dragging his chains, living on the scantiest of diets, among rats, in darkness, heat, or cold, he languished for five years. Yet he faced his ordeal with courage, and as Evelyn Underhill remarks, with a kind of wry humor, writing once:

> 'Although by day and night I lie
> As fattening pigs within their sty,
> I fear the Christmas is not nigh
> When they shall make good pork of me.'[59]

And again he remarks: 'If only the friars who come to Rome in search of bishoprics were put on this diet their sermons would not be so long.'[59]

Then one day in October 1303 the pope was dead and a new pope, Benedict XI, was on the throne. Jacopone was released. On the day that he stepped forth from the dungeon into an Italian autumn with the sun shining on grapevines turning yellow, on cypresses and poplars and olives, he broke out into song, '*O Amor*', *amore divina*. . . .' (O love, love divine).

By easy stages he found his way, first to a hermitage on the Tiber, and finally to the convent of the Brothers Minor at Collazzone, half-way between Todi and Perugia. There in contemplation and in writing he spent his remaining years. There, it is thought, he wrote in Latin the famous *Stabat Mater Dolorosa* and the *Stabat Mater Speciosa*.

Toward the end of 1306 Fra Jacopone became ill. His brothers wished to administer the last sacraments. He refused. He wished to receive these rather from his friend, Fra Giovanni of La Verna. But La Verna was far away to the north and east, and Fra Giovanni did not know of Jacopone's illness. Still Fra Jacopone refused. Toward evening, however, the brothers saw in the distance two friars coming, and as they drew nearer, they recognized one as Fra Giovanni. It was a miracle, they thought. Fra Jacopone and Fra Giovanni had suitable discourse, then Jacopone received from his friend the sacrament. Just as midnight ushered in a new Christmas Day, Jacopone's spirit took leave of his body. In the neighboring church, the legend relates, the priest was intoning *Gloria in Excelsis*.

No one has said so, but it would be no wonder if then the monks surrounding his bed had broken out singing one of Jacopone's own Christmas carols:

> '. . . . .
> In a piercing major key,
> Yet with soft timidity,
> Sweetest singing charms the ear;
> Now ensues a minor strain,
> Gently floating down again
> Sweeter still, and still more clear.
> Such a descant, pure and keen,
> Never sure was heard or seen,
> So divine in harmony.
>
> . . . .
> . . . .
> Humble men, and innocent,
> Upright men and diligent,
> Come before him, come and sing.
> Let him not in vain entreat,

Come and kneel before his feet,
Giving glory to your king.
Ye shall have your heart's desire,
Tasting with the heavenly choir
Feasts of love eternally.'[59]

(Lauda 64, pp. 413–419)

16

Orvieto

To MANY people the name Orvieto unfortunately means just one thing—wine. They may have heard vaguely that the town boasts a cathedral of some merit, but they are sure it boasts a wine of more merit. Several of the towns of this region have for long been rivals for the tributes accorded their vintages. Montepulciano on the southern edge of Tuscany likes to quote a couplet:

> 'Give ear and give faith to the edict divine,
> Montepulciano's the King of all wine.'

> FRANCESCO REDI, *Bacchus in Tuscany*
> Trs. Leigh Hunt

Over at Montefiascone, a few miles to the west, high above Lake Bolsena they have a legend proving that theirs is the best. A certain German bishop, Johannes Fugger, it is said, on his way south, sent ahead a servant-connoisseur to taste and report on the wines along the way. If the local wine was good, he was to write EST (It is) on the wall by the gate of the town; if it was very good, he was to write EST EST. When Bishop Fugger arrived at Montefiascone, he took a room and settled down to enjoy himself. The inscription read EST EST EST. How much or how long he imbibed, the story does not say. But the happy bishop realized before the end that it was the end and he made a last request, that once a year a cask of Montefiascone wine be poured upon his grave. It is said that the city fathers, undoubtedly realizing the value of advertising, were still carrying out his request some seventy-five years ago. Anyhow the bishop's grave is there, on the floor

of San Flaviano's lower church down the hill from the piazza through
which one passes. At each side of his rather crudely carved figure is
carved also a large flask. What might have happened if the servant had
got instead to Orvieto is hard to say; he might himself have got no
farther.

The soil of the slopes around the town is fertile. Anyhow white
grapes grown there seem to have a special something. Volcanic ash
well weathered by centuries is usually good growing soil; it is full of
lime, magnesium, iron, various trace elements, probably of phosphates.
Orvieto itself stands high (one thousand and sixty-six feet), above the
Paglia. It is on a volcanic flat-top or *mesa* several miles around. Once, in
geologic ages past, this whole district was covered with volcanic ash
and then with lava. Gradually rain and frost made cracks, streams cut
through soft underlying shales, and great portions of the lava cap
spalled off, leaving cliffs such as we see today at Orvieto, at Orte to
the southeast, at La Civita not far from Lake Bolsena, and elsewhere.
These heights needed no walls for protection, and the early peoples
were quick to take advantage of the situation.

The Etruscans spreading inland from the coastal towns of Caere
(Cerveteri) and Tarquinia found this rock to their liking. There they
established a well-ordered and proud civilization, at least to judge from
the treasures found there since and in the neighborhood. Called
Volsinii, it was one of the twelve towns of the Etruscan confederation,
and may also have had special significance as a religious center. That
there was at least one temple there we know. Its stone foundations are
traceable in the Belvedere beyond the *pozzo*. The upper part was
probably as usual of terra cotta and wood painted in red and other
colors. Statues, and fragments of terra cotta belonging to it were found
during the excavations there forty years or so ago. Other temples may
also have existed on this hilltop and have been destroyed by the
Romans when they conquered Orvieto in 265 B.C. or thereabouts.
Pliny, the Elder, in his *Natural History*[43] reports that at that time two
thousand statues are said to have been carried away by the Romans.
Some of these may have been from the temples; some were probably
looted from tombs, may even have been the decorative tops of
cinerary urns, such as one sees in the Etruscan museum at Chiusi. At
that time many survivors are supposed to have fled to the new Volsinii

Orvieto

(Bolsena) on its hilltop to the west. From that circumstance the present Orvieto may have derived its name, *Urbs vetus* (or *vieto*), the old town. In wandering about Orvieto one comes upon many Etruscan things. Even individuals there have become minor collectors. No doubt farmers still bring in occasionally bits dug up on a sidehill or a vineyard. There is, of course, the archaeological museum (on a top floor, as always) across from the *duomo*. There those things found at the Belvedere are housed as well as others brought from tombs in the hills not far away. There is a notable sarcophagus, for instance, carved with the story of Ulysses. Almost beside this museum, in the Faina Palace, is a still more impressive collection. There are many fine figurines, some bronze pots, some black *bucchero*, case after case of ancient coins. It is especially rich, however, in red and black Greek vases from Etruscan tombs. Many vases, by no means all, of course, formerly supposed to be Etruscan, are now being identified as Attic, traded by the Greeks no doubt for other types of things of Etruscan manufacture. Anyone with artistic or classical interests or even with normal curiosity could spend hours here examining the delicate paintings on these vases, hunting scenes, chariot races, festivals with musical accompaniment, banquets, sacrifices. One often wonders, as did Keats:

> 'What little town by river or sea shore,
> Or mountain-built with peaceful citadel,
> Is emptied of its folk this pious morn?'
>
> *Ode on a Grecian Urn*

There are a few simple Etruscan tombs part way down the hill just off the road to the railway station. If you have seen those at Chiusi or Tarquinia, these are not worth bothering about. They are in a row, of great blocks of stone heavily grown-over with sod. Within their dark interiors there are no paintings, just stone benches where sarcophagi were once placed.

In two of Orvieto's churches there are Etruscan evidences. In San Lorenzo it is an altar from some Etruscan temple, cylindrical and of stone; on it now rests the top of a Christian high altar. Over all is a high, pointed, and carved stone canopy of the twelfth century. Deep underneath Sant' Andrea in the Piazza della Repubblica some years ago there were found traces of a church probably of the sixth century; below it again, archaeologists discovered what appeared to be an Etruscan street, some buildings, and a well.

In exploring the narrow streets one might as well look at some of the small churches. More than in many places they give one a feeling of the Middle Ages. San Lorenzo, just mentioned, is full of fourteenth- and fifteenth-century frescoes of saints, some fragmentary, some restored. Behind the high altar, in the darkness of the apse, eyes of saints stare down. The figures are Byzantine in style, tall, thin, and slightly metallic, never of this world. So it is at San Giovenale at the western end of town. There sometime in the twelfth, thirteenth, fourteenth, and fifteenth centuries almost every wall or column or pilaster was frescoed, probably by local artists. It is almost as if each painter had hastened to make his frescoed offering to his Lord before another had pre-empted all the space. It is an ancient church, begun supposedly in the early eleventh century (1009), and simple. Even the columns are rather crude. In San Giovenale the medieval period seemed not far removed. Even the custodian contributed a certain atmosphere; shabby and elderly, with a black shawl and sweeping skirts, she limped along, using an umbrella, to be sure, as her cane. The church was all hers. She knew its every cranny, and it was dear to her.

Afterwards we walked out to the piazza in front where one looks down from the parapet onto small gardens and to the road winding through the green valley from the hills beyond. Nearer, to the left, was what is considered 'the old quarter'. There are low houses of tufa, many roofs angling into one another, a church tower beyond, the cliff dropping off below. Close by, under a roof weighted down by rocks as in Switzerland, was a window full of blooming plants. Smoke curled up from a chimney there, no doubt from a fire built of gathered little sticks.

Around the corner is San Agostino, now no longer open. It has, however, a beautiful Gothic doorway. In the Piazza della Repubblica the campanile of Sant' Andrea rises from the ground, quite separate from the church. It is dodecagonal. More than halfway up it is pierced by three rows of twin-light windows, and under the crenellated top by three other rows of small square holes. One rarely sees a tower like it. Sant' Andrea itself is old, was important in the days of the commune. In it many solemn occasions were celebrated, the sermon urging the fourth crusade, for instance. One pope was crowned there. Boniface VIII, of inglorious fame, first was made a cardinal there, as was Nicholas IV. In the arcade beside the church there is now a flower market. The visitor to Orvieto may wish to walk down to San Domenico, now in a state of disrepair, where is the cosmatesque tomb (Arnolfo di Cambio) of Cardinal Guglielmo de Braye, and where in the attached monastery Thomas Aquinas once lived for a while.

Orvieto is a town in which it is fun to walk around discovering things, old palaces looking comfortable but unimpressive yet rather lovely with their flower pots on a rain-washed sunny day; doorways, checkerboard window frames such as those in the bishop's palace (once the place where popes stayed); shops where lace is sold; views out along the cliffside or of the cathedral between the walls of Via Maitani, from the courtyard of the Clementini palace, now the public library, or from a high window in the Faina palace where you see to great advantage the whole pattern of the Piazza del' Duomo. There once were many towers, it is said, in the days of the Guelfs and the Ghibellines, the Monaldeschi and the Filippeschi; there are no longer. Now one looks up to the Torre del Moro or to the Torretta dell' Orologio, where, standing, as it were, over the Piazza del' Duomo the old (thirteenth century) bronze statue of *Maurizio* still beats out the hours.

Everyone should see the Palazzo del Popolo (thirteenth century) with its handsome three-light windows, its great arches with heavy recessed moldings, its stairway at one end. Even in the early morning when the piazza may be thronged with people marketing for fish, fruit, flowers, and vegetables, the *palazzo* is beautiful, golden in the sunshine. Perhaps, if you are staying at the Hotel Reale, a place itself of interest and charm, you will see it many times in many lights.

The lines of the pope's palace near the *duomo* remind one of it, though more severe. Orvieto was for long a favorite sojourning place of popes, and besides the bishop's palace, which they had often occupied, they needed a palace for the entertaining of visiting prelates. It was built at various times but most of it probably in the thirteenth and early fourteenth centuries. One often wonders how builders of that day managed to make additions with so little evidence that they had been again at work. They fortunately had not yet learned short cuts, knew nothing about lean-tos or such appendages. Today the palace houses the Opera del Duomo, a museum of objects belonging especially to the church, reliquaries, chalices, ancient vestments, a bronze or two, old architectural drawings of the cathedral—one somewhat doubtfully attributed to Arnolfo di Cambio—statues, statuettes, and paintings. There are two works by Simone Martini of Siena, several small figures by Arnolfo, and others by the Pisani. Those who worked on the cathedral in various capacities, Lorenzo Maitani, Ippolito Scalza, Signorelli, and others undoubtedly left behind them trial efforts and these have been treasured. Some of them are good, most not significant.

Probably most visitors will wish to go down to see the famous *pozzo*, off the Piazzale Cahen, near the funicular, and at least to look down into its depths. It was built by Antonio da Sangallo, the younger, at the order of one of the popes who having fled from Rome to Orvieto (1527–1528), realized how vulnerable the town was to siege because of lack of water. Two spiral stairways were constructed wide enough and easy enough for donkeys single file to descend and carry back up casks of water. The two stairways opened at the spring and there was always one-way traffic. At the foot there is nothing to see except the place of the spring and a great central shaft to the opening above. The stairways are lighted by windows opening on this shaft.

Of course it is the cathedral in Orvieto, one of the best in Italy, that one really comes to see. All these other things but set the stage. To appreciate its story fully one must live for the moment in the age in which it was created, must try to accept the mood of the time and place, to forget about such things as buses for everywhere lined up in the Piazza della Repubblica or scooters bumping along narrow alleys, and think instead of a Bohemian priest in the 1260's, so the story goes, travelling slowly on his way to Rome. He was young, probably, and very much a human being, for he was secretly sceptical of the doctrine of transubstantiation. This was heresy, he knew. As he passed through Bolsena, the people of Santa Christina asked him to officiate at mass. He did. As he held up the host, he saw blood dripping from it on the sacramental linen. He put it down untouched. He could go no farther. This was the miracle for which he had subconsciously hoped. Pope

Urban IV was in Orvieto. So was Thomas Aquinas. The priest hastened there, telling of the miracle and of his own sin. The local bishop was at once dispatched to bring back the host and the stained linen. Later in honor of the miracle the pope instituted the feast of Corpus Christi, instructing Aquinas to compose the appropriate office. Then he declared that a great cathedral should be built in Orvieto to commemorate the occasion and make a place for the sacred evidence. How Bolsena must have felt let down! It was not until 1290 or thereabouts, however, that the first stone of the new *duomo* was laid, in the reign of Pope Nicholas IV.

Many architects, sculptors, and painters had a hand in the building and its ornamentation, for after all from start to finish the work, inside and out, occupied well on to three hundred years. Lorenzo Maitani of Siena must be given major credit for its design and probably for the design of much of its detail; he worked on it for at least twenty-five years. Antonio Federighi, also of Siena, is said to have completed the top of the façade. Andrea Pisano and Andrea Orcagna worked especially on carvings.

People liken it to the cathedral of Siena. Actually it is much simpler and more beautiful than that. The façade has greater organization and unity of design. Vertically it is divided into three sections, one central gable to which the others are definitely subordinate. Under the rose window ('St. Catherine's wheel') a gallery runs all the way across the front. The four buttresses ending in pinnacles draw the eye upward. There are statues in the square framing the rose window, and some elsewhere, but no multiplicity of them. Above the piers are the symbols of the evangelists, the angel of St. Matthew, the lion of St. Mark, the eagle of St. John, the bull of St. Luke. Mosaics, to be sure, are everywhere, above the doors, in the gables.

But the glory of the façade is, in the opinion of many, in the carving on the four marble piers. There between the tendrils of vines are bas-reliefs, scenes from the Old and the New Testament. Though in marble, the work is in many ways comparable to that of Ghiberti's bronze doors in Florence. It is, however, earlier (approximately 1320–1330). The first pier begins with Genesis, with the creation. The fourth is of the last judgment, the rising of the dead, the escorting of the blessed to heaven, the hideous dragging of the evil to a nether world.

On the two intervening piers are the stories of kings and prophets, of the Virgin and of Christ. Though the design and possibly some of the carving are usually attributed to Maitani and his pupils, there are those who think that Andrea Pisano may also have worked on these piers. One of the incidental marvels is that the figures are still relatively clear and fresh. Yet in the United States one can hardly read the inscription on a marble tombstone after one hundred years.

Even the inside of the cathedral, despite its stripes of black and white, is satisfying. The proportions create for one a sense of height and spaciousness. In the apse a Gothic window of four vertical divisions with tracery at the top gives emphasis to this. The arches, to be sure, are round. Above each is a simple lancet window, part of alabaster, part of stained glass. The whole effect is of quietness and peace rather than of great magnificence.

Yet there is art to be seen within these walls. Many persons contributed. There is a *Pietà* (1579), for instance, by Ippolito Scalza, one of Orvieto's native sons, a sculptor and an architect. It has four figures, the limp body of Christ stretched across his mother's lap, the mourning Magdalene caressing a hand and foot, Nicodemus standing and looking down in deep distress, still grasping in one hand the ladder. It is Christ's mother only who seems to have risen above her immediate sorrow; in her face and attitude there are reflected life and hope. There is another of Scalza's works in the cathedral, an *Ecce Homo*, carved when he was seventy-six.

In the choir there is beautiful carved woodwork, and frescoes in the apse by Ugolino di Prete Ilario, another Orvietan. Near the main entrance, to the left, is a *Madonna and Child* by Gentile da Fabriano, an artist of the Marches. In the chapel of the Corporale there is a painting by Lippo Memmi of Siena, of the Madonna adored by church fathers, saints, and angels. There are wrought-iron gates, too, worth notice at the entrance to the two major chapels.

Perhaps one should go first to the chapel of the Corporale to the left. On the walls frescoes by Ugolino di Prete Ilario record the story of *The Miracle of Bolsena*. On the high altar within a marble *tabernacolo* is the reliquary. It is in silver, enamel, and jewels in the shape of the cathedral and was made by a Sienese, Ugolino di Vieri, and his assistants, possibly after a design of Maitani's though after the latter's death. Once a year, on the feast of Corpus Christi, it is carried in procession through the streets.

The chapel in the opposite transept, that of the Madonna di San Brizio, is one made famous by the frescoes of Fra Angelico and Luca Signorelli. They were begun in 1447 with the help of Gozzoli and others, but only two sections of the vaults were completed before Angelico was called elsewhere. These two frescoes were of a stern and powerful Christ sitting in judgment on the world and of a group of prophets posed on a triangular bank of clouds (to fit the vault of course). They are, most of them, holding manuscripts or gesticulating, and nearly all conform to the popular conception of a prophet, even today, a person with a long face and a longer beard, though they are all individuals in expression. There are a few younger ones, just to show that even in a new generation there is hope. When Signorelli took over finally in 1499, he followed Angelico's plan for the vaults, with choruses, of the apostles with the Virgin, of the patriarchs, of the doctors of the church, of the martyrs, and of the virgins.

Signorelli knew well the scriptural story, had read his Dante also, was familiar with the classic conceptions of Charon and the River Styx, of Pluto and his realm, and he drew upon all these for inspiration in his frescoes on the walls. They gave him ample scope for the depiction of the human figure under various kinds of stress, in every sort of movement and attitude. In the first fresco the Antichrist, prompted by the devil, speaks to the people. Groups stand around. (In one the profile of Dante is recognizable.) In the background much goes on; people are killed and tortured; others flee as the Archangel descending in a rain of fire falls upon the Antichrist. Then there is a vivid picture of the end of the world, when the sun and moon are darkened, fire shoots through the sky, buildings are overturned by earthquakes, and the ground is littered with the dead and dying. In the next scene, the resurrection of the dead, Signorelli showed himself a literalist. Above, the angels blow the last trump, and then the bare skeletons begin to push up out of the ground, gradually becoming clothed with flesh. In nakedness but with joy they greet one another, looking toward the sky in thanksgiving. There follows a picture of the damned at the mouth of hell, while above three angels guard to see that none escapes. In the next Charon in his boat pilots the damned across the river while others on the bank await their turn. But there are the blessed, too, accompanied by music, garlanded with flowers, before the gates of heaven. Below these frescoes are medallions, one of *Empedocles* as if contemplating the destruction of the world, others of poets, *Homer*, *Lucan*, *Horace*, *Virgil*, *Ovid*, *Dante*. Each of these is accompanied by miniature scenes from his poems and is framed in arabesques. In a niche by itself on the right wall Signorelli painted a *Pietà*, considered one of his most powerful and sympathetic works.

Before leaving Orvieto every visitor is almost sure to go again to the public gardens where the old *fortezza* stood. There he will look out along the bastions, over which a great pine hangs its plumy head, to the Umbrian hills, the valley of the Paglia, and, farther away still, the Tiber. He may watch a loaded donkey coming up the road beneath the wall, or, in the spring, see slopes full of flowering fruit trees. In the park there is little left to remind one of the old fortress built by Cardinal Albornoz in 1364, a gate, a tower, and these sustaining walls. He came, a representative of the pope, to have surveillance of the city, though it still had certain of its communal rights and was not finally taken over by the church until 1450. The scene there almost inevitably recalls another, though at first perhaps one cannot place it; then it all comes back—it is the view from the high garden at Avignon where one looks across the Rhône and a great pine leans over the parapet. Probably it is purest coincidence, yet in 1364 the popes were still in Avignon. Could it be that Cardinal Albornoz chose this site because he, too, saw a likeness?

If one is in an exploring mood, Orvieto makes a good center for trips to the south and west. From it one could easily drive one day to Viterbo, see its medieval (Pellegrino) quarter, the balconies, and outside stairways, its papal palace and its fountains. Bolsena is not far away and the lake also of that name is beautiful and set round with fishing villages. Tarquinia, of course, is farther away, yet one should not miss it. It is an old town full of towers. Its Vitelleschi Palace, now the museum, dark and ill-lighted as it is, has many carved Etruscan sarcophagi and paintings from the tombs. Of major importance are the tombs themselves just out of town. There you will see many wall paintings: banquet scenes, wrestling matches, priestly rites; musicians with flutes and lyres; animals real and mythological, leopards, bulls, horses, snakes, and others. In many, Etruscan vases are shown as a decorative feature on the walls. The church of San Flaviano at Montefiascone has already been mentioned. It is a gem, two churches really, one above the other, facing in two directions. Its simple Lombard interior, the loggia all across the front, at the top of the lower church, the deep well in the center between the upper and lower edifices, the proportions of the upper church seen from above, all give it distinction.

Then at the end of a day as you come back and top the hill, you stop —you cannot help stopping—for there ahead is Orvieto, high on its cliff, seen as you see it nowhere else, and there, too, the cathedral rising above all the roofs of the town and shining in the sun.

Liguria

17

Porto Venere

OF THE villages of the Italian Riviera none is more alluring than Porto Venere. It is a fishing village where men go out to sea by day, and even at night, at certain times of year, with lanterns, to scoop up schools of sardines or of anchovies; where others hunt among the rocks for that delicacy, *frutti di mare*. The houses on the waterfront are built like a wall, six, seven, eight stories high, and are tinted in all the colors dear to Mediterranean peoples, pink, green, blue, orange, red, and yellow. Beyond these is a long promontory rising gradually to a rocky point on the ocean front. There stands the church of San Pietro braving the winds and waves, for Saint Peter was himself a fisherman if only on the Sea of Galilee. Along this front whether one is resting on the terrace of a *trattoria* or sitting on a rock looking out to sea, there is no urge to move. Nets may be drying in the sun, a washing of many colors may be dangling from a house, someone somewhere behind an open window may be singing; and always there are the waves almost at one's feet. Time seems to stand still, at least to the casual visitor.

Up in the town itself you follow a long narrow street, lined with shops and the entrances that must lead to the upper stories of the tall houses down below. Here and there over an ancient doorway there will be a carving, perhaps only a simple IHS such as San Bernardino made popular in Siena, occasionally a bas-relief of some winged mythological creature or maybe a sea monster. You look down long narrow stairways to the wharf or up other stairways to get a glimpse of sky or tree, or the tower of San Lorenzo. If you follow some of these stairways uphill, you will come out perhaps on a small piazza where some fisherman has built a patterned pavement of shells before his door, or a miniature garden. In some window you will see perhaps a ship's model, or at the end of a path a lantern hanging from its bracket, old stone walls grown full of spindly grasses and weeds, or an agave reaching out its jagged spears. Occasionally there will be a view over rooftops to the sea. Everywhere, but especially, of course, down near the wharf there will be cats of varying ancestry. Once Porto Venere may have had only a thousand cats but all of them have had kittens at short intervals. They are around every corner, on doorsteps, walls, burying their heads in bowls specially set out for their refreshment. Still higher, if one follows the path above the village, there are the ivy-grown walls of the ruined fortress, its round towers at the corners, windows made for archers, a fine old fig tree branching across the path, and a view 'that maketh the heart glad' over the village, bay, islands, and sea. Occasionally on a sparkling day one can see, it is said, the dim outlines of Corsica.

At the end of the village itself, lower down, you come out on an esplanade of marble in the raw, it would seem, veined with red and black and yellow, and then you climb up a little way to the black and white San Pietro. It is a church of many traditions, made over in recent years from the crumbling ruin of one built probably in the twelfth century. Part of it, however, is said to date from the sixth century and to have been mentioned, along with the once-adjoining Benedictine monastery, in letters to the bishops of Milan and of Luni by Gregory the Great (590–604). This part is a little chapel built, so the legend goes, by fishermen seeking Saint Peter's protection on treacherous seas. It is entered through arches from the main church. There are old slot windows, some original pavement, and in the rather crude rounded apse a black statue of Saint Peter, seated. On the far side a door leads to a terrace. There, through windows reminiscent of Venice, you look out over sea and headlands, up to the *campo santo* on its high ledge and to the fortress.

From the esplanade another narrow street leads uphill to the Piazza of San Lorenzo. There in a setting of trees is the parish church, also of the twelfth century. Over the door is a bas-relief of the saint himself on his gridiron. Within are many small items, a few paintings, none of great importance, a baptismal font, and against the wall a large log, all dear to the people of the town. The log is, according to the story,

Porto Venere

cedar driftwood from the Orient washed ashore at Porto Venere in 1204. Inside was found a tarnished parchment, on which there appeared to be a painting of the Madonna. This 'white Madonna', having miraculously regained its colors in the fourteenth century, was enclosed in a reliquary, and is one of the treasures of the village.

Yet though there may be little else to see specifically at Porto Venere, its situation and its surroundings all recall much from the shadowed and the shining valleys of the past. The little harbor out in front is sheltered. Across a narrow inlet no wider than four hundred feet lies the large island of Palmaria, once obviously of a piece with the coast and the low mountains at the back of Porto Venere. Beyond is the smaller island of Tino, a great rock with a lighthouse on its top, and yet beyond the still smaller Tinetto. The little bay, part of the greater bay of La Spezia, is fortunately around an obscuring corner from the naval and shipbuilding activities of the latter.

During ages the beating waves have hollowed caves in the rocks along these shores. In these no doubt smugglers could and did hide out. To early stone-age man, however, they were home. In the Grotta dei Colombi on Palmaria in the last century there was found evidence of his one-time habitation there—stone arrow heads, cooking vessels, long bone needles, presumably for putting together the skins of animals he used for clothes, shells pierced and polished probably for the adornment of his womenfolk. (See the archaeological museum in La Spezia.)

Around the headlands to the right, only a few miles over the hills behind are the Cinque Terre, the five small towns, famous for their wines, Monterosso, Vernazza, Corniglia, Manarola, Riomaggiore. The towns themselves cling to the rocks or cluster in narrow valleys, houses piled together. Above on steep terraced hillsides grow the grapes. Though not far away, they are almost inaccessible except by sea, by foot, or donkey-back, although they may be reached by the stopping train from La Spezia. The wines, however, are available all along the coast. One can sample them at Porto Venere at the *albergo*, where one can also enjoy the local shellfish, *datteri*, and other specialties of the sea.

Who the first Ligurians were who occupied this long, narrow coastline no one really knows. Some think they may have been colonists from Spain. There are those who suspect that they may have been closely related to the Elymians of Sicily. In Liguria there is an Egesta (Sestre), in Sicily a Segesta, first Elymian, then Greek. There was a temple of Venus at Erice, a legendary temple to her (though it may well have been Roman) at Porto Venere on the spot where now stands the church of San Pietro. (Venus, who rose from the foam-flecked sea, besides being the goddess of love and beauty, was also the protectress of fishermen.) All this is surmise. All that we certainly know is that some of the Near Eastern peoples, notably the Phoenicians, were great travellers. They might have colonized both places. For the shores of Liguria, like those of Sicily, have an equable climate.

Early in the Christian era Porto Venere, we do know, had become a Roman port. Claudius Ptolemy so records in his geography in the second century. Even before that time the Romans had a thriving town at Luni, then Luna, at the mouth of the Magra. There they had an amphitheater seating several thousand persons. From there they may have shipped marble from the Carrara quarries or even from some of the nearer hills.

In the course of the centuries many other peoples came and went, the Celts, the Saracens raiding the coastline from bases in Sardinia, the Lombards in the early Middle Ages, the Normans in their time. In the twelfth century the Genoese took over Porto Venere and held it intermittently for several centuries. It was a port, however, that others craved, especially the Pisans who had fortified themselves in Lerici across the bay. The Genoese fortified also Porto Venere. Old prints show not only a heavy wall leading out along the promontory to the point but another along the landward waterfront and angling up the hill to a great fortress above. Three towers marked its course, and these became a part of Porto Venere's escutcheon.

It was, of course, for centuries a convenient way station for travellers by sea to the north and south. Sometimes they were driven in by storms. Yet many others, individuals, have discovered for themselves its attractions and those of the whole region. Franco Sacchetti and Boccaccio were familiar with it. So was Petrarch. But many in more modern times have held this shoreline dear. There is a cave at Porto Venere, the Grotta Arpaia, where Byron came. There listening to the ocean he found inspiration, it is said, for the writing of *The*

Corsair. He loved the sea in all its wildest moods, and understood the stormy men who rode its waves. But he loved it also in its milder aspects, once cast himself into it and swam the bay to Lerici. In *Childe Harold's Pilgrimage* he wrote:

> '. . . and my joy
> Of youthful sports was on thy breast to be
> Borne, like thy bubbles, onward: from a boy
> I wanton'd with thy breakers—they to me
> Were a delight; and if the freshening sea
> Made them a terror—'twas a pleasing fear,
> For I was as it were a child of thee,
> And trusted to thy billows far and near,
> And laid my hand upon thy mane. . . .'

(Canto IV)

George Sand, too, came to Porto Venere. So did Henry James. Shelley knew well this shore. He lived for a while in the arcaded Villa Magni at San Terenzo, almost next door to Lerici. It was from there that he sailed off in the *Ariel* for Livorno and his tragic end near Viareggio. Down the shore from Lerici only three kilometers on the high road (above Lerici the sign indicates Tellaro) to the south is a cove, Fiascherino. There D. H. Lawrence and his Freda once took a house, and in his letters he speaks of it as one of the most beautiful of places. He was right. There is no village there, just rocks and sea and trees, ilex and pine and olive groves, a tiny beach, and an occasional house hidden in the woods. At Tellaro, a small fishing village three kilometers farther on, even the road ends. If one wishes to stay a while and explore this whole region, this 'divine bay' as Shelley called it, one could not do better than to make one's headquarters at Fiascherino.

> 'The whispering waves were half asleep,
> The clouds were gone to play,
> And on the woods, and on the deep
> The smile of Heaven lay.'

PERCY BYSSHE SHELLEY,
The Pine Forest of the Cascine Near Pisa

Lazio

18

Nemi in the Alban Hills

'O Moon! the oldest shades 'mong oldest trees
Feel palpitations when thou lookest in:
. . . .
Thou dost bless everywhere, with silver lip
Kissing dead things to life.'

KEATS, *Endymion*, Book III

EVERY visitor to Rome finds himself repeatedly at the foot of the
Spanish stairs. It is not one thing, of course, that attracts, that
makes the picture unforgettable for all who once have seen it, but
rather the combination, the high wide sweep of steps, tier upon tier,
the church at the top, the rusty houses at the side with their association
with Keats, the green branches and vines reaching out from between
walls, the fountain in the piazza in the foreground, the umbrella-
covered flower stalls at the base. In season, blooming in vases and
buckets there, are daffodils and marguerites, anemones, ranunculi,
asters, snapdragons, sweet peas, carnations, irises, lilies, roses, mimosa,
violets—basketfuls of great deep purple violets from which to choose,
each bunch surrounded by its halo of green leaves. The carnations, one
is sure, came from the terraced fields of San Remo on the Riviera.
Where, one asks, do the violets come from? 'Nemi,' the *contadina*
answers, reaching down to lift a bunch from the basket in which all
of them look as if the dew had scarcely dried off their petals. Nemi in
the Alban hills, from the shores of Lake Nemi, deep blue itself like

these violets, round like these bunches, and all enclosed in green! It is itself a bouquet.

For Nemi is one of the loveliest spots in the lovely Alban hills. Even in the time of Cicero these hills to the south, ranging from one thousand to better than three thousand feet, were a haunt of Romans seeking escape from the heat and miasma of their plain, or even from the tensions and hurly-burly of life within the city. Any visitor to Rome should take a day to go to these hills and their villages, the Roman *castelli*. They are not far away, fifteen to twenty miles. From the top of Monte Cavo, that highest hill on the horizon to the south, one looks on woods, lakes, villages, the plain to the dome of St. Peter's, and the burnished sea at Anzio to the southwest. Up the side of this hill wound the Triumphal Way (portions of it still to be seen) to the temple of Jupiter Laziale on the peak. For to him, mightiest of the gods, thanks must be rendered lest angered he hurl his thunderbolts on ungrateful man.

One may go by several ways, of course, making a kind of circuit. One of the best, however, is to take the road toward Palestrina first, from the Porta Maggiore. To the right will be the Claudian aqueduct stepping high across the campagna on its way to Rome. Then there will be little else to see but fields and small farmhouses, each in its group of eucalyptus trees, till one begins to climb into the hills. At the end of the day you can then come back along the old Appian Way, marked by pines and cypresses and Roman tombs, and enter the city by the Porta San Sebastiano close to the catacombs.

These hills are thick with villages, with orchards and vineyards, with woods of ilex, beech, and nuts. One goes not just to see specific things, palaces or ruins or gardens, but to get the flavor of these hills, to feel what they must have meant to each succeeding period, what they mean even now. I've seen them at various seasons, looking out at Lake Nemi, for instance, in the spring through a mist of blooming mimosa trees, sitting out in the sunshine of a February day on the terrace of a *trattoria* eating spaghetti or *risotto*, and roasted chestnuts. In the fall, on all the slopes men are gathering in the grapes, loading the mules or donkeys—in Tuscany they would be white oxen—with great baskets. In every village one meets the pack animals climbing up the steep stair-streets to have their paniers unloaded. The doors to the dark wine

Nemi

cellars are then wide open and the vats are lined up. Frascati, of course, is famous for its white wine. If you are courageous, though one cannot advise such temerity, you'll taste the new wine from one of the spigots. You'll learn, too, how *vino santo* is made, from several colors of selected grapes. It may be holy wine indeed, but nearly everyone has his own supply, and there is nothing much better for lunch occasionally than *vino santo* with hard-crusted Italian bread and *prosciutto*. If you know the right person and are there at the right time of day, you might be lucky enough to see the men and girls assemble for the pressing of the grapes. They first wash off their bare feet at a convenient faucet, then climb the ladder and step into the huge vat to tramp out the juice. It's a method still in use in some excellent wineries.

There are many of these Roman *castelli*. Frascati has been known for centuries for its magnificent villas, the Aldobrandini, which the German Kesselring used as his headquarters in the last Great War, the Mondragone, property of the Roman church, the Falconieri, the Lancellotti. All have great formal gardens, with terraces, pools, fountains, and statues. Because of the German occupation Frascati suffered from bombing; and in others of these villages one can still see the pockmarks of war. Above Frascati was ancient Tusculum, to which a wooded avenue leads. It was Cato's birthplace. Close by, Cicero is supposed to have had a villa. They point out now stones of its foundations. On that quiet hilltop he might well have found the peace in which to compose essays on old age or friendship, or some of his orations. There are still tiers of seats of the old theater built into the hillside. Palestrina, too, has Roman ruins, a temple of Fortune; it has also the Colonna-Barberini palace, and on the top of the hill the remains of an old citadel.

There are other towns: Rocca di Papa climbing steeply up the back of Monte Cavo; Monte Compatri, at more than nineteen hundred feet, with a small hotel which Romans of today find useful; Grottaferrata, known for its abbey and for its wine; Albano looking down on Lake Albano; Castel Gandolfo where the pope has his summer palace; Ariccia—sunsets can be wonderful from its high viaduct; Genzano from which one takes the road to Nemi and its deep crater lake.

Nemi in Roman days was the peculiar haunt of the goddess Diana, daughter of Jupiter and sister of Apollo, and there on the slopes above the lake was a temple dedicated to her. These wooded hills were grateful to her eye, for she was goddess of the chase, and here roamed probably some of her favorite animals, especially the deer. She was, first of all, however, the moon goddess who drove at night her silver chariot across the sky; and as she looked down at Lake Nemi, in its placid waters she saw herself and her chariot reflected. So the lake became known as her mirror (*specchio di Diana*); it was round indeed like an ancient mirror. It was fed by springs, by one especially which gushed from the hill below the town. This was fit place for the chaste Diana and her nymphs to bathe. Even today the little restaurant in the town of Nemi bears the name, Specchio di Diana.

On this lake the emperor Caligula (A.D. 6-41) had two boats, each approximately two hundred and thirty-three feet by sixty-five feet. Whether these were houseboats possibly used for hunting parties or whether they were for ritualistic use in the service of Diana, no one knows. Fishermen first discovered them, looking down through the clear waters. (There were fresh-water eels in Nemi.) In the early 1500's the first attempts were made to investigate these sunken boats and to raise them. Those and later efforts were in vain, until in the time of Mussolini someone hit upon the plan of draining the lake temporarily. The ships were cradled and brought out. Along the shore a special building was erected to house them and there they stayed, museum specimens of Roman shipbuilding, until in 1944 the Germans burned them. There is little left there now to see except incomplete reproductions. On these there have been affixed whatever was left of the originals, bronze ornaments particularly. There are heads of a wolf, a panther, a lion, of the Medusa, some mosaic flooring, and various small parts. Fortunately, however, archaeologists have pictures and records.

Down in this hollow of the hills, too, one finds violets growing. Sheltered from winds, catching and holding the warmth of the sun, provided with moisture, the shores of Lake Nemi are a natural greenhouse. Reporting in his *Memoirs* in the 1400's Pius II speaks of the medlars, apples, pears, plums, quinces, cherries, as well as chestnuts, walnuts, and filberts, grown along its banks. It supplied, he adds, all Rome with fruit. He does not mention strawberries, for which it now is known almost as much as for its violets. In season from those fertile fields women carry upon their heads great basketfuls of luscious berries. In June, in fact, there is a strawberry festival.

The village of Nemi where this festival takes place lies on a narrow bench on the cliff's edge immediately above the lake. The road to it leads along the high southern margin, crosses the viaduct over a gorge and comes directly into the piazza. On the lakeside this is shut in by an old castle with its forbidding round tower and by the Roman wall into which houses have been built (note on the far side the thin brick which denote its Roman construction). Through this wall there is an arch. The castle once belonged to the Orsini, the Colonna, the Braschi, later to the Ruspoli. Around this the village centers. There is a colorful fruit stand, a bakery, the *ristorante* placed up and a little to one side to command a view. Up the hill a short way is the church. There is little else save houses, and narrow streets where children and dogs romp, chickens hunt for whatever they can find, and men, women, and donkeys find their way home at night from the valley far below. At one side of the piazza one looks over a parapet. Tier upon tier of narrow terraces range down an almost perpendicular hillside. How many times in Italy, as elsewhere, one exclaims at the husky men and women who have built them with their hands and are still tending them. Like mountain goats they go up and down, wresting from the soil its tribute of food. Yet in Nemi these terraces seem more than in most places spectacular. Each one at best is no more than four to six feet wide, enough only for a few rows of lettuce or of onions. 'The garden that I love', Norman Douglas quotes an Italian as having once said to him, 'contains good vegetables.'

Because of these terraces and for other reasons the piazza at Nemi seems memorable. More than once I've stood there watching, looking toward the high arch. Through it one sees sky and clouds, but through it, too, come the men and women from the lakeside fields of fruit and violets, along the road beneath the Roman wall. There may be a mule and his driver following slowly up behind. There may be a woman, tall and strongly built, a basket brimful of purple violets on her head. She moves over the cobblestones with the grace of a goddess—though my acquaintance with real goddesses is rather limited.

Here come first the violets one finds on the Piazza di Spagna in Rome, on the Via Veneto and in other places. Once when we were about to leave our *pensione* bound again for home, Sabatina appeared at our doors bringing to each of us a bunch of violets in their green haloes. Sabatina, tall herself and graceful, with a lovely face, had all the while been making up our rooms, performing many little services. She hoped we would come back, she said. Violets from Nemi! They were a more potent magnet than any coin tossed into the fountain of Trevi.

Campania

19

Ravello

THERE must be somewhere a fairy tale whose setting is Ravello. It was made for one. But come to think of it there is, in Boccaccio's *Decameron*. It is about a certain Landolfo Rufolo 'exceeding rich', who lived 'on a hillside overlooking the sea, which the country folk call Amalfi Side, full of little towns and gardens and springs and of men as rich and stirring in the matter of trade as any in the world'.* One of these little towns, it goes on to say, was Ravello. But go read the story for yourself (second day, fourth tale). Not everyone taken prisoner, then shipwrecked on a rocky coast, floats off upon a chest, is rescued by a woman cleaning pots and pans along the coast of Corfu, and finally gets back home with a bag of diamonds round his neck, more wealth than he had ever known before.

The name Rufolo is right. The description of the country around Amalfi is right, the background, too—a merchant prince, pirates, enemy ships, the return (he was clothed again by fellow citizens, merchants at Trani). Amalfi was once a great maritime power, finally overrun by Pisa. Ravello in the hills above was in its domain. It was full of wealthy families dealing with the east especially, in fancy dyed goods, cotton, fustian, and wool. There were depots of the goods not only in Palermo, but along the coast opposite to Greece, Barletta, Trani, and elsewhere. The sea lanes everywhere were beset with enemy ships and pirates. To lose all and again to win it back was not uncommon. Boccaccio had been to Ravello. How these people in the Middle Ages did get about, by ship, by donkey, and by horse! They had time to stop along the way and pass the time of day, to learn the local legends

* Translated by John Payne, with an Introduction by Sir Walter Raleigh, p. 87.

of who ran off with whom and why. And in this they had a great advantage over us who travel fast.

Evidently Boccaccio had found Ravello no less enchanting than we had. We arrived there just at dusk one night, having dodged all afternoon around the corners of the Amalfi drive, a breathtaking experience, not only because of the beauty of the outlook but because we never knew just when on the narrow, crooked way we'd meet a bus head-on. When we drove into the little piazza in front of the Caruso Belvedere after that last steep, switchback road, we breathed a sigh of genuine relief. Upstairs the steam was just beginning to hiss. It was November and the evenings at eleven hundred feet were cold. Out in front was a glassed-in terrace. We ordered drinks and a few moments later were sitting out there watching the moon come up over the mountains, illumining all the bay beneath. Several fishing boats were out, their lanterns bobbing up and down. We thought we'd never move again, just stay there. Such was our introduction to Ravello.

That night we rested quietly, after a delicious dinner, including a *rosé* wine made on the premises and a specialty of the house, chocolate soufflé. Before we went to bed, however, we walked out to the end of the long terrace beyond the arbor, and looked down on the lights of the little towns of Minori and Maiori hugging the sea and mountainside. Up the hill in the other direction, the people in the villages, Scala and the others, had, most of them, blown their candles already. In the morning we'd see what there was to see.

We found much more than we had expected. The palace we were living in, for the past seventy-five years in the hands of the Carusos, had been that of the d'Afflittos, one of the first families of Ravello as far back at least as the twelfth century. Its doorway was a gem. There were ancient bits everywhere. Across the piazza was the church of San Giovanni consecrated in 1069. Its pulpit is a marvel, similar to that in the cathedral, though different in detail. Its mosaics, animals, birds, arabesques, geometric designs, its carved capitals, give it a Byzantine look.

We proceeded down the street, a footpath really. The ridge was lined with palaces, many of them now hotels. Through the open archways we caught sight of gardens full of oleanders, fig trees, palms and lemon trees, huge ornamental vases and amphorae. Turning right,

Ravello

down a steep street, along which a mimosa was just coming into bloom, we reached the main piazza, almost empty of people. It was hard to believe that this once had been a town of thirty-six thousand persons. Here was the cathedral built into the side hill. Its bronze doors immediately got our attention. They were made by Barisano da Trani, in the late 1170's. The small panels with figures of saints, apostles, and others are each framed by arabesques with rosettes in bronze at the corners. The designs are very similar to those at the side entrance to the cathedral of Monreale near Palermo. Those, too, were made by Barisano at almost the same time.

Once inside the cathedral we were excited. Here were two extraordinary pulpits, across from each other on either side of the nave. That to the right was given by a Rufolo in the thirteenth century and made by Niccolo di Bartolomeo da Foggia. Underneath it, behind the columns on their snarling lions was the private chapel of the Rufolos. The pulpit itself is a magnificent piece of carved marble friezes, cornices, capitals. The heads of a man and woman in profile are set at either side of the stair entrance. Above this door is a bust, the identification of which has baffled art critics through the years. It is of a beautiful woman, crowned. The mosaic panels on the sides are sometimes of geometric design, sometimes of animals or graceful birds in greens or blues. Even the grooves of the spiral columns are inlaid. Across from this is another lower pulpit and lectern, an *ambo*, as it was called in early Christian churches. It is still earlier, made, it is thought, by a sculptor from Narnia (Narni). It has two approaches, a stairway at each end. On the marble screens of these are mosaics, on the one side of Jonah being swallowed by the great fish, on the other of his being regurgitated. As he is halfway out, he is already gaily waving a hand, I suppose to his friends on shore, just as one does on arriving at a dock. The fish is a stylized sea serpent, probably a medieval landlubber's interpretation of the Scriptures. It has wings, horns, a forked tail, and coils.

Aside from these two pulpits the cathedral offers little of much interest, bits and pieces embedded in the walls, a Roman sarcophagus, the tomb of one of the d'Afflittos. The caretaker shows one, however, the chapel of Ravello's patron saint, San Panteleone. A phial of this martyr's blood, he explains, is here preserved and every year it liquefies, in July. One is reminded of the comment of the fourteenth-century Sacchetti, in one of his *Novelle:*

'Faith is a good thing, and saveth all who have it; but truly the vice of avarice causeth much deceit in the matter of relics. It may be said that there is not a church which does not pretend to possess milk of the Virgin Mary! If it were so, there could be no relic more precious, seeing that nothing of her glorious body remaineth upon the earth; but there is so much milk shown in the world, said to be hers, that it would suffice for a fountain flowing many days!'[56]

We went next to the Villa Rufolo (entrance through the square tower on the cathedral piazza). Here Wagner came and is supposed to have found his inspiration for parts of *Parsifal.* Surely his description of the garden of Klingsor is recognizable. Here is an ancient villa, pretty much a ruin, with Saracenic interlacing arches of blue (in the *cortile*), a great Norman tower amid luxuriant trees and shrubbery, a Virginia creeper clambering up its sides. There are terraces, one after another, down the precipitous hill. They were still ablaze in November with fall flowers in patterned beds. There were woodland paths along which crocuses had just finished blooming and daffodils were coming up. There are great flights of steps, balustrades, stone benches where one may sit in the sun and look down to the sea past the Moorish domes of Santa Annunziata just below. As one sits there, looking at mountains and sea as far as Paestum on the flats to the south, one thinks not so much of Klingsor, however, and of Parsifal's wresting of the lance from him, as of the landings on the beaches of Salerno during the last Great War. The smoke of battle must have been clearly visible from here. Indeed, a waiter at our hotel told us that he had watched from there and listened to the bombardment.

There is another villa, too, the Cimbrone, on another farther promontory of Ravello's ridge. It is well worth seeing for its Saracenic loggia, its tiny cloister, its views through arches to the sea, its gardens, trees, and hedges, and the long alley flanked by marble busts on pillars, leading to the end of the promontory and a sheer drop to the rocks and sea.

If one were staying a while in Ravello, one should go up the hill to

Scala, once an important town; and there are little villages all around which one can explore, on the hill and by the sea. There is Atrani, Positano, an artists' colony, Amalfi, of course, with its cathedral; and there is the drive along the shore and over the ridge to Sorrento, a spectacular drive which no one should miss. In the other direction one may visit Salerno, take the autostrada to Herculaneum and Pompeii, or drive down the coast to Paestum, where there are some of the best Greek temples in Italy. It was once a Greek city, about 500 B.C., Poseidonia, dedicated to Neptune. I remember as a youngster picnicking there with my family one spring day and picking violets among the ruins. It was then, and is still, a lonely place. There were flocks of goats pasturing on the weeds, and some farmers plowing. As we walked on the fresh ground I picked up bits of old terra cotta pottery, iridescent glass, and one tiny bit of lapis lazuli. So far as I was concerned, they were a bag of diamonds to hang around my neck.

Sicily

20

Erice

THERE is a haunting quality about all Sicily. Its gray villages on the hilltops fade into the landscape as if they had been carved from the rock of the mountainside itself; they are hardly visible from a distance. There is a sense of timelessness one can't escape. To this many things contribute: the shepherds on the slopes guarding their sheep and goats, the gnarled olive trees bent by the winds of centuries, the agave spears everywhere as if no one had dared to touch them, the scrub pines on the hillside, the cloud shadows drifting over untended fields. One is almost surprised to find in a field a family of children astride a donkey, or on a road a painted cart drawn by a mule with red tassels and brass-knobbed harness, taking a load of dun-colored pots into town. The names that inevitably come up add to the feeling. Aeschylus was here witnessing some of his plays. Empedocles wandered along the southern shore and far up on the smoking slopes of Etna. Dionysius, the tyrant, from his post above the cave in which his slaves were incarcerated, enjoyed listening to their laments. Here Aeneas, legend says, landed on his way to Latium and the founding of Rome; here the sirens coaxed Ulysses; here are the rocks thrown by the one-eyed Polyphemus. One hardly knows which were real and which mythological, for the aroma of mythology can be very heady.

Besides the prehistoric tribes, the Siculi (from whom Sicily derives its name), the Sicani, the Elymi in the far northwest, many people have lived and fought over the land of Sicily, Phoenicians, Trojans perhaps, Greeks, Carthaginians—a mixture themselves of Phoenicians and African tribes—Romans, Saracens, Normans, Spanish. There are even two Albanian towns, dating from the fifteenth century, whose people still adhere to the Greek Orthodox church, still have their own customs and festival costumes. I shall never forget seeing at Piano degli Albanesi a woman striding along, her black skirt practically sweeping the pavement and a great bunch of yellow chrysanthemums in her arms. Like lava peoples have flowed across the land giving it a character unique. So there are Greek temples, gigantic structures made for the worship of heroic gods, Moorish domes and interlacing arches, Byzantine mosaics, Roman columns, Norman towers. There are tall men with the chiseled faces of Arabs. There are Christian church towers that look as if their builders had for some long moment forgotten they were not erecting minarets. With all of this, in the spring when floating almond petals fill the air and when yellow broom is in flower, one looks past all these to blue sea surging white against the rocks, and one knows that this is a land of make-believe.

Yet Sicily swarms with real people in great cities, Catania, Palermo, Siracusa, Messina, rich in business and industry. From them many ships go to and fro. There are many little towns, too, through which one threads one's way, with extreme caution, be it said, among hordes of children, curious and voluble. From doorways babies, chickens, goats ook out, and women on whose faces is stamped eternal resignation. In the south nowadays there are flourishing orchards and market gardens, and young citrus plantations, furnished with irrigation plants, modern equipment, and storage barns. There men with trucks, not donkey carts, pass one on the road. So after many days the land of Sicily renews itself.

All this was background when we went to Erice in the far northwest corner of the island. As soon as we had passed Marsala, reeking of wine along its streets, we began to see Erice atop what seemed from that point of view an inaccessible mountain. It was only a gray nest of buildings nearly twenty-five hundred feet above us. 'I will lift up mine eyes unto the hills from whence cometh my help', wrote the psalmist David. The priests of Baal (Phoenicians) placed their altars on high places. Great Zeus, or Jupiter, had dwelt on Mount Olympus. And here on a mountain rising almost out of the sea was Erice, a citadel and a sacred place since before time was being counted. It was of this that Virgil wrote in the fifth book of his *Aeneid*:

Erice

'Aeneas guiding with his hand a plough,
Marks out the city's ground, gives separate lands
By lot, and bids within this place appear
A second Troy. Trojan Acestes takes
The kingly power, and with benignant joy
Appoints a forum, and decrees just laws
Before a gathered senate. Then they raise
On that star-circled Erycinian hill,
The temple to Idalian Venus dear;
And at Anchises' sepulchre ordain
A priesthood and wide groves of hallowed shade.'*

Long before, however, Venus Erycina had made this craggy, pine-crested mountain-top her own. It was of limestone, and no doubt there were caves which the goddess of love found convenient; she was not likely to be caught out there except by such random flyers as Daedalus —and he held a close patent on his wings. Anyway the heather-loving (Erycina) Venus once fell in love, the legend says, with a famous Athenian beekeeper and Argonaut, Butes, and carried him off to this mountain-top above Trapani. Their son was Eryx, king of the Elymians and a hefty wrestler. Aeneas who came from far-off Troy was of course half-brother to Eryx. His mother, too, was Venus, his father Anchises. On the way, the story runs, the Trojan ships had put in at Drepanum (Trapani) and there, nearby, Anchises had, fittingly, died and been entombed. They had found relatives there, Trojans who had preceded them, headed by Acestes. No wonder that Erice was sacred to the Romans, as it was indeed to other Mediterranean peoples.

Legend says the Greeks had worshipped Aphrodite there (Greek counterpart of Venus) and the Phoenicians, Astarte, and that even before their arrival the native tribes had had an altar on the spot. Sailors rounding the corner looked to the mountain for guidance. If it was shrouded in fog, they must stop, climb up, and offer sacrifices to an indignant goddess. If it was clear, they could safely go on. Even in medieval days the present campanile built by the Aragonese in 1312,

---

* From translation by Theodore C. Williams, Houghton Mifflin Co. (Boston 1908). By permission of the publishers.

before the cathedral, served as a watchtower and a primitive lighthouse for passing mariners.

Perhaps because it was a holy spot, more probably because it was so good a lookout over the islands nearby and the sea, it was a place forever fought over. One would have supposed it almost impregnable before the days of artillery and airplanes, for only on the northwest side could it be approached. The motor road today switches back and forth up this side, and here, too, the cable car swings up. Surely it must have been easy to starve out an enemy there. The only water would have had to come from rain and condensed fog; the only food from animals pastured on the gentler slopes, from berries, maybe nuts, and fish and grain brought up the long trails from the sea and fields below. Something of the record appears even in the names by which the mountain was called, first Mount Eryx, then Heraclea, again during the Arab domination Gebel Hamed, then Monte San Giuliano after a Christian saint. Finally, since 1934, it is Erice.

Yet it is the town itself and its people that fascinate one now. Guidebooks insist that its women are more than usually beautiful, daughters of Venus. Be that as it may, on a November day of scudding fog a group of men in black hoods and long black capes pulled close, breasting the wind with shoulders bent, makes one stop and look. They are like gnomes out of some story book.

In the morning early fogs often close in. Then one plods in faith up the long street beside the cliff's edge toward the fortress at the top. From time to time there will be a sudden glimpse, a gray dome perhaps at the top of a side street, San Giuliano's tower through the trees of the Balio (the park at the top). The square Norman towers of the citadel stand out for a moment, then are blotted out. Through a slot one sees patterned fields below, then one is alone again, the wall beside one, the pavement underfoot.

One wonders where the people are—safe inside their doors no doubt on such a morning, or gone to work, by cable car, in Trapani. To be sure, as we explored the back streets, an occasional woman smiled at us through an open window. A nun scudded across the path much like the fog itself. Someone was getting water out of a town faucet in a piazza. Men were making a great dust inside a church, repairing it. A boy was driving a donkey up the street. There were occasional shops, one especially, a grocery (door closed) with a large green cauliflower on a bracket at either side, a very decorative marker. There was an abandoned church reconstituted as a factory. Here women were hooking rugs and handbags in designs distinctively their own, geometrical, resembling slightly Navajo rugs. This was Erice's only home industry. Someone on this bleak day started singing 'O Sole Mio', and with gay abandon they all joined in. It seemed a very quiet town. Yet in summer, one is told, Erice becomes something of a resort, will probably become more of one now that it has a Jolly hotel. People have summer homes up there, and in August there are several festivals.

Nearly every house is built around a patio, Spanish style. Paved roughly with stones, there have been adequate places left for a tree or two, nearly always a fig tree, sometimes a mimosa. There are fuchsias, too, and potted plants of many kinds. Usually there is a stone basin to catch water from the roof, occasionally a wellhead. A stone stairway leads upstairs, and maybe there is a balcony with vines. There will probably be a cat or two; possibly a washing on the line. The patios are the family living rooms and many of them are beautiful.

Never would one find more distinguished doorways in one small town. They are of every kind and baffle description. In their varying detail, however, they must represent the many layers of population that have been Erice's. One sees occasionally the Greek triglyph, often acanthus leaves, some fluted columns, plain Doric and Ionic columns, Moorish arches, Byzantine tracings, shell decorations, masques, both tragic and comic, heads reminiscent of Medusa. How many ancient buildings must have contributed to the making of these doorways! Over almost every one is a balcony of stone or wrought iron.

The pavements, too, of streets and sidewalks all over town are worth a look. They are of squares of a foot or so in size. Small sharp stones in slivers more or less, all laid in one direction, constitute the center. These are framed by larger limestone blocks mitred at the corners. They are not easy on one's feet but definitely give character to the town.

Of course the Norman fortress dominates everything. Its walls and towers are beautiful, especially seen at a distance through a framework of trees or wisps of fog. There is an inner courtyard, too, with distinctive bronze doors. Once inside the old citadel, one climbs up stairs and down, over bridges, looks down into dungeons; its chief interest, however, is the site itself, overlooking mountain, sea, and plain. Through it one reaches the Temple of Venus, of which there is little left to see, the *pozzo*—either well or granary—and foundation stones. Pieces from it long ago found their place in the walls of the fortress and in the right wall of the cathedral. Several other bits, too, are to be seen in the local museum, notably a Greek head of Venus.

In the museum one finds, also, the most noteworthy art work of the town, a marble *Annunciation*, really a lovely thing, by Antonello Gagini, a Sicilian artist of the sixteenth century. The churches offer little inside save a few Madonnas by Sicilian artists, reliquaries and chalices by Erycinian goldsmiths. The cathedral one should visit for its interesting exterior and doors and for its bizarre interior; San Giovanni at the far end of town if for nothing else than its superb setting and its doors to east and west. Near the Porta Spada one may see the prehistoric cyclopean walls, somewhat altered in later ages. Mythology attributes them to Daedalus, he who winged his way from Crete, fleeing the wrath of Minos. He is supposed to have left also a votive offering to Venus, a golden honeycomb, appropriate enough since Eryx' father had been a beekeeper.

There are other things worth doing while one visits Erice. There is Marsala, the ancient Lilybaeum, with its wineries founded, it is said, by an Englishman. There is Trapani with its salt pans, rectangular basins where sea water is evaporated, its museum with its fine examples of Trapanese coral and gold work. And there are the three Egadi Islands out in front to which little boats make regular sailings. One of these, Favignano, is a center of tuna fisheries. Another, Levanzano, has prehistoric cave paintings. Segesta, too, is no more than two hours away by motor car. Its Greek temple is one of the most impressive in Sicily. There is an amphitheater, also, on top of a hill. One can picnic there and be back in time for tea and sunset at Erice.

For Erice is above all a place of views. In a sunset sky the mountainous Egadi Islands are deep blue against a shining sea. And the salt pans of Trapani in the foreground catch on their glistening surface all the reds and golds that tinge the clouds around the setting sun. Then darkness comes and the lights far down below and at sea come out. Finally and distantly one discerns other lights, those on the high headlands of Tunis at Cape Bon. Carthage after all was not far away. Of all the Italian hill towns gray Erice will always be for me one of the most haunting. It is timeless and mysterious. Ghosts walk there.

Bibliography

1. Aldington, Richard, *A Wreath For San Gemignano* (with translation of Folgore's 'Garland of Months'). William Heinemann Limited (London, 1946).

2. Arnold, T. W., *The Little Flowers of Saint Francis of Assisi.* Translated by T. W. Arnold. J. M. Dent & Company (London, 1904).

3. Arnold, Matthew, 'Pagan and Medieval Religious Sentiment', *Essays in Criticism,* First Series. The Macmillan Company (London, New York, 1891).

4. Berenson, Bernard, *The Central Italian Painters of the Renaissance.* G. P. Putnam's Sons (New York, 1909).

5. Berenson, Bernard, *Seeing and Knowing.* The Macmillan Company (New York, 1953).

6. Berenson, Bernard, *The Passionate Pilgrim.* Thames and Hudson (London, 1960).

7. Burckhardt, Jacob, *The Civilization of the Renaissance in Italy.* Translated by S. G. C. Middlemore. The Phaidon Press (Vienna, 1937), Oxford University Press (New York, no date).

8. Calvino, Italo, *Italian Fables.* Translated by Louis Brigante. The Orion Press (New York, 1959).

9. Campbell, Sir Neil, *Napoleon at Fontainbleau and Elba.* J. Murray (London, 1869).

10. Caxton, William, *Golden Legend or Lives of the Saints,* as Englished by William Caxton. J. M. Dent & Company (London, 1900).

11. Cles-Reden, Sibylle, *The Buried People.* Translated from the German by C. M. Wodehouse. Rupert Hart-Davis (London, 1955).

12. Cruikshank, J. W. and A. M., *The Umbrian Cities of Italy.* L. C. Page & Company (Boston, 1907).

13. Cruttwell, Maud, *Luca Signorelli.* George Bell & Sons (London, 1901).

14. Cummings, Charles A., *A History of Architecture in Italy,* 2 vols. Houghton Mifflin Company (Boston and New York, 1901).

15. Dennistoun, James, *Memoirs of the Dukes of Urbino, Illustrating the Arms, Arts, and Literature of Italy from 1440 to 1630*, 3 vols. Longman, Brown, Green, and Longmans (London, 1851).

16. Galbraith, Edith C., 'Malaspina's Voyage Around the World', *California Historical Quarterly*, Vol. 3, No. 3, page 215 ff (October, 1924).

17. Gardner, Edmund, *The Story of Siena and San Gimignano.* J. M. Dent & Company (London, 1902).

18. Giannitrapani, Emilio, 'L'Elba', Note Geographiche, pp. 933–954, *Universo*, Nov., 1938 (Firenze).

19. Gragg, Florence A. (translator), and Gabel, Leona C. (editor), *Memoirs of a Renaissance Pope: the Commentaries of Pius II.* G. P. Putnam's Sons (New York, 1959).

20. Grifi, E., *Saunterings in Florence.* R. Bemporad & Figlio (Florence, 1904).

21. Hare, Augustus John Cuthbert, *Cities of Northern and Central Italy*, Vol. 3. G. Routledge & Sons (London, 1876).

22. Hewlett, Maurice, *The Road in Tuscany.* The Macmillan Company (New York, 1904).

23. Heywood, William, *A History of Perugia.* G. P. Putnam's Sons (New York, 1910).

24. Heywood, William, *Palio and Ponte.* Methuen & Company (London, 1904).

25. Heywood, William, *The Ensamples of Fra Filippo, A Study of Medieval Siena.* Enrico Torrini (Siena, 1901).

26. Hutton, Edward, *In Unknown Tuscany.* Methuen & Company (London, 1909).

27. Hutton, Edward, *The Cities of Romagna and the Marches.* The Macmillan Company (New York, 1913).

28. Hutton, Edward, *Siena and Southern Tuscany.* The Macmillan Company (New York, 1910).

29. Hutton, Edward, *Assisi and Umbria Revisited.* David McKay Inc. (New York, 1958).

30. Huxley, Aldous, *Along the Road.* Chatto & Windus (London, 1948).

31. James, Henry, *Italian Hours.* Houghton Mifflin Company (Boston, 1909).

32. Malaspina, Assolino, 'I Malaspina di Ascoli Piceno', *Revista Araldica* (Rome, Sept.–Oct., 1952).

33. Mariani, Valerio, *Arnolfo di Cambio*. Tumminelli (Roma, 1943).

34. McBride, Robert Medill, *Hilltop Cities of Italy*. R. M. McBride & Company (New York, 1936).

35. Misciatelli, Piero, *The Mystics of Siena*. W. Heffer & Sons Ltd. (Cambridge, England, 1929).

36. Norton, Charles Eliot, *Historical Studies of Church Building in the Middle Ages*. Harper & Brothers (New York, 1880).

37. Olschki, Leonardo, *The Genius of Italy*. Oxford University Press (London and New York, 1949).

38. Ozanam, Antoine Frederic, *The Franciscan Poets in Italy of the Thirteenth Century*. Translated by A. E. Nellen and N. C. Craig. D. Nutt (London, 1914).

39. Parks, George Bruner, *The English Traveler to Italy*, Vol. 1, Middle Ages (to 1525). Stanford University Press (Stanford, California, 1954).

40. Perkins, John Ward, 'The Church of San Salvatore at Spoleto, Some Structural Notes', *Papers*, British School at Rome, Vol. 17 (New Series, Vol. 4) (London, 1949, pp. 72–86).

41. Pevsner, Nikolaus, *An Outline of European Architecture*. Charles Scribner's Sons (New York, 1948).

42. Pliny, The Younger, *Epistles*. Translated by William Melmoth. William Heinemann Limited (London, 1915), The Macmillan Company (New York, 1915).

43. Pliny, The Elder, *The Natural History of Pliny*. Translated by John Bostock and H. T. Riley. Henry G. Bohn (London, 1857) (Vol. VI, p. 62. Pliny's Book XXXIV, Chap. 16(7)).

44. Poultney, James Wilson, *The Bronze Tables of Iguvium*. American Philological Association (Baltimore, 1959).

45. Pulgram, Ernst, *The Tongues of Italy*. Harvard University Press (Cambridge, Mass., 1958).

46. Randall-MacIver, David, *The Etruscans*. The Clarendon Press (Oxford, 1927).

47. Rosenzweig, Irene, *Ritual and Cults of pre-Roman Iguvium*. Waverly Press Inc. (Baltimore, 1937).

48. Santayana, Silvio George, *Two Renaissance Educators: Alberti and Piccolomini*. Meador Publishing Company (Boston, 1930).

49. Schevill, Ferdinand, *Siena, The Story of a Medieval Commune*. Charles Scribner's Sons (New York, 1909).

50. Sedgwick, Henry Dwight, *Italy in the Thirteenth Century*, 2 vols. Houghton Mifflin Company (Boston and New York, 1913).

51. Seymour, Frederick H., *Up Hill and Down Dale in Ancient Etruria*. D. Appleton & Company (New York, 1910).

52. Simpson, Frederick Moore, *A History of Architectural Development*. Longmans, Green and Company (London and New York, 1911).

53. Sismondi, J. C. L., *History of the Italian Republics in the Middle Ages*. Recast by William Boulting. G. Routledge and Sons (London, 1832), E. P. Dutton & Company (New York, 1906).

54. Sforza, Count Carlo, *Italy and Italians*. Translated by Edward Hutton. E. P. Dutton & Company (New York, 1949).

55. Staley, Edgecumbe, *The Guilds of Florence*. Methuen and Company (London, 1906), A. C. McClurg Company (Chicago, 1906).

56. Steegman, Mary G. (translator), *Tales from Franco Sacchetti*, with an Introduction by Dr. Giulio Biagi, Director of the Laurentian Library, Florence. J. M. Dent & Company (London, 1908).

57. Symonds, John Addington, *Italian Byways*. Henry Holt and Company (New York, 1883).

58. Toor, Frances, *Festivals and Folkways of Italy*. Crown Publishers (New York, 1953).

59. Underhill, Evelyn, *Jacopone da Todi, Poet and Mystic*. J. M. Dent & Sons Ltd. (London, 1919), E. P. Dutton & Company (New York, 1919). Translation of Poems by Mrs. Theodore Beck.

60. Vasari, Giorgio, *Lives of 70 Painters, Sculptors, and Architects*. Edited by E. H. and E. W. Blashfield and A. A. Hopkins. Charles Scribner's Sons (New York, 1911).

61. Vittorini, Domenico, *The Age of Dante*. Syracuse University Press (Syracuse, New York, 1957).

62. Wall, Bernard, *Italian Art, Life and Landscape*. William Heinemann Limited (London, 1956).

63. Williams, Egerton R., *Hill Towns of Italy*. Houghton Mifflin Company (Boston and New York, 1903).

64. Wittkower, Rudolf, *Architectural Principles in the Age of Humanism*. A. Tiranti (London, 1952).

65. Wolff, Sir Henry Drummond, *The Island Empire: or, Scenes of the First Exile of the Emperor Napoleon I*. T. Bosworth (London, 1855).

66. Young, Col. G. F., *The Medici*. E. P. Dutton & Company (New York, 1924).

Index